BROKEN ROADS

James Patrick

First published in the United Kingdom 1st February 2022 by:

Broken Roads

Copyright© J.J. Patrick (James Patrick) 2021, 2022

All Rights Reserved.

Cover Art

Copyright © Cynefin Road 2021, 2022

All Rights Reserved.

The author has exercised his legal and moral rights.

Broken Roads is a work of non-fiction, exploring the case of convicted serial killer Robert Ben Rhoades and seeking the solutions which could prevent truck-driving offenders from doing harm in future. 42.5% of the net profit from every copy of this book goes to the Cold Case Foundation, a charitable organisation based in Utah which helps investigators solve cold cases, bringing long awaited closure to families.

Cynefin Road is a small, independent publishing house with a heart, so thank you for buying an authorised edition of this book and refusing to feed the pirates (not the rum loving kind) by copying, scanning, or otherwise distributing this brilliant work without permission. It also means you'll steer clear of the long arm of the law. Without you being a goody two-shoes, we wouldn't be able to bring you amazing things to read. Writers deserve your support and ours, so give yourself a pat on the back for doing something wonderful and enjoy the story.

The views and opinions expressed in this book are those of the author and may not reflect those of the Cold Case Foundation.

Knowing you've read this small print makes us happy enough to throw some shapes while nobody's watching. We hope you have a nice day, wish you multiple lottery wins, and want you to find infinite joy wherever life's rich journey may take you.

First Edition

Print ISBN 978-1-7398770-0-2 | Electronic ISBN 978-1-7398770-1-9

Cynefin Road is a trading style of JJ Patrick Limited, a company registered in England and Wales

Company Number: 11931051 | Vat Registration: 381483873

Registered Office: The Stable Yard, Stony Stratford, MK11 1BN, UK

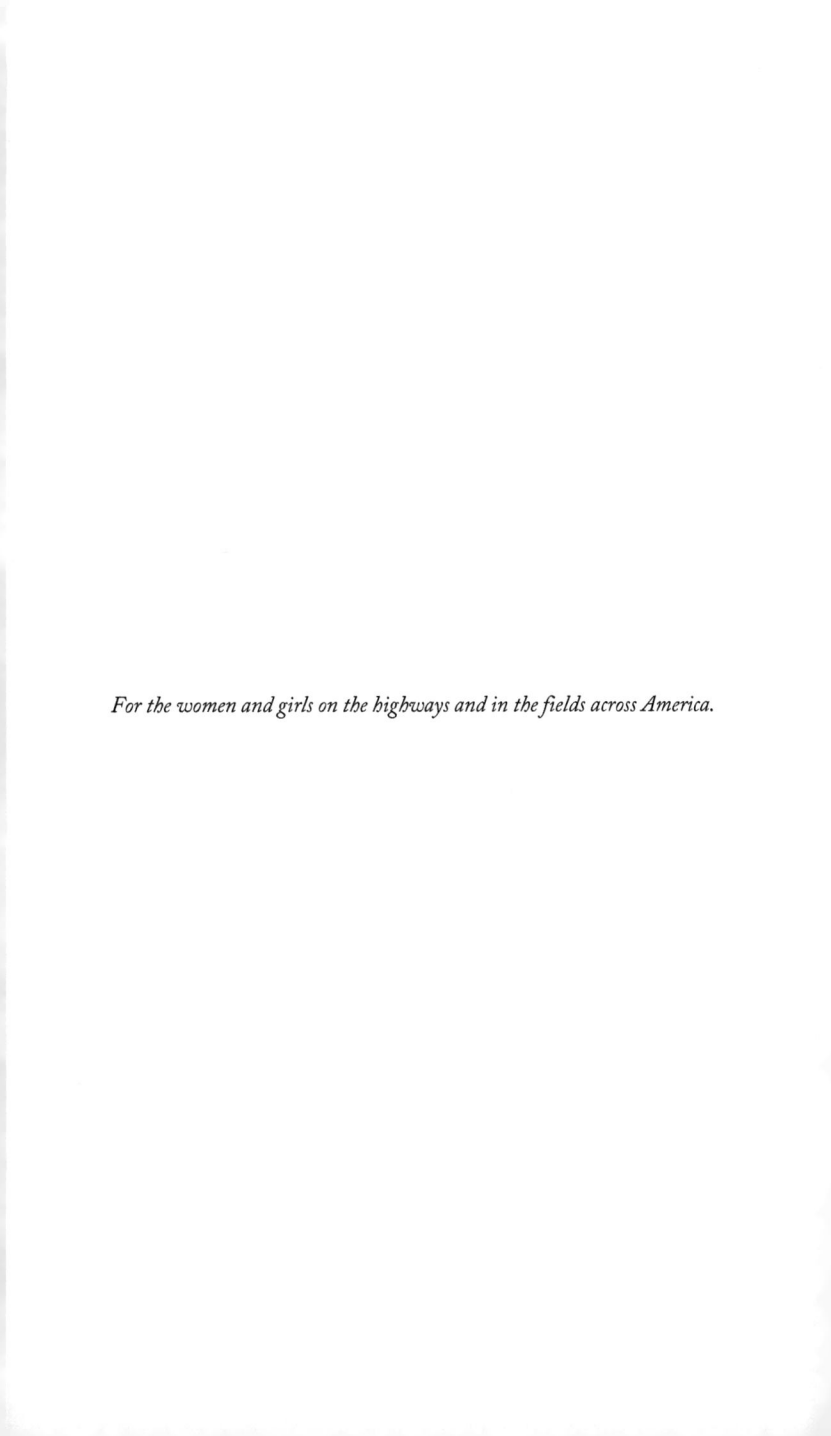

For the women and girls on the highways and in the fields across America.

AUTHOR'S NOTE

Hopefully this book will help to stop bad things from happening in the future. There's nothing else to say.

James.

IN THE UNITED STATES, OVER 600,000 PEOPLE ARE REPORTED MISSING EACH YEAR. RIGHT NOW, THERE ARE AROUND 90,000 PEOPLE IN AMERICA WHOSE WHEREABOUTS ARE UNKNOWN. SOME PEOPLE DISAPPEAR AND NOBODY EVER CALLS IT IN.

EACH YEAR THERE ARE 20,000 HOMICIDES IN THE UNITED STATES. JUST UNDER HALF OF THOSE CASES WILL NEVER BE SOLVED AND YOU WILL NEVER HEAR ABOUT THEM. BETWEEN 1980 AND 2008 ALONE POLICE FORCES ACROSS AMERICA AMASSED SOME 185,000 COLD CASES. SOME OF THE VICTIMS WILL NEVER BE NAMED.

THERE ARE BETWEEN 25 AND 50 ACTIVE SERIAL KILLERS IN AMERICA TODAY. MANY OF THESE KILLERS HAVE NOT BEEN IDENTIFIED AND AUTHORITIES HAVE NO IDEA WHEN OR WHERE THEY WILL STRIKE NEXT.

THE GIRL IN THE PHOTOGRAPH

It is an old photograph staring up at me, taken some time in the mid-80s to early 1990s judging by the hairstyle and the surroundings. Pre-digital. From the time before life was this fast. Before information was as instantly pliable as it has become, back when we used to make calls from phone-boxes and if you made an appointment to meet a friend a few weeks down the line, you would both turn up at the designated spot, on time, and without any syncing calendars or sending confirmation texts.

The young woman in the picture has a mane of glossy black hair spilling over her shoulders and hanging against a grey hooded top. Her face is moon pale due to the flash of a camera, which causes her tired eyes to squint. I can still make out enough of her features to recognize she's Native American. Whether she is smiling or grimacing is up for debate. The way it verges toward an uncomfortable half smile is the universal language of women in a vulnerable position when confronted with a man whose intentions are not known. She appears to be in her early twenties, sitting in the passenger seat of what looks like a truck, right on the threshold of a door which hangs open into the dark night. The paintwork looks white or cream, it is hard to tell with the age of the photo, but there's brown trim on the interior door panel. The curtain between the cab and the sleeping compartment is in the frame, as if it has been pulled open. Whomever is using the camera, presumably also the truck driver, is not in the picture of course. Because of the door being open there is no reflection of them to zoom in on and laboriously tidy up with Photoshop, but that is okay. I have another batch of photos of that individual to look at later, along with some of the "cargo" they were carrying during the relevant period. This photo of the girl has a story all of its own. One which was not resolved until very recently.

Pamela first saw a photograph of her younger self in 2015 when it was circulating on Facebook with a note asking for anyone who knew that girl to get in touch. Now in her early fifties and based in Alberta, Canada, Pamela is a Thunder Child First Nation woman who started hitchhiking in the early 80s. She made her way from Saskatchewan to White City, about four-hundred kilometres south - near Regina – as the day was heading towards late evening. By her recollection, it was about eight or nine pm, meaning the sun was down, when she managed to finally flag down a semi-truck and ran to where it pulled over on the side of the road.

"Hey, jump on in here," the American driver said, giving her a hand with a heavy bag and putting it behind the curtain as she climbed into the cab. Before she even got to close the door he snapped the picture.

"What did you do that for?" she asked, according to her telling documented in a 2019 article by APTN News reporter Holly Moore[1].

The driver replied: "If you rip me off, I can tell the cops that you stole from me."

They talked on the three-hundred-and-fifty-kilometre journey to Brandon, Manitoba, through the dark Canadian night and, at one stage, the driver pointed out the sticker on his dashboard which read "cash grass or ass no one rides for free." Pamela did not have any money or drugs so, she states, she settled on sex in the back of the cab before eventually being dropped off another two-hundred-and-fourteen kilometres away in Winnipeg. The truck driver told her his name was Robert.

For thirty years Pamela Lee Milliken, who lives in Moose Jaw, Saskatchewan, had no idea just how lucky she was to be alive. I tracked her down using the same social media platform she found her younger self's picture on in 2015. Proud of her heritage and with a lot of wisdom to share, she's contemplating a future leading the community. She now uses both of her names – she is Kitwatino Muskiti Bishiki Equay (giiwedin mashkode-bizhiki ikwe, according to the Ojibwe People's Dictionary), which means

---

[1] https://www.aptnnews.ca/national-news/alberta-woman-recognizes-herself-in-photo-found-in-u-s-serial-killers-truck/,

Alberta woman recognizes herself in photo found in U.S. serial killer's truck, APTN News, Holly Moore, 24 February 2019

North Buffalo Woman in Ojibwe. Over the years I have spoken some truly fascinating people from burglars to politicians, but Pamela belongs in the top segment of that list. And she also shares a profession with Robert.

"I'm First Nation from Canada - Thunder child, Saskatchewan. I'm fifty-three years old. I have three daughters, ten grandchildren. I'm a truck driver and I do heavy equipment operator too," she told me. "My grandchildren keep me busy," she giggled, and you could hear love and good nature and crows-feet laughter lines squeezing together as she did. "You wanted to hear my side of the story of what had happened between Robert and I?"

I did. That's why I had reached out to her and why we were talking over the internet, our voices travelling under thousands of miles of sea and arriving at each other's ears at the same time they would have if we were sat in Pamela's garden. It was back in 1984, when she was just eighteen. I found out quickly that Pamela not only has crystal-clear recall but also has a knack for storytelling, weaving events of mid 2010 with the 80s in a seamless style which would put any movie writing team to shame.

"2015 I was on Facebook going through my browser while on my Facebook page and I was just reading and scrolling. And then all of a sudden I seen this picture of a native girl and it said: Anyone know this young lady whose picture was found in a serial killer's truck? When I looked at it, and it just like it was a flashback. It was just like I was back in that truck," she said.

The day that Robert had taken that picture, she was only just about to turn away to close the door behind her after climbing into the cab. She was in the middle of telling him thanks for picking her up as she had been on the road all day and had only just sat down when she looked at him. "He clicked a picture of me and then that's when I said well what was that for? And then he said, just in case you rip me off. I'm going to keep this picture. And it's going to be verify who you are if you ever tried to steal off me. So I didn't question, I just thought okay, well, that's a safety precaution kind of thing. You know. I wasn't quite actually eighteen - I would say I was turning eighteen because in Alberta I wasn't old enough to get into the bar. Bar ages are eighteen and I wasn't old enough, that's how I know."

Seeing a picture of your younger self you didn't know existed is strange enough – a cousin of mine did this to me recently – but discovering that picture of you was taken by a serial killer when you hitched a ride a few decades in the past and lived to tell the tale might seem unbelievable. People close to Pamela at the time she found the Facebook post certainly struggled with the idea and this led to some detective work of her own, until she tracked down childhood photographs she didn't know existed and matched them back to the Facebook post she had, by that point, lost access to.

"I told my common law boyfriend at the time. I had said: this is me. And then he looked at it, and he says, oh, get out of here. And I said, no honestly, God, this is me this, I remember this picture. He didn't believe me, but I took a picture of me, right there. And then, like what I was wearing, I had long hair at the time and I tried to match it up with the picture in the truck, but it was it was the age difference which meant he couldn't really match it up. So then, after that, it was just like I was searching for this picture of me when I was eighteen years old. I couldn't find any picture of me until I went to Thunder child, where I'm originally from and I was looking. I was visiting with my niece, Peggy, and she had pictures of family on her wall. And I was looking at all of them and then said, who is this? And then she looked at it. And she goes, you can't even recognize yourself? And I said, when was this taken? And she said that picture was taken when you first came back to the reserve, remember? Remember when you were at uncle Stephen's and you were visiting the family? And then I said, Oh, cool. So I took a picture of the picture." Memories of the exact conversation fell out of Pamela like quarters on a won slot machine.

She explained why the picture mattered, telling her cousin about the 2015 post she had seen on Facebook with her and the serial killer, Robert. This was the picture Pamela had been looking for all those years - this was 2018, three years on – but she had long since lost the post. The thing with Pamela, though, is that luck seems to walk around after her like a shadow. "Now I didn't have the post. But I had the picture and, in 2019, I was in camp, in St. Paul's. I was telling my colleague about it: I have the picture, but I don't have the post. And I had told him like because we were having lunch together. And then it was after that I said: if I ever find that post again, I'm going to upload it and tell people that I'm okay and I'm alive. So, he said: Yeah, well, that's a fascinating story. He was telling me he didn't believe me, so I went back to my dorm and I turned on my Facebook on the shared computer and it was the first post that was on my Facebook, right there on my newsfeed."

With browser cache her lucky charm, Pamela sent a private message to the lady behind the Facebook post, writing "Hey, this is me," and the reply was perhaps an unsurprising "Oh get of out here." If I'm honest, most of us would have thought it was a joke, but Pamela persisted and they ended up texting each other. Pamela sent her that picture of uncle Stephen's, captured when she was around eighteen.

"She went: holy cow that is you! And I said I know." Pamela laughed, more deeply this time. "And then I said how do I get rid of this post and let people know that I'm okay. And then she said that I should get a hold of somebody on the murdered and missing Indigenous women page. So, I went on there. And then I had told them and all of a sudden my inbox lit up with better than over five hundred messages. And the post itself had six hundred comments and over one thousand shares all over the world. Like, I had people from Australia, everywhere, Germany, saying that they were praying for me and wondering what had happened to me. And it just blew my mind. Like it scared me, actually. I had to phone my adopted parents and told them I opened up a can of worms that I can't close."

Having spoken to her, Pamela genuinely had no idea who Robert was until the Facebook post. Since then, she has researched his case and even retraced her own steps on that incredibly lucky hitchhiking expedition in the 80s. She was picked up outside of town called Regina, a word I'd become very familiar with while researching this case for reasons you'll come to understand. Pamela's whole story is one of odd coincidences and happenstance.

"I was like just going through his documentaries and you know, some of the things that were what he had done and you know where he had travelled, but he had picked me up outside of Regina. There's a town called White wood. I thought it was White Star City or something like that. But I went for a drive down there just this past spring and found the exact place where he had picked me up and I was just like, you know, kind of reminiscing and it didn't really dawn on me at the time. He was a very dangerous man. It just didn't dawn on me. When I jumped in, he seemed like a real nice man, you know, and then we were talking and he had asked me where I was from and where I came from. And I said, well I've been on the highway since seven o'clock this morning and I'm running away from my biological parents."

She told Robert the truth, that she was on her way to Winnipeg to go and find her brother who she had never met in her adult life, as she was taken away from their family when she was eighteen months old. She wasn't even entirely sure he was there but had heard on the grapevine he was. Winnipeg is where she said she was going and that is where she fully intended to get.

"Don't your parents know where you are?" Robert asked her.

"Well, my adopted parents know that I'm going to Winnipeg," she told him. That was her safety precaution, as she put it. She told Robert she was expected and that relatives were waiting for a call from her at a certain time – one set back where she was leaving from, and the other in Winnipeg. She felt comfortable enough to tell Robert about her life, that she was adopted and later went back home, working her way through culture shock, and that she couldn't really understand her life at the time. "I just want to run away, and I just don't want to come back. I'm going to want to pick between two lives and be with my brother, and I want to stay with him for a while and sort things out," she carried on telling the trucker. Rather than a safety precaution, this should have been a welcome mat. At the time when she was hitching, Pamela describes her lifestyle as transient. Her circuit, as she describes it, was Thunder Child to Saskatoon - which is around two and a half hours away - and on to Prince Albert - another hour and twenty minutes. Her road trip from Thunder Child to Winnipeg was around twelve hours in all, giving her a long period of exposure to the friendly trucker with the camera. She relives that day in her head often and her unusual gift for the recall of details makes hearing the story an immersive experience. Talking to her about something which happened when *Flashdance* was a billboard number one provides a more detailed account than most eyewitnesses will give you for events in the last twenty-four hours.

On the day she met Robert, Pamela left Thunder Child at seven o'clock in the morning and had made her way to Regina by early afternoon. She walked as far as White Wood and managed to flag down a ride – a truck loaded with cola, which she agreed to help unload in exchange for the lift. By the time the job was done, Pamela was tired and the driver took pity on her.

"We unloaded the van and we turned around and came back," she said. "He had dropped me off and I told him I was really tired. He said that he would give me a room. I'll get a room for you for helping me and you can stay there and, you know, feed you too and then you can just carry on from when you wake up, he said. So that was about, I don't know, I think maybe about four o'clock when he had dropped me off at the hotel room. And then I woke up when it was about eight o'clock and I had something to eat, then jumped back out onto the highway trying to get to Winnipeg, because I knew I had still quite a ways to go and it was still daylight. It was in the summertime, eight o'clock at night and it started getting dark about 10 o'clock. But I was walking from White Wood for about two hours when I finally got picked up."

She describes the truck which stopped for her that night as a flat nose semi-truck. She wasn't expecting a truck to stop because in her experience they rarely picked up hitchhikers. Nonetheless, she heard the engine, stuck out her thumb and gave a half look over her shoulder. It went past her without stopping and she carried on walking, dejected. Then she saw the taillights come on and the truck pulled over.

"I said: oh right on, cool, right on. I took off and went running, opened the door, naturally, and I saw Robert. I was telling myself I thanked God for him picking me up. I'd been walking with this heavy bag all day." She remembers seeing a tall man with brown hair and glasses in the cab, wearing a grey, button-up cowboy shirt.

"Where are you heading?" he asked her, and she told him Winnipeg. "Hop on up here, that's where I'm heading – I'm going through there on my way to Florida."

"Oh cool," she replied and heaved her hockey bag up into the cab. By her recollection, it weighed around seventy pounds. Robert grabbed it half-way and lifted it away from her like it weighed nothing at all. "Holy cow, you're pretty strong!" she told him. He threw the bag over the back of the seats, onto the back corner of the bed then Pamela climbed up and sat down, telling the affable driver she had been hitchhiking since seven that morning - making it from Saskatoon down to Regina and now the road out from White Wood. The photograph of Pamela in the truck was taken from the driver's seat before she even had a chance to shut the door. It took her by surprise. "I don't even know where he got the camera from, because there was a light up in there. He must have had it on his lap because, suddenly, when I jumped in, I turned and I looked at him and I just smiled. I was just going turn and grab the door then I look back at him and that's when he snapped his picture. I asked him what that was for. I always like to say it was a Polaroid but I'm not quite sure on that. I don't know, like, I don't think it was a digital. I don't even think digital existed in those days."

This is the compelling thing about Pamela and her story. She doesn't obviously try and flesh out memories she does not have on tap but, if she does remember something, it is in full HD. Despite the passage of time, she can truly talk in detail about what happened on almost any given day.

Listening to her describe the exchange which took place with Robert, in which he accused her of being an underage runaway, I got a potential insight into a victim selection process which I have not seen documented anywhere else. Robert was looking for early options to dominate and seeking signs of weakness or opportunities to gain compliance through fear of authority. Afterwards, when that failed, he changed tack to share dreams and sympathy. The same exchange explains to me at least why Pamela is still walking around: she simply wasn't scared so, for him, there was no sport.

"On the journey I was telling him about me being adopted and my dad being a Court of Queen's Bench judge, telling him a little bit about my family life - like I'm the third youngest of the adopted kids and I was out in Thunder Child where I met my biological dad and all my cousins. You know, just a quick glance of what my life was about. And that, more or less, gave him the impression that I was kind of lost and seeking someplace to go," she said. "That's why I was heading toward Winnipeg, to try to find some kind of security or something." She says that Robert sat in near silence and listened to her until they were a few miles outside of Brandon, Manitoba – around two or three hours from White Wood depending on whether you take the Trans-Canada Highway or the MB-16 East.

"You, you're a runaway!" Robert broke his silence, probing. Running through his selection script. "You're thirteen years old, you're a runaway."

"I'm not thirteen!" Pamela replied. "I'm eighteen years old. I was born in 1966, do the math!"

He tested her. "I'm going to take you to the Brandon RCMP and drop you off and let them deal with you."

"Go ahead," she said, holding firm. "Go ahead, drop me off and I'll be back out on the highway in fifteen minutes."

"You don't even have any ID," he pressed.

"I don't have any ID, but I have a phone number for my mom," she threw back as the truck rolled towards Brandon where the police station sits on

Veteran's Way and 17th Street East, off the highway. He kept on at her, pushing her to admit she was a teen runaway until she shrugged "Drop me off." He was gearing down and, when they saw the RCMP station picture on a highway sign, he was trying to convince her he would turn her in. Pamela stared him down. "Go ahead. I don't care. Go ahead."

She won the battle of wills and Robert accelerated, passing the stops and turn offs. She knew he wasn't going to take her into the Mounties.

"I don't know, it must have been less than two or so hour later," she told me, "Maybe not even about an hour later, and we were in this one stretch where there was no cars at all. This is probably now about two o'clock in the morning and he asked me if I was hungry. And I said, Yeah, I was hungry. He said, there's a cooler in the back with some submarine sandwiches in it. And I said all right and sat in the front and ate. After we were done eating, he just said did you ever want to drive truck, and I said yeah! Then I drove his truck, somebody like me!"

"Do you drink?" he asked her, which she replied yes to. "Well, there's some back there, underneath the bed. Slide them out so you can have a beer."

"Okay," Pamela replied and grabbed the beers from under the bed. She sat in the front seat drinking as he drove.

Robert began to open up, telling her he had been driving trucks for years and years, taking routes from everywhere including Edmonton to Florida and back. He told her he stayed on the road for about six months or so a year, doing nothing but driving. He drip-fed her a story about his wife, peppering it across all the other chatter in broken pieces to weave a narrative. Seeding a sob story to facilitate intimacy.

"After I finished my first beer, he said I could have another one and then that's when we're in this stretch of road - it was just two lanes and it was no cars on the highway whatsoever," she told me. "And then he points out the sign on his dash and it says *cash, grass, or ass, nobody rides for free*. And then I looked at it and I was just like: man, no way! I was just thinking that in my head. I was looking at the front window no cars, I looked in the door mirror out the side window, no lights. It was pitch dark and it was a wooded area. And I was just like I can't get dropped off out here in the middle of nowhere, no vehicles and freaking total darkness." Pamela was stuck. She was in the middle of nowhere, had no money, and did not take drugs so weed wasn't an option. "I guess tonight's your lucky night," she said to Robert. Though there was clear coercion, she perceives that she willingly consented to sex in exchange for the ride.

"Get another beer," Robert said to her. "Have another beer and relax. Jump in the back and put on something comfortable." She did as he asked.

"I knew what it was gonna be, we were going to have sex anyway," she told me. "So, I just took off my clothes and I put on one of his cowboy shirts with a button snap on the front and sat in the front seat in my underwear and put my feet up on the dash. I drank my second beer and I'm not a very heavy drinker, so a second beer was already making me feel kind of woozy."

Robert eyed her up. "You want to drive the truck right now?" he asked. She nodded. "Come on over here sit on my lap." She moved across the seat and sat on his lap, he let her take the wheel of semi. There was still nobody on the highway, so she steered back and forth between the two lanes until he said: "All right, that's enough. Now get back in your seat." He said the lane changing would probably roll his truck, so she sat back in the passenger seat, feet on the dash, and drank a third beer.

"I can see you're really tired," he said.

"Yeah, I've been up quite a few quite a few hours already," Pamela replied.

"This is where you end up in the back and go to sleep. If you want to wake up later, I can drive for a couple more hours."

"Sure," she said and climbed into the bed. He drove, Pamela fell asleep.

She woke up to hear the truck slowing, Robert gearing down. She opened her eyes and looked out of the little window on the side of the sleeper cabin. She saw the sun was coming up. "Where are we?" she asked.

"We're in a truck stop outside Winnipeg," Robert replied. From Brandon, Winnipeg is between two and three hours, so it would have been around five am by then, Pamela guessed. "I'm gonna go and have some breakfast. Do you want anything?"

"Yeah, I'll have and a sandwich and a coke."

He said "okay," and Robert left the truck. Pamela fell asleep again until he returned. He handed her a wrapped-up sandwich and a drink, which she put in her bag because, she says, she knew she would need it later in the day, then the trucker crawled into bed. You might expect, as I did, that sex would have been the first thing on his agenda, but it was not.

"What do you want? What do you look for? Do you do have any future plans?" he asked.

"Sure I do," she replied. "I have plans to have kids. I want three girls five years apart." This actually happened, years after the truck ride - Pamela has three girls, five years apart.

"What kind of husband are you looking for?" he asked her.

"Well, I want I want one with curly hair, broad shoulders type physique, and a dimple in his chin." Robert laughed at her vision of the perfect man, but again this came true for Pamela in the years that followed and she stayed with that man for fourteen years - she calls that another chapter. She was feeling bold in the morning light of the truck though, and asked Robert: "If you love your wife so much, how come you don't go back there?"

"Because she cheated on me with my best friend," he replied, expanding on the story he had seeded over the course of many hours.

"Well, if you love her a lot, how come you can't forgive her?"

"There's no forgiving," he said. "I built this business around me for her. Everything. All my time and effort went into this business for her. And when I came back early from Florida that time and found her in bed with my best friend…there's no way I am ever going back." Robert told Pamela he walked in on her as a surprise because he was a couple days early from a run, then found her in their marital bed with his best friend. According to his story, he looked at both of them, took in the scene, turned around and walked out the door. He said he never went back. "I've been driving truck six months straight now. I haven't stopped once."

After that he said that he wanted her and they had sex in the sleeper, after which the driver slept for a couple of hours. He told her he would give her money for a bus if she needed it and would drop her off at the bus station.

"We woke up about ten o'clock and then he drove me into Winnipeg," Pamela told me. "And he was trying to get me to stay with him. *Are you sure you don't want to come with me to Florida?* he said and then I said no, I want to stop and see my brother. He went quiet again. He was still driving. I said let's talk about how long and how big Winnipeg was, because it seemed like it took us forever to get to a bus stop. And then we're at the bus depot and, suddenly, he says to me: how about if we phone your brother, we'll go visit your brother for a couple of hours, I'll sleep some more, and then we'll go to Florida. I looked at him and I said, you know, I didn't want to stay for a couple hours, I want to stay for like six months. And then he was like, he was really trying to ask me to go with him, but I didn't want to go with him. And then we got to the West depot. I opened up the door, and he said: well use the bus depot and don't talk to any strangers." Pamela laughed as she told me this, a stranger on the end of an internet line, thousands of miles away. "I have a hard time not talking to strangers. Ever since I was a kid. Anyway. He says, do you have any money? I didn't want to take any of his money because I figured, you know, he gave me a ride, fed me, gave me drinks. You know, I was pushing my luck to have asked you for money. So, I said no, I have money, but I only had a dollar seventy-five in my pocket."

They parted ways there in Winnipeg.

"Take care and I hope your dreams come true," Robert said.

"Yes, you too. And drive safe," she replied, and he drove away.

Pamela stood in the bus depot and then made her way to the phones. She had to skim through the phone books looking for her brother's name, C Baker, and she remembers four pages of six little columns of Bakers back-to-back. She had refused the trucker's money, leaving her with less than two dollars in her pocket, so she muttered a prayer under her breath, closed her eyes and let her finger walk down the column, then dialled the C Baker it landed on. "Sure enough, it was my brother's number," she told me, still giggling.

We chatted a bit longer. I probed a few details of the sleeping compartment. And Pamela recalled a suitcase being under the bed with the case of beers. She remembers crushed velvet textiles on the bed. She also pointed out that she used to shave her pubic hair to try and encourage it to grow. And that Robert told her he liked this. Many years later, when she watched the documentary, the truth of the person she remembered sleeping with came as a surprise. Like most monsters out in the real world, people never notice them until it is too late. "I was just, like, I was kind of mind boggling. Because he didn't give me the impression he was that kind of a person. Like, after watching his documentaries and everything. And, you know, like he didn't seem to be this monster like the way you saw in the documentary. He never once made me want to do you know, like…he didn't force me to do anything. I drove the truck, you know? And it's just like, I don't know," she trailed off. "It's just when I actually like, read his documents and read up on him, there's a way he must have changed. Because it was oh man…it just it just blew my mind. Like, the whole story is so surreal."

I asked Pamela repeatedly if she was certain it was him.

"There's that one picture of him where he was wearing that brown cowboy shirt and his glasses. And his hair is, well, that's how he looked but he was wearing a grey shirt. I looked at him when he smiled at me, there was that kind of like the crooked smile. He was like a cowboy, a cowboy trucker. And when I read the other lady's story from the GQ article and she had said cash, grass, or ass, nobody rides for free, I said yeah that is the exact same sign that he had pulled out on me." She's referring to an article by Vanessa Veselka, written in 2012, though she mentions a bumper sticker as opposed to a sign in the cab, which is a seed of doubt in the story. "It was dark on that highway and I thought that we were just going to be like, people that just met on a dark night, thanked each other, and never saw each other again. Out of billions of people in the world, how would we ever see each other again? Two ships sailing in the night. That's what I figured. Nobody will know. Nobody will know what happened, nobody will care, you know, I feel relieved and all that. It could have went totally different. I could have never seen my children grow. I could have never met my future husband, I could have never been a truck driver myself. You know, and I've done a lot of things, like being a heavyweight boxer. I've done a lot of things I never thought I could do. And to think that it could have been non-existent if the tables were turned a different way." Pamela was lucky. She got to live an interesting life in the years since. And this is something which I personally think is genuinely important: victims of murder should have gone on to live their lives. They should have all have had the opportunity to giggle through stories like Pamela's one about the time she randomly became a champion boxer.

She chose to become a youth worker and attended the University of Chicago Indian Teachers Education Program, but in her view they wanted to be too authoritarian. So, she branched off into community youth work. "My reserve needed youth workers, so I worked at the youth centre there. And every session I'd take the kids out to the store to go buy them treats before I drove them home at night. One day there was a sign there and it was called the *Are You Tough Enough Circuit*. It was forty dollars to play and a thousand if you walked away. So anyway, I was up there buying candies, telling the kids come on you guys I want to go home, let's go. One of the little boys says: hey, auntie, can you do that? And I said, what? And he points at the poster and I'm looking at the poster but I told them I didn't have the entry fee. We're going to get your entry fee and you're going to go represent Thunder Child, they said and, sure enough, that's what they did. They collected forty dollars of change and an extra thirty for gas and sent me to represent Thunder child at the very top of the competition. My first fight was twenty-seven seconds to a total knock out, so I just sat and watched all the fights all night till the very last one, then I beat her too and won a thousand bucks. All I had to do was fight for thirty seconds and then the three minutes and that was it. I told my adopted dad that. I said: Hey, Dad, I got your name in the boxing circuit."

Her adopted father laughed at the idea she had won a thousand dollars in under four minutes: "Those are lawyer fees! Being a judge those are lawyer's fees for Christ's sake," she remembers him saying. She defended her title several times, winning each. But not everything is luck and not all roads lead to a happy ending.

Pamela has watched her community suffer and even lost close relatives - young women like her who went missing and were found deceased many years later, discarded. Her niece, tragically, was one of them. Ultimately, she doesn't understand why Robert, who she believes to be a serial killer, let her go alive. That may always cast its own shadow.

"Oh yeah, I'm grateful I wasn't a statistic. I've always said that I wasn't gonna die from the hands of a man or die from drugs and alcohol. And I don't know what made Robert not do what he did, you know. I don't know what made him not kill me or what made me different from any other girl, or how you even know. I just thank God that he was walking with me that day. It was really totally miraculous how I didn't get killed."

We keep in touch, by Facebook Messenger. After I spoke with Pamela, she became resolute as regards getting an answer from Robert as to why he hadn't killed her. She wanted to write to him in prison and, in my view, if that brings her closure it is the right thing to do. Open-ended questions are psychologically harmful so, if you can get answers, you should. Her account left me with a lot of work to do. A lot to vet and verify, as you never simply take something at face value. So, I at my desk and reviewed her testimony alongside the available facts. I don't doubt her account, that in the mid-80s she hitched a ride with a trucker named Robert. I don't dispute anything she said about what happened, how many beers she drank, the route they took, the conversation they had, or that she honestly believes he was Robert Ben Rhoades, having later seen pictures of him. The problems I stumble into are administrative, really. Arising simply through following the *checkable facts, provable lies* mantra, which springs from following the evidence and applies to witnesses just in the same way it does to suspects.

The photograph of the girl in the truck was, depending which account you read, on the end of the roll of film seized in 1990. This bothered me a lot because it seemed improbable there would be a five-year gap on one film, especially given that the convicted killer in question, Rhoades, was taking photographs all the time – many of which I've seen and most of which I will never forget, no matter how much I might want to. But this is problematic because prints of photos were retrieved from Rhoades' apartment and there's no sure answer as to whether this one was on a roll of film or in a stack of physical prints. If I'm honest, I lean towards a physical photo, not for convenience of hypothesis but more for probability because the time gap makes less sense. This tiny conflict puts Pamela's story in an immediate limbo, where it could be true yet might not even be possible simultaneously. There is also the photograph itself and the comparison image of Pamela, taken by her uncle. They are undeniably very, very similar, down to the unevenness of the eyes and the shape of the mouth, but I could not hand on heart say they are the same person by looking at them side-by-side – which, incidentally, is one of the most infuriating things I see being claimed as definitive identification evidence on the internet all the time. To try and get through to the truth, I first overlayed the two images, setting the opacity on the top layer so I could match the images together. The eyes, nose and mouth do align perfectly, but comparative distance measurements help much more, because they are biometrically distinct from person to person – which is how face recognition technology works. The distance between the eyes, eyes to ears, eyes to nose, nose to mouth, and mouth (corner to corner) is identical, give or take a handful of pixels. The caveat to this is simply that what I did with these photos on my desktop computer isn't forensic science, it is informed research which, again, led me straight back to: her story could be true but might not be. This may sound frustrating, but this is what investigative work is really like and it is important to be honest about that. It's dull detail work, nothing like the movies, but those dull details inform both your investigative strategy and any forensic analysis you request. In short, I did the leg work and found the photographs did not leave me with facts or lies. They left me with maybe. Pamela's account is neither ruled in nor ruled out.

The photograph deals with who, but the second problem faced is where. Which is perhaps just as frustrating, if not more so. Robert Ben Rhoades drove for Empire Truck Lines out of Houston – they don't exist anymore, having been bought out, and nobody currently there has been able to provide information from thirty or more years ago. However, through Greg Cooper at the Cold Case Foundation, who worked the Rhoades case, I have the mapped trucking routes based on Rhoades' Empire driver logs for 1984, 1987, 1988, 1989, and 1990. These do nothing to confirm Pamela's account. In 1984, Rhoades was driving relatively local (in the grand scheme of America) routes which kept him circling Texas, Oklahoma, Arkansas, and Louisiana. There was a gap of three years, and he was back operating a loop in 1987, this time around Texas, Louisiana, Mississippi, and Alabama. It was not until 1988 he can be traced driving Florida, but the route ends in Chicago. In 1989 it ran as far up as Washington State but Florida had dropped off his map altogether. It was only in 1990 that his driving became truly trans-American. It turned out the Empire drivers logs work against Pamela's story and, to seemingly put a final nail in the coffin, the one thing a member of staff at Empire Truck Lines was able to tell me: they've never run routes on the thirty-eight-hour drive to Edmonton, Canada. But there is that gap in facts. A big glowing hole where 1985 should have been and it was Rhoades' wife, Debra Davis, who filled in that blank when speaking to

Veselka for the GQ article[2] in 2012. In the summer of 1985, Rhoades was not driving for Empire. He was, as it happens, working for an operation in Georgia, based on the I-95 itself – which puts his home-plate that year on the stretch running from Savannah in the North to Jacksonville, over the Florida border in the south. Most of the Georgia freight companies in that area, even over thirty years later, are still advertising the cross-country route to Edmonton. Suddenly, Pamela's story comes back from the dead and once again is walking around in limbo, where it might be true but might not.

This left me caught between a witness I believe is credible and surrounding facts which act both to support and contradict her story in equal measure. I had also made the safe decision to set aside her identification of Rhoades and her mention of the cash, grass, or ass sticker because she had clearly been open to the external influence of other sources over many, many years. This did not leave a lot of avenues open to shore up what she told me, so I decided on one last course of action.

The NaMus (National Missing and Unidentified Persons System) database[3], administered by the National Institute of Justice, is open for anyone to search. I use the system a lot, even train others to use it to, so I cracked my knuckles and entered the details I felt were pertinent. Namely, I was looking at the photograph of the girl in the truck on the basis it wasn't Pamela and searching for unidentified bodies which matched up with Rhoades year-by-year driver's logs from Empire Truck Lines. I set the criteria as: female, either white or American Indian/Alaskan Native, Adult pre-30, estimated year of death between 1984 and 1990, and found in Texas, Oklahoma, Arkansas, Louisiana, Mississippi, or Alabama. I kept the timeframe, based on the facts of Rhoades's truck routes, constrained to 1984 and 1987 to begin with, which gave me the selection of states. Of over

---

[2] https://www.gq.com/story/truck-stop-killer-gq-november-2012, The Truck Stop Killer, GQ Magazine, Vanessa Veselka, 24th October 2012

[3] https://namus.nij.ojp.gov/

thirteen thousand unidentified bodies listed in NaMus, the search returned only eight results and I felt a familiar flutter in my stomach: that instinct which says something might be there.

The first case was a female found in an abandoned building in a city location, which did not fit Rhoades' pattern. The second and third were discounted too for similar reasons. Number four was a different story. Case number PA87-061 was that of a dark-haired white female, aged twenty to twenty-one and found out in the sticks of Kingsbury, Guadalupe County on April 3rd 1987 - within spitting distance of the I-10 and only a couple of hours from Houston. It was close to Rhoades, I could feel that, but it still wasn't him. The logs had him over in East Texas the whole time, driving between Dallas and Houston before heading into the neighbouring Eastern states. Number five was out for the same reason, too far West, number six was back to being an urban centre, and seven did not fit the truck route either. I was starting to wonder what had sparked my instincts when I clicked the last record, PA84-0009. The young girl in the composite sketch was about fourteen or fifteen by my reckoning, though the record expanded the age range to twelve to twenty. Not all of her body was intact in the field where she was found, near Vidor, Texas on the 1st of January 1984. In the sketch she had shoulder-length brown hair but then I saw it - the thing which was there to be found. Her hair had been cut, according to the records, and was no more than two inches long as if it were growing back from being shaved off. Rhoades cropped his victim's hair. The location, near 1005 Ridgewood St, Vidor, was only yards from the I-10 and only fifteen minutes East of Beaumont. Rhoades dropped the bodies of his victims in secluded spots along his routes without going far off track. His 1984 driver logs took him directly along this route, but 1983 was another unfilled hole.

I shifted the search into missing persons, looking nationally for girls aged twelve to sixteen who had disappeared between October 1983 and December 31 that year. One case stood out, that of Sondra Kay Ramber – a brown-haired fourteen-year-old who disappeared from Santa Fe on October 26th.

Details are slim and there's some confusion between whether she vanished from home or while walking to school, so I decided to get in touch with the Institute of Forensic Sciences at Harris County who own the unidentified body case. I asked for whatever information they could provide on the deceased - the cause of death, and that mention of cropped hair - and to cross-check the records with Ramber's missing person case, to see if the medical examiner had noted a mole on the right cheek during the autopsy. These things normally take a long time to resolve, especially when the case papers have been bundled off to the archives as was the case here. In the end, the wait was only a day and Harris County were amazingly helpful, sending across the autopsy report on the deceased girl as a PDF.

Joseph A. Jachimczyk M.D. was the forensic pathologist who conducted the autopsy for Harris County on the 21st of April 1984. I knew straight away this meant the remains weren't just partial, they were skeletal. Four months was too long a time between the discovery and the medical examination for any other explanation. It was confirmed in black and white, additionally stating the cause of death could not be determined. Helpfully, though, this did rule out the Ramber missing person case as being connected, and the autopsy verified my thinking on why, stating death had occurred at least a year before. What little there was of the body arrived with the medical examiner in a carboard box, in what was noted as a "random array." The reporting officers map showed the bones were spread out over quite a large area in the field. The poor girl's remains were found in a pasture as a resident checked their fence-line after repair work. There was not much left of her – suspected to be due to animal predation – and the remains consisted of a skull but no mandible, some of the shoulders and ribs, and spine, most of the right arm but not the hand, and the left pelvis. Many of the teeth in the top half of the skull were missing – the front teeth noted as "post-mortem" absent, and the only anomaly found in X-ray were the fillings in teeth 13 and 14, meaning somebody had cared for the girl once, at least enough to take her to the dentist. A black nylon belt was found near the body, along with a green and white terry cloth Present Company blouse and some matted red-brown hair which was about two inches long and noted as being fine.

It wasn't a Rhoades case, just a badly worded NaMus record, but it was still a desperately sad tragedy. I adjusted the search criteria, shifting the date ranges, trying again and again, with and without the description of the clothing. Looking for girls with braces on their front teeth. All that came up was a handful of improbable matches, which I eliminated one by one. I turned back to the description of the girl in the photograph which started all this and came up with no useful matches in the unidentified bodies which might provide an alternative identity to Pamela as the girl in the photograph. Frustrated and left with nothing more to pursue -and no closure for the poor kid in the pasture - I eventually closed the browser and sat quietly for a while, gathering my thoughts. This stuff will haunt you if you don't take the time to process it before carrying on with the work.

Reviewing the facts around Pamela's account of her truck ride with Rhoades had not ruled out her version of events yet had not fully corroborated them. If she were to give that statement in a court environment it would be down to a jury to determine where it was true or not, beyond reasonable doubt. As an investigator it is not my job to make those determinations, only to pursue the evidence to its ends and put the result forward for consideration. What I personally think really doesn't matter but, if you were to ask for my professional opinion, I would simply say: I believe she had a truck ride with a man named Robert in 1985, she believes it was Robert Ben Rhoades, and there is no evidence available to me at this time which firmly contradicts her account.

Until I spoke with Pamela, the file of research on the Rhoades case with the photograph inside was just hard facts, court records, data, and some wild internet speculation. Afterwards, though, the case of Robert Ben Rhoades, The Truck Stop Killer came to life in all its darkness. And, sometimes, you must stare into the dark to understand the light.

COUNCIL BLUFFS

One hundred and thirty miles away from Des Moines, just a couple of hours if you take the I-80, lies Council Bluffs. Down in the south-west corner of Iowa facing the Missouri River and the Nebraska border, it is the most populated city in that part of the state. Up until the 1850s it was called Gainesville, originally the head of the thirteen-hundred-mile Mormon trail leading to Utah. It was also an intersection of the emigrant trails which lead out into the West and saw America grow ever outwards into the country we know today. The place has an interesting past and a surprising number of interrelated entries span from encyclopaedia to Wikis [4].

They say history is a tapestry but, in the case of Council Bluffs, it is one of the richest patchworks in North America. Across the river in Nebraska, about twenty miles further north, the original Council Bluffs sat at Fort Atkinson and got its name when the Corps of Discovery Expedition - led by Captain Lewis and Second Lieutenant Clark after the Louisiana Purchase - met the Otoe tribe in 1804. It wasn't until the 1830s, when the Chippewa, Ottawa, and Potawatomi tribes were forced to leave Chicago to make way for the incorporated city, that the Iowa side of the river became a reservation. The group were referred to as the members of the Council of Three Fires, the Pottawattamie being the largest of the three. Before finally arriving, they attempted to settle in the territory between Kansas and Missouri until that was bought out by settlers too. In truth, they had only been trying to avoid conflict with the Sioux, but American progress had other ideas. Led by Sauganash, the son of William Caldwell – an Irish immigrant who fought against American Rebels as a soldier in the British Indian Department during the revolutionary war – they arrived in their assigned reservation in

---

[4] https://en.wikipedia.org/wiki/Council_Bluffs,_Iowa, Council Bluffs, Wikipedia, CC BY-SA 3.0

late 1830s and established a village for which became known as Caldwell's Camp. The nearby fort personnel just called them the Bluff Indians.

Ravaged by the whiskey trade, the area was policed by the US Army operating out of Fort Croghan which was built in 1842 and, by 1846, the Pottawattamie had been forced out again. This time being pushed to Kansas. Then came the Latter-Day Saints - using the spot as a crossing point of the Missouri river - and its transformation from Caldwell's Camp to Kanesville (Thomas Kane was the man responsible for negotiating federal permits to encamp there over the 1846-47 winter and the two became the hub for outfitting the wagon trains of the Mormon Exodus). It was also the launching station of the Mormon Battalion during the Mexican-American war, and the first place where plural marriage was practiced. Then came the gold rush and the town changed shape again. In 1852 it was renamed Council Bluffs – the name it retains today as the heart of Pottawattamie County. Abraham Lincoln designated the city as the official starting point of the Transcontinental Railroad, finished in 1869 and Mile Zero is still marked by a golden spike at the junction of 21st Street and 9th Avenue. The spike itself was allegedly used in the promotion of the 1930s movie Union Pacific. There's one of the iconic and slightly haunted looking railway bridges crossing the river, the last connection point of Council Bluffs and the railroad which was completed in 1872. It's now the home of casinos, electronics, food processing, and even a Google server farm. It also holds a dubious record for high lead measurements in the air and several violations of the Clean Water Act. The quirkiest thing about it is the rotary jail, or Squirrel Cage, which was in use right until 1969. I'd never even heard of this kind of layout, where the cells are set over three storeys and are cranked around by a jailer until the cell door matches up with a doorway on the landing. It bemused me a little to hear that the cylinder mechanism was disconnected in 1960 but the jail itself remained in use for 9 years afterwards. It is exactly the kind of tortuous misery you would want to avoid if you were a criminal in the area while it was open. And Council Bluffs does have more than its fair share of crime and criminality.

Public data[5] shows motor vehicle theft, larceny, and property crime well above national averages between 1999 and 2017. Robbery statistics are in line with national averages but way above Iowa state's and Homicides are in an uncomfortable sandwich between the two trends lines, peaks and troughs in a roughly two-year cycle. There are some oddities though – and I say this as one of the few global experts with bona fides in sniffing out trouble with the crime figures.

Before I go on, I feel like I should probably explain, at least briefly. I joined the police in 2004, starting as a constable in Derbyshire, working as an intelligence officer and qualifying as a Sergeant before transferring to the Metropolitan Police in London in 2009. By 2013 I was working on a force-wide improvement programme having beaten down the Assistant Commissioner's door in 2012. It was there, carrying out analytical work for the top echelons of Specialist Crime and Operations, that I raised the alarm over the under-recording of serious offences. This put me in direct conflict with Scotland Yard, so I did the only thing I could do and sparked a select committee inquiry into the crime figure which saw police recorded crime stripped of its status as an official national statistic and led to permanent change in the way offences are recorded and reported. In turn, this also led to change in the way police whistle-blowers are dealt with on the orders of then Home Secretary Theresa May. If I listen back to the parliamentary speeches and news coverage now, it all feels distant. Like a voicemail message from the past.

"We are indebted to PC Patrick for his courage and speaking out in fulfilment of his duty to the highest standards of public service, despite

---

[5]https://www.macrotrends.net/cities/us/ia/council-bluffs/crime-rate-statistics#:~:text=Violent%20crimes%20are%20defined%20in,a%206.89%25%20decline%20from%202015, Macrotrends.net, Council Bluffs IA Crime Rate 1999-2017

intense pressures to the contrary," said Sir Bernard Jenkin, chair of the committee, in a clip broadcast across multiple channels and repeated in most of the national newspapers back then. The same quote is in the final parliamentary report itself, a permanent public record of what happened. I sometimes wonder if would do the same thing again. Ultimately, I think the answer is yes because I am awkward like that. Most importantly, the whole sorry affair left me with a skill set which doesn't really exist, because nobody wants to admit that is needed. Every now and then though, it does come in handy, and that unique experience does have a minor part to play in this story.

Rape offences in Council Bluffs, for example, start being recorded properly in 2013 with one-hundred and twenty-one cases per hundred thousand population which is four times the national average and nose-dived to thirty-eight cases per hundred thousand people – under the state and national average by 2017. Sheer drops like that are anomalous. It's not just rape offences. Assault plummeted from three times the national and state average in 2012 to an unusually low plateau below the averages, which has stayed stable at one-hundred and eleven case per hundred thousand people since 2015. Burglary followed an almost identical trajectory between 2013 and 2015 before escalating again by 2017. If you see a pattern of steep decline in one key area, it is generally indicative of good policing. If you see it in serious offences but not others it is either a good sign the figures are being fudged to meet targets or that under-reporting is taking hold due to an erosion in public trust or a failing policing strategy. I have a lot of questions about the Uniform Crime Recording system in America and will revisit them repeatedly with the Themis project, a software program I am developing which is designed to help smaller agencies capture crime data effectively and identify serial offending patterns across state and county lines. In the meantime, thoughts of a national crime review I did in Mexico a few years ago buzzed around in my head - in some states you could see corruption flowing from the election of certain officials and streaming down into the crime data. Where murders went down, accidental deaths leapt up in the public health data. You get the picture.

The 1977 annual release of Iowa Uniform Crime Reports[6] made available by NCJRS tells a good story about Council Bluffs too.

"While this report contains information both on the raw number of crimes reported and the rate of crime per 100,000 population, much more attention has been given to rates per population than to raw figures. The latter, obviously, are significantly affected by population, even within groupings of cities of a given size. Thus, based on raw figures, Davenport, with 6,834 reported Part I offenses in 1977, possesses a larger crime problem than Council Bluffs, which reported 5,599 offenses. Using rates per population, however, one finds that Council Bluffs, with 9,026.9 crimes per 100,000 population, possesses the highest crime rate for cities of more than 50,000 population, while Davenport's rate of 6,845.2 is below the average," it says. Part I crimes are the serious offences like burglary, rape, robbery, and murder. Even back then, Council Bluffs – which had the lowest population of the cities with over fifty thousand residents – had a significant crime problem, reporting the highest crime rates in the state, and had been above average for a few years.

There is good information which goes back even further too, covering the period between 1920 and 1941. I found a fascinating digital library entry in the form of a dissertation by Douglas Wersch[7], studying for a doctorate at Iowa State University. Written in 1992, it is entitled "Resisting The Wave: Rural Iowa's war against crime," and in it I found reference to a study of Iowa's rural offenders dated 1944 by an academic called B. Clinard. It read: "Clinard interviewed sixty Iowa Reformatory inmates who came from farms to determine the importance of mobility, "differential association" with

---

6 https://www.ojp.gov/pdffiles1/Digitization/52801NCJRS.pdf, US DOJ, Uniform Crime Reports Iowa 1977

7 https://lib.dr.iastate.edu/cgi/viewcontent.cgi?referer=https://www.google.com/&httpsredir=1&article=10965&context=rtd,

Resisting the wave: rural Iowa's war against crime, 1920-1941, Iowa State University, Wertsch D, 1992

criminal behaviour and "criminal social type and conception of self in the lives of rural offenders." His interviews disclose farm offenders to be unlike their urban counterparts, unusually mobile even though they do not see themselves as being so. Nomadic drifting and occupations like truck driving are common in all their backgrounds. They share an impersonal view of the world and revel in their "emancipation" from the confines of their farm life. Differential Association, defined as habitual social joining with criminals played no part in the lives of these farm offenders. Two thirds of them never associated with boys' gangs and an equal percentage were alone when first arrested. Most important, Clinard found that farm offenders "do not exhibit the characteristics of a definite criminal social type." Their criminal activity started after their teen years, long after the time when basic attitudes normally form." This neatly took me back to the reason I was even reading about Council Bluffs in the first place: Robert Ben Rhoades, the seemingly amicable trucker who, it is claimed, gave Pamela Milliken a ride in the 1980's. An atypical criminal and a nomad.

He was born on November 22nd 1945 as the second of four children in Council Bluffs. He grew up there and attended the Thomas Jefferson High School which first opened its doors in 1922. By the limited accounts about his growing up which are out there, he seemed to be a normal kid - playing football, wrestling, singing in the choir, and even attending French club. That is conflicted, however, by statements in many of the public reports on him which say he was arrested for tampering with a vehicle in 1961 (when he was sixteen) and again a year later for public fighting. He graduated high school in 1964. In a few of the profiles of Rhoades on the internet, it states he graduated from Monticello High School. This isn't quite right; the school was Thomas Jefferson and the 1964 Yearbook "The Monticello." Council Bluffs library has a copy of it online[8] - it opens with a dedication to John F

---

[8] https://www.councilbluffslibrary.org/archive/files/original/a24bfd5f909a8b7c4cf761cb18ff7a23.pdf, The Monticello '64, Thomas Jefferson High School Yearbook, Free Public Library, Council Bluffs, Ia 373C-C83t

Kennedy. The colour scheme of the book is a vibrant orange and a deep brown, very much of its day, but the most striking thing in the faculty pages, where Mrs Ralston, science, page 26, and Miss Wolfe, English, page 29, both struck me as having obvious physical similarities to people Rhoades would later meet, kidnap, and kill. The whole Rhoades clan appears in the book too, and I started to think it was the wrong year, wrong school, or wrong town altogether when I found him. *Rhoades, Bob. Vocational, Football, Wrestling, Choir, Boys' Glee Club, French Club.* There he was on Page 216 - dark coloured suit, neat pencil tie, thick-rimmed black spectacles, neatly combed hair on the young version of a face which hasn't really changed shape over the years. That picture of him was not previously out there in any of his many listings and profiles on the internet, I had found something new. Unsurprisingly, given a clear military presence in the school, Rhoades joined the Marines on graduation but by 1968 had been dishonourably discharged, allegedly for his involvement in a robbery. He tried college and dropped out, tried to join law enforcement but was rejected – a pattern which repeats in several serial killer cases, as the craving for authority is a common trait. His work history after the military was a mess of low paid jobs, from supermarkets to warehouses, until he settled on truck driving. He married in Council Bluffs, divorced, married, had a child again, and divorced again, then finally found himself in Houston, Texas. It is not clear when he moved from Council Bluffs to Texas, but public genealogy site searches give a long list of relatives in the area, which is where he met and married divorced mother of three Debra Davis as the mid-1980s approached. FBI Profiling legend Roy Hazelwood, guiding light to the Cold Case Foundation's Greg Cooper, interviewed Debra for his book *The Evil That Men Do*[9].

Born in Talahoma, Tennessee in 1957, according to Hazelwood's book, Debra was the youngest of six sisters and was raised in a working-class

---

[9] The Evil That Men Do: FBI Profiler Roy Hazelwood's Journey Into the Minds of Sexual Predators, Roy Hazelwood with Stephen G. Michaud, St Martin's Press, ISBN: 978-0-312-19877-0

family, moving to Houston, Texas when she was four. At the age of six she was molested by an eighteen-year-old neighbour who moved away the following week. Debra became withdrawn, self-loathing, and suffered periods of depression throughout her life. She married her high school sweetheart at 17, gave birth to her third child in 1981 and made a serious attempt at suicide in 1983 using medication. In the wake of that, and too poor to divorce, she shared her residence with her ex-husband even though it was over. She met Robert Rhoades, who introduced himself as Dusty and was dressed as a pilot, in a club. He was charming and she fell in love with him quickly because he treated her well and listened when she spoke.

Over time, Rhoades admitted he was a truck driver, not a pilot, and told her something about his past which isn't found in The Monticello. He said his father had been a soldier, stationed in West Germany when Rhoades was born, and returned after a few years taking up work as a firefighter in Council Bluffs. By 1964, the year Robert was graduating, he said his father was arrested for molesting Robert's cousins – one male and one female. He then allegedly committed suicide. It has taken a little while to unpick some of the family history because the detail is light and largely not source-referenced across the internet, the yearbook being a prime example - as if nobody every bothered to look properly and just contented themselves to repeat whatever was already written there. All I had to go on were the names Ben and Betty Rhoades and it took about four minutes to discount Betty completely. Ben Rhoades apparent gravestone[10], in the Fairview cemetery in Council Bluffs, shows a date of death as February 24th 1966 but doesn't give a cause. It just states his service in World War 2 and gives his age as fifty-two. After painstakingly trawling genealogy websites, I was able to piece most of his life together.

Ben Rhoades was born on March 13th 1913 to Elmer Rhoades and Bessie Bailey. He was one of thirteen children, closest in age to his younger brother

---

10 https://www.findagrave.com/memorial/35169528/ben-rhoades/flower, Find A Grave

Harry, whose nickname was Dusty and who moved to Florida in the late 1950s. Ben enlisted on August 14th 1944 at Fort Leavenworth and became a fireman in Council Bluffs after the war ended and he left the military. He married Fay Helms on Lake Manawa at some point in the early 1930s and their first son, Roger, was born on April 9th 1933. Robert Rhoades was born in 1945 and their younger brother Richard was born in 1948. Judging by photographs in various family trees, war changed Ben. By the sixties he had lost his skinny frame and bulked up, his expression was serious, and he wore his hair in a military buzzcut - Robert is the dead spit of him. Before the war, he was skinny, floppy haired, and less stern. He collected coins most of his life, which Fay kept long after his death – this was last mentioned in 1998. Fay apparently used to hang out in speakeasys, at least according to happy family rumour. She was also the first woman hired at the Union Pacific railroad during World War Two and even applied to work on airplanes – though she ended up packing munitions in Nebraska. According to the family tree, she loved music and taught kids to play instruments. Something wasn't right though. You could see that in family photographs of the family together in what must have been the fifties. She looked haunted. The boys however, Robert in particular, seemed happy. There's one photo of them all together on the steps of a brick building with Robert Ben Rhoades smiling ear to ear in a checked suit jacket. Beaming despite an obviously broken left wrist. There's nothing about suicide. Nothing about molestation at the end of the trail. Just an obituary and a service date, February 28th 1966. The hymns at Ben's funeral were Just a Close Walk With Thee and It Is No Secret. The only other thing I can find in the local papers about him is a May 10th 1953 article about his ten years in the Fire Department and his wish that everyone would drive as carefully as he drove the fire truck.

Robert intimated to Debra Davis, Hazelwood wrote, that his father had also molested him. In many ways, this would make sense of some of his teenage behaviour. The alleged lashing out. The failure to find North. Even, potentially, the collapse of the first two marriages and his later actions. But none of this can be confirmed. My gut feel, from a policing point of view, is that there was something wrong in the household - the photographs tell that story - but they can't say *what*, which leaves us with the third-party account of what a convicted murderer once said, much the same as Pamela's. It is compelling, looking at the totality of the situation and having a much better understanding of the family tree than ever before, but Debra's words are still only hearsay.

Casting the net wider still, in hope of finding some record of the child abuse allegations against Ben Rhoades, I came across something else instead. Iowa implemented the sex offender registry some thirty years after Ben Rhoades' death - in 1995, in the wake of the Jacob Wetterling Crimes Act which has since been updated and amended by new legislation in the form of Megan's Law in 1996 and the Adam Walsh Child Protection and Safety Act in 2006. Jacob Wetterling was kidnapped, sexually assaulted, and murdered in Minnesota in 1989. He was 11 years old. It was not until 2016, after DNA from another case led to an arrest, that Danny James Heinrich confessed and led police to Jacob's remains in Paynesville.

The Iowa registry[11] is accessible online and a quick search on Council Bluffs brings up a list 106 currently registered sex offenders in the central city alone. The local and regional news is full of cases dating back years, as if Council Bluffs has something in the water beyond the pollution the EPA worry about, but there is nothing at all about Ben Rhoades. So, I searched the cold cases databases which are dotted across the internet and easy enough to find. One jumped out at me, but not because of Ben.

Seventeen-year-old Judith Kaylene Pleas was reported missing on August 10th 1973 in Council Bluffs and her decomposed body was found strangled and discarded in a cornfield just outside the city limits in October the same year. A young suspect was arrested for this, convicted even, but this was

---

[11] https://www.iowasexoffender.gov, Iowa Sex Offender Registry

overturned in 1975 by Iowa's supreme court[12] and the case remains open today. Council Bluffs Police Department did not cover itself in glory in the investigation, keeping the mentally vulnerable suspect Steven Lybarger awake for a prolonged period – twenty-six and a half hours - having initially extradited him from San Francisco for cheque frauds. He was polygraphed and interrogated over a period of nine and a half hours, with a hard interview at the very end "breaking him." The confession which came from that is clearly coerced and utterly unreliable, and the court was so peeved they dragged the specific section of Lybarger's interview out in the judgment: "As far as anybody else being with me, I can't — I don't think we did. I just don't know whether I did or didn't. From there was night, I guess. I don't know if I had my car or my bike but probably a car, I don't know, my car was screwed up...It might have been a bike. I remember being out there. We were goofing around, I think it was my car." The Lybarger kid was not a credible suspect at all, and Ben Rhoades had passed away almost a decade earlier, but what leapt out at me was the method, the disposal, and the location.

Robert Ben Rhoades' first marriage, it turns out, happened before 1970 in Council Bluffs but by February 18th 1970 he was married for the second time. It was in this relationship he became a father in late 1971. This goes against a whole host of internet entries on his background and goes to show that you really cannot just take any of it at face value. But it did lead me to understand that Robert's long-haul trucking career might not have started until the later 70s, so he was apparently local at the time of the Pleas murder. Rhoades always claimed to have committed his first murder in the mid-seventies, though he has never given specific details, and I cannot help but wonder if this Iowa cold case was it. Judith Pleas' smiling face, framed by shoulder-length brown hair, stared back sat me from the screen for a long time.

---

12 https://iowacoldcases.org/wp-content/uploads/2011/02/judith-pleas-supreme-court-decision-3-19-75.pdf, Iowa Cold Case, Pleas J, Supreme Court Decision 3-19-75

By the time Robert met Debra Davis, he certainly had a well-developed need to be in control and had mastered the techniques to facilitate it, which indicates practice. Process refinement. In Debra's own words, as their relationship blossomed he would treat her like his personal "paper doll" - dressing her exactly how he wanted to her to look. Staging every aspect of her appearance, from lingerie to make-up. Taking his time because these are the aspects he had come to master and revel in. He also started financially supporting Debra, making her feel protected in a world which had repeatedly kicked her. Nowadays, all of this would be flagged as coercive control and trigger several alarms. Back then, the world was still trying to find the legs which would eventually lift thousands of women out of domestic violence and elevate the issue to a matter of international debate and consensus.

His controlling nature became more evident as time went on. He took her to a swinger's club and eventually persuaded her to engage in group sex. She drew the line at BDSM, rejecting his introduction of devices such as nipple clamps into their bedroom, though her rejections did not stop him from bringing an array of items home to show her. Their home was full of violent pornography and he racked up huge phone bills on sex lines. He even ordered a "love slave" to turn up at her door on his orders. By 1986 Debra knew Rhoades's dark side intimately and she could see his addiction to pain and suffering went beyond sex toys and books. When she was ill he would lie with her, just to watch her suffer, and when she was hospitalised due to Lupus, the pain she was in aroused him so much he clambered into the hospital bed to have sex with her. She subsequently left him, or tried to, and the charm offensive began with carefully crafted love letters while he was away on a solid drive of three months. He sensed her growing confident and independent without him and pulled out all the stops to keep control. It worked. When he returned, they married within two days, on St Valentine's Day. The marriage only lasted a few years.

Debra is very clear about Rhoades' ultimate fetish. "His thing was control," she told Roy Hazelwood. Even when drunk he never lost it. My opinion is he was really his own paper doll. A carefully put together composition where a person should have been. And you can see this flowing through almost every ounce of him. He broke his arm in an industrial accident and the first thing he did on waking from graft surgery was tear the IV from his arm so he could never lose his grip on himself. I read this as being at least partly driven by concern about what he would admit while his inhibitions were lowered by medication. He stayed away from the truck for a year while he recovered from that injury and the end of his marriage to Debra came when his mask finally fell away in 1989. She refused to let Rhoades have anal sex with her, so he raped her and completely lost control of himself, revealing the animal he had otherwise kept tethered. He violently beat her then took himself off to the living room when she refused to give him the satisfaction of breaking. As a parting shot, she hit him with a baseball bat and left with her belongings.

For Debra, it was over until a year or so later. Despite everything, *in spite* of everything, she took the circumstances life had thrown at her and refused to be a victim. Rather than be controlled, she set fire to Rhoades' paper doll and became a speaker on domestic violence and a counsellor to abused women.

Council Bluffs, that small high-crime city in the south-western corner of Iowa, has always been the start of a journey, Mile Zero. It should not really come as a surprise that the trail of the Truck Stop Killer began there too.

- Broken Roads -

ARE YOU LOST?

After exploring Robert Ben Rhoades early life in Council Bluffs, putting his family history straight, I was left curious about that area of the United States. I was also deeply disturbed by the apparent ease with which American girls either disappear or are left unidentified in fields across the country. I wanted to understand. Wanted to see if the societal undercurrent, the sheer scale of America, and the lack of welfare safety net were combining to create this perfect storm, leaving lost souls in its wake. That unspoken call was answered by Della, who contacted me through the Cold Case Live site. While not specifically related to Rhoades, she told me a story which paints a picture of the vulnerable side of America which serial killers like the truck driver exploit only too easily.

"I work in a government position," Della told me. "And it's…basically I work for a mental health hospital. Oh gosh. This is always the hard part James. It's talking about myself. I can hide from it all day long. Currently, I basically just work, I have a family - a husband and three children, two of them grown and the other one about to graduate high school. He's in his last semester. I'm just living my life."

A blond-haired, blue-eyed American Girl, Della's upbringing did not really raise any alarms or set out a clear path which led directly to where it did. She grew up in Omaha, Nebraska having moved there with the whole family when she was ten years old. "We travelled out of a back of a station wagon," she said. "If you could imagine in the back end of the 70s, my dad and four blonde, blue-eyed girls in a panel station wagon, traveling all over the United States. Mostly on the West Coast, up and down there and most of the states on the western end of the US. So that was kind of an interesting little life and then we just settled in Omaha when I was ten. I grew up pretty much in Omaha all my life and did a little bit of traveling when I got older - to Colorado -and that was really about it."

Omaha may well be in a different state to Council Bluffs but, as Della explained to me, the state line is rather blurry due to the local geography.

"Council Bluffs is, well...if you're in downtown Omaha like when I was growing up, put it like this, the bars in Omaha would close it one, so you could leave and the bars in Iowa would close at two. You could literally leave at last call in Omaha and get to Council Bluffs just right across the bridge, over the Missouri River, and be there in time for a couple of drinks and then last call. I guess it depended on how fast you drove, if you were driving - though that's not very responsible in hindsight. But it's literally a stone's throw, right across the bridge." Local knowledge is always more important than research – that option we all seem to default to in the digital age, which would tell you it's eleven minutes in a car to traverse the four and a half miles between the two places. It is what you might call a modernized city, Omaha. Similar in size to Atlanta – both heading towards a population of five hundred thousand people and a long way from the handful of folks now living in the old western boom towns like Tombstone, down in Arizona. Omaha was a perhaps unexpected early success in telemarketing, becoming a hub for that industry when it was in its infancy. I wanted to know more, to get a feel for this interconnected area and its odd-looking crime statistics, so I asked her whether the area could be described as safe.

"It still has a small town feel but it also at the same time has a big town feel. I guess it just depends on if you look at it as a whole – I mean it feels like a big city but, depending on the neighbourhood or part of town that you're from, it feels like a small town," Della told me. "Where I grew up, to me, was safe. I grew up in the south Omaha area. I just think, in my opinion, I just don't feel safe anywhere unless I've been there and know the area. Like, even today, if I don't know the area on the other side of the town I'm living in now, you know, as a grown woman I won't go over there alone. I just I don't feel safe no matter where it is."

This is where Della's story takes its twist, having safely lured you in with her idyllic, summer-coloured childhood, the settled family life, the small town feel and its innocuous telemarketing successes. She was a normal kid with a warm life, and she fell off the edge. Nobody was there to catch her.

"I know with serial killers and a lot of their victims, they depend on easy prey. And a lot of their easy prey are, you know, prostitutes or working girls and that sort. And it just so happens I am one of those girls," she said, matter of fact. "Previously, you know. I have a history and for the grace of God but there I go, you know, still to this day I'm lucky I'm not in that life anymore. I've you know, escaped a few of those situations myself." She listened to the Out of The Cold podcast, catching the Council Bluffs episode almost by random accident. "It's rare that anyone does any podcasts on my area, so immediately my thoughts went to Deb, I don't know how popular her case right now in Omaha but, to me, it's still a really big case. It will always stay with me until it's solved. Deb was one of my friends. At the time I had come back to Omaha from Denver, I believe it was around 1998 or 99 and I had met her probably a year after I got back. She was just one of those little ladies that you just kind of you want to draw her in and you want to take care of her, you know. I've always had this thing…of course, it's weird, but even in the seedier world it's like high school. You have the girls you get along with and you have the girls that you don't get along with. And that was just one of those girls that I liked, and you just wanted to protect her. That's just how I felt with her. She was cute and adorable. I felt like she was someone that people would take advantage of, just given her situation and choices."

I had heard this exact psychology many times before, explained to me by the girls working the streets in Peartree where I learned how to police. Whatever the situation, humans will generally still behave in the way they are socialised to behave. Our nature is to survive but our nurture, at least in western cultures, is to establish community and pecking orders. The understanding of this is littered across psychological study, from Moscovici's theory of Collective Common Sense (essentially how we define norms through our social interactions), to Solomon Asch's paradigm of social conformity which showed that people will go to extremes to fit in within a social group.

"Deb was a working girl as well," Della continued. "She was addicted to crack cocaine. And so, she did…She was a…I hate the word: prostitute, so we'll use Sex Worker, it's the more modern word, I suppose. She was a sex worker. And she did that to make money for to purchase crack cocaine. So yeah, that's what her issue was, along with all of us, the rest of us out there basically. I don't really know whatever situation had gotten her to where she was, she would just say that's where she was, you know, and we just kind of looked out for each other."

Deb was Debra Ann Gutierrez Barajas, a brunette who disappeared in Omaha on May 25th 2006. She was last seen heading towards Park Avenue in Leavenworth. Della told me that Deb had been released on bail close to the time she disappeared.

"She had gotten picked up; I don't know what her charges were. At the time, could be any anywhere from failure to appear on a previous case or a sex worker ticket, anything like that," Della said. "But her bail was small, but it looks like this is where it gets weird, because the guy that had gotten her out of jail was a manager to this big apartment slash low-income housing which was not far from Council Bluffs. That guy had bailed her out and said she was able to stay in one of the empty apartments that were there. She had a friendship with this guy, I guess. So, he would let her stay in an empty apartment when she needed somewhere to go. The police were already looking into him because his wife had been killed, like I want to say about fifteen or twenty years prior, and she was found in a barrel. They always suspected him of doing it, but I believe they eventually got near more evidence, to where they could actually file charges against him."

The man who bailed Debra out was Thomas Tomich, a building manager at the Rorick Apartments in Omaha. He divorced his wife Lois in 1981 and killed her in 1983, after she embarked on a relationship with his brother. There was a history of domestic violence between the pair but, after she was reported missing by her father, there was no physical evidence to link Thomas to her disappearance. That was until twenty years later, when her body was discovered in a barrel by men foraging for mushrooms in 2006. Her secret coffin was a fifty-five-gallon drum, filled with eight hundred pounds of construction grade concrete, linked to Tomich by his employment at the time she was murdered. Police initially identified Lois by comparing her description and clothing to the original missing person reports and later confirmed it with a comparative DNA sample taken from her daughter. The case was handled by Pottawattamie County officials and the autopsy showed she had been strangled with a metal coat hanger – an item which was found inside the barrel.

"Deb was bailed out of jail and she was staying at that apartment building," Della told me. "But then she came up missing and her family had filed a missing person's report for her. I believe it was like six months later I heard, as I had already left when I'd gotten sober in 2003. So, once I got out of that world, I just completely cut everyone off. I think it was like six months later that she was found. Now, when she was found they were looking for Thomas at about the same time for his wife's murder. I think there were either one or two other girls that had been found murdered or were missing and they were trying to link him to those. It ended up where they could not link him to Deb's murder, but he ended up jumping off the Rorick apartment buildings and committed suicide rather than go to prison."

Tomich really did commit suicide by jumping off the roof of the Rorick apartments on November the 16th 2006, the day after his wife's remains were formally identified, and it was at this point the local police began to look at him in relation to Debra's missing person case. She wasn't quite missing though. Her remains were found in a ravine northwest of Glenwood in Iowa. Two days before Tomich jumped, on November the 14th. The ravine is about half an hour from Omaha if you cross the bridge and drive south on the I-29 from Council Bluffs. This location was only a few miles away from the ditch were another Omaha sex worker, twenty-five-year-old Brianne

Flowers – also known as Brianne Smith - was found dead on June 10th 2006. She went missing a month before Deb. Tomich was linked to Deb by both the Rorick building and the two-hundred and fifty dollar bail he paid for her on May the 16th and Flowers' husband confirmed Tomich was known to Brianne and several other sex workers. However, while Lois's case was closed and attributed to Thomas, the cases of both Deb and Brianne remain open and can be found on the Iowa cold cases website[13]. The coward who threw himself off the Rorick apartments rather than face his consequences is still considered a person of interest in both murders. There are countless other stories of serial offences against sex workers in the area, including that of the brutal rapist Todd Mills - a volunteer firefighter who raped two prostitutes at gunpoint in Omaha in 2010 and pled guilty to three more sex offenses in Council Bluffs in 2012. Mills drove his victims to remote area north of Council Bluffs to carry out truly horrific offenses, which included raping one woman with a gun barrel. For his Nebraska crimes, he was sentenced to one hundred and forty years in prison, and another fifty in Iowa on top of that.

Della herself had been on the receiving end of savage treatment and learned to trust her instincts to keep herself safe in the hardest possible way.

"In Colorado, I had a gun put to my head," she told me. "I'm at a car lot. You think you're safe in those situations because it was his place of work. You're not. Just because it's somewhere that they're familiar with doesn't make it any safer. No safer for you, it only makes it safer for them. I was really lucky to get out of that situation. I've been beat up several times. I've been raped multiple times in. Yes, you can be raped if you're a sex worker, I don't care what anybody says. I've had a knife put to my throat in Omaha a couple of times. And of course been beat up in Omaha. Yeah, I can't tell you how many times. You know, you don't know who you're getting in a car with. You don't know whose house you're going into. Your gut is never ever

---

[13] IowaColdCases.org

wrong. Ever. If you feel something wrong in your gut, go, go, go. Walk away, run away."

I've seen these stories. Investigated similar cases. The reality of it lurks in almost every town and city. It is painful to know that, for all our advancements in technology, this is everyday life for women worldwide. And the background reasons they end up at risk are often similar. The same can be said of the system defects: the way that crimes aren't properly recorded or investigated, leaving suspects free to offend and again; the lack of budget which leads to rape kits and forensic samples being left untested for years, producing the same result; the attitude of some investigators towards sex workers and the perception that when they say rape, they just mean they haven't been paid. There are signs of change, of course - the attitudes of detectives are shifting because of training for one, and significant progress has been made in processing rape kits – but that can never fix the past. I talked with Della about life events. What led her to sex work. Her story is that same one I had heard countless times before. And that weighs on me.

"When I lived out in Colorado, that's where the lifestyle kind of started happening for me on accident. It was because of a bad relationship that I was in. I'd gotten really bad into the alcoholism. The guy that I was in this relationship with was very abusive and, you know, emotionally, physically, they just kind of tear you down. You think you just can't do any better. Blah, blah, blah, you know, all that, you know, the history that comes with the abuse. Oh, you wouldn't believe how fast that spirals," Della said. "Man, that relationship started actually in Omaha. And I just don't know what drives a person, whether female or male doesn't matter, that when you do find out that that person is abusive you still stay with them. I look back at myself and I'm like, how did I ever, ever fall, you know? How much I must have felt bad for me not to think of myself but this man. I was abused that much. And I went back, and I would keep going back until I was beat down physically and emotionally enough that I just did not care what happened."

I could have been speaking to any one of the thousands of domestic abuse victims I have dealt with and taken statements from over the years. Even a cursory look at the statistics section of the National Coalition Against Domestic Violence website[14] is enough to break your heart on your best day. A quarter of women experience some form of domestic abuse and violence caused by an intimate partner accounts for around fifteen percent of all crime in the US. This saddened me, in part because it further deconstructs these safe notions of perfect, enlightened democratic societies we often hide behind the flags of. That comfort blanket gets torn away from you quickly when you start policing, which is why so many law enforcement personnel end up scarred by cynicism, jading their dealings with others as exposure compounds over a few decades. In the main, however, all this tells you something grim about humans in general: our societies can be separated by thousands of miles, but the awful things people do to one another manifest in the same ways again and again, and always have. The spiral is important too, because it weaves into situational behaviour and the impact of adaptation to new norms – those core elements of psychology which underpin everything. As normal changes, what people will do and accept adapts along with it, leading to increasingly chaotic responses and skewed compliance. Addiction and substance abuse is a heavy foot on the accelerator, removing inhibitions and clouding judgement, creating further distortion which erodes both decision-making ability and that most fundamental thing of all: hope.

"We all have choices and we think each choice we can make consciously, you know, until we can't," Della continued. "That's where all that came to one day. It was in June 1994, when OJ was all over the news. And I remember the TVs, and everything being focused on him in his Bronco. This ex-boyfriend and I were out at a bar, and we had gotten into an argument, of course we had, because we were drinking and I had went home, and I

---

14 https://ncadv.org/

thought everything was going to be okay. Well, apparently, he thought he might pull a legendary OJ move and he busted in through our basement door. We lived in a ground floor apartment. And he busted in and took a piece of the glass and came to my throat with it. And luckily the neighbours intervened and called the police and he fled. Well, he came back later that night. And of course, I forgave him. And he says, well, let's move to Colorado that'll make everything better. Oh, sure, you know, of course I agreed. But it did not make anything better. It just made things worse. And it isolated me even more from my family, which is exactly where he wanted me."

Thirty years later, we finally seem to have a much better understanding of coercive control and the role isolation plays in increasing risks in domestic abuse situations, but there is no point pretending these patterns of behaviour are not still recognisable. The lockdown year of the pandemic resulted in increases in domestic violence too, directly connected to increased isolation. Many victims were left unable to access the services which help protect them, and children were taken out of schools, where they are clearly visible to the professionals who know when something is going on. We have not fixed this problem. It hasn't gone away. When people such as Della tell their stories, they are not just historical accounts of a different world, these stories are the mirror we all need to stare into until nothing stares back.

"I got a job. And the first, you know, first pay check, we got that…I got that, of course, because he's not gonna work. We went out and celebrated and of course, ended up fighting," Della spoke more softly now, with this odd kind of bemusement, as if she still can't believe how quickly her slide down the hill happened. "I woke up the next morning with a dollar in my pocket. He had left me, and I took the bus downtown trying to look for him. But I couldn't find him. So, I thought I'd take the bus back to the area from where I came earlier that day, where we had stayed the night before in a motel. I'm walking down the road, this is like the main road in this part of Colorado that we're in and it was kind of dusk out when this car pulls off to a side road. He keeps hitting his brakes so the lights flash. And I'm like, well, maybe this guy is lost - I was extremely naive to this stuff. I don't have anything better to do, so I walk up to this stranger, to this car, and I go up to his driver's door and I'm like, are you lost?"

That simple question opened this whole new chapter in Della's life. A much darker one. "He's like, no! Do you want to ride somewhere? And I'm like, I really don't have anywhere to go. No thanks. And he's like, well get in we'll just drive around and have a beer. And I'm like okay, that sounds fine. So, I get in and we're driving around and this guy is like making these sexual comments and hinting around and, and in my head. I'm freaking out and I'm like: Oh my god, I'm about to be you know, assaulted or something. I'm gonna die. You know? And, finally, he just blurted out, he goes: will you have sex with me for fifty bucks? and I'm stunned. I'm completely floored. I've never been asked this before. And I think to myself well, here I am in Colorado. I know not a soul here. I have nowhere to go. I have nowhere to sleep. So, I said you have a condom? I ended up making enough money that night to go back to Omaha to my family, and I never spoke to that again for a long time."

Where I grew up, in a small town in East Midlands of England, drug use is common. When I started in the police, I very quickly came across people I had known from being out in town at the weekend, many of them ravaged by crack and heroin addiction. One guy, who used to be in an all-weekend clubbing group, was one of the first burglars I happen to have caught in a garden. I also once walked into the police station for a night shift and got ribbed by another officer because he met my "girlfriend." She was someone I knew from school, who had fallen into heroin addiction because of a bad relationship and eventually become a sex worker. Talking with Della brought all of it back. I had not thought about any of it for years.

"Drugs destroy you from the inside out. They literally destroy everything. And that's all you have left, it's the quickest way to make money by doing the most degrading thing you can ever imagine. And that's putting yourself out there to be vulnerable," Della said. "I actually got pregnant in 2003. I was off and on again, trying to get sober. I just had enough of the life you know, I was tired. In the beginning, you might think it's fun. To me though, the sex work was never fun. It is the most humiliating thing I have ever had to do. The first time I did it as a means of survival. Just to get home. All I wanted to do was get home that first time. And then once I made the mistake of telling the boyfriend, when he came crawling back, it became a way to support us. And then when we broke up it became about self-support. I had started crack-cocaine back up then and that's when it becomes it's no longer a choice. Because you're so addicted to the cocaine, you're not controlling what's happening to you anymore. And people can often sit there and say, well, that's, you always have a choice. And I'm like, no. Go smoke crack for a year and come back and tell me, you have a choice."

You can escape addiction, of course. If you have the desire to do so and get the right support. I've seen it happen with one of the first sex workers I ever developed as an intelligence source. She got clean and even got her children back over the course of the five years that I served in Derbyshire. I still remember the first time I met her, handing over my coffee on a bitter winter's night because I didn't know what else to do - telling her she should find a way out because she deserved not to be stood on that corner. But she did not just wake up one day and it was all over. It took years, the intervention of multiple agencies and services, and numerous slips. Della did the same eventually, against the odds I have to say, but she took ownership of her addiction and her lifestyle, then worked herself back to a point where making a choice was possible. Unapologetically too.

"I conquered that bitch for, for lack of a better explanation," Della said, her natural toughness on full display. "I got sober in 2003 and I gave birth to my son. June 20th was my original sobriety date. Unfortunately, though I did use some - I mean, compared to spending four or five hundred dollars a day on crack prior to pregnancy, I guess I was spending only fifty a week while I was pregnant. None of it is forgivable, mind you. None of it is justifiable in any way whatsoever. But I did ease up on the whole thing. Social services got notified because I told the hospital: you're going to find I test positive for cocaine and so will my son. You know, and that's a really hard thing to admit is to tell them you're positive for drugs and you're pregnant and giving birth. He went to foster care and I had to get, quote unquote, my shit together."

The birth of her son was a transformational moment, in which Della rose above her circumstances. But in her telling of how she overcame, I finally saw how she fell to begin with: a martial breakdown and a bitter custody fight. Over the years, a tendency has developed to over-simplify, leading to misallocation of public resources. Gateway Drug Theory is a good example of this, walking budget allocation up a garden path for a long time by focusing attention on a substance rather than people and underlying circumstances. Had it been the other way, we might have drawn a more direct line to loss of employment, family breakdown, and financial problems as risk markers for negative behavioural choices and funded safety net interventions instead. When you do not have a need for sub-economies to rise in the absence of welfare protections, you don't have to fight wars on drugs because the industry behind them has no market forces to prey on. At the human level, if we remove the incentives for people to destroy themselves and forget their problems, they are less likely to do it. It is a mess, but not an irretrievable one.

"I will let you know I have two older children," Della continued. "I lost them in my divorce back in '90. It was '94 that I met the boyfriend after I was divorced in 1992 from my first husband. He ended up getting custody of my two older kids and he would never let me see them. He didn't follow the custody arrangement or the visitation arrangement. That's where I started drinking. And then, of course, my scheduled visits would stop. I didn't go because he wasn't letting me go. And I didn't bring it up to the judge. So that's where my drinking spiralled and it was hard," she said. It is almost an understatement really, alcohol addiction is more common that

- Broken Roads -

most of us care to admit - leading to almost one hundred thousand deaths a year in America, shortening lives of those trapped with it by an average of nearly thirty years according to the CDC[15]. "It's not, it's not easy to just quit something cold turkey but I'm a strong woman," Della added. "That's one thing I did learn. I thought, you know, through that one relationship that I had over those years with that guy, I will never to this day understand how I let someone treat me that bad, because I am not that weak. I'm a strong, strong alpha. I got through so much. I have prevailed over so much. I've done so much. Never will get that. And I got custody back of my youngest boy within a year. We fight, of course, we're parent and child, but we're living a perfectly normal life. He's doing great in school; he doesn't have any signs of it affecting him mentally or physically. He came out just fine."

What is truly astounding about Della is that she didn't just stop at leaving sex work, overcoming addiction, and settling down to be a mother. She came out of that situation swinging.

"My passion has always been with the criminal justice field, believe it or not," she told me. "I've always admired law enforcement. I've always admired homicide detectives. It's just stuff I've always wanted to do. And obviously, I never pursued that because of obvious reasons. Which is always something you know, that's going to kick me in the butt. So, I went on to get an associate degree, and a bachelor's degree and a master's degree in criminal justice. I went and did a short internship with them Dr. Mary Dudley, she was the medical examiner in Jackson County, Missouri. And I was able to hang out with her for a weekend. She invited me to her house. And she let me go and not actually assist on autopsies - I didn't do any cutting - but I got to hold, you know, the parts, I guess you could say. That was, I don't know, if you've ever had a moment in your life where you have walked into

---

[15] https://www.cdc.gov/alcohol/fact-sheets/alcohol-use.htm#:~:text=Alcohol%20Use%20and%20Your%20Health,-Espa%C3%B1ol%20(Spanish)&text=Drinking%20too%20much%20can%20harm,an%20average%20of%2029%20years, Alcohol Use and Your Health, Centers for Disease Control and Prevention.

a room and the clouds parted and the angels started singing. That was my moment in the autopsy room, you know, it's that kind of stuff that I've always wanted to do. Unfortunately, the sad thing is Nebraska's is so antiquated - we still run on a coroner system - and I have lack of experience and age plays a factor, so by the time I graduated with my master's the odds were kind of stacked against me career-wise. If I find something in those fields anywhere, that'd be amazing. I want to be able to utilise that information that I have up in my head. To be able to get any experience in that to be able to help in any way, in whatever capacity, that would just be bonus."

Speaking with Della was as inspirational as it was upsetting. Having talked about all the vulnerabilities which make people ideal targets for serial offenders like Tomich, Mills, and Robert Ben Rhoades, we ended up discussing how to stop more people becoming victims, how to break the cycles which lead women to domestic abuse, drug addiction, and sex work. There are no easy answers, and this is something well known across research and study. The work of Fritz Perls is good point of reference, for example, the core of his theory being that humans can only accept a truth they discover for themselves. As you might expect, it is more complex than this and comes back to personal experience. The discovery of this ultimately led to the creation of the Gestalt therapy process, which reframes thinking to create choices for the subject as a mechanism for changing behaviour. Out in the world though, where people are being backed into corner, not everyone has had the therapy, so the behaviour is still on its default setting.

"The thing is, it comes back again and again to choices," Della said. "You can tell everybody as much as you want, you know. I go to meetings, and I share my story but I don't go to speaking engagements or anything like that. Teenagers are teenagers, I would love to drill it into their heads: hey, you know, this is what happened to me. And most every teenager, nine out of ten, will go oh, that ain't gonna happen to me. And you just want to take them in, you want to hold them in, you want to say no, don't go out there. Because chances are one of them's not going to come back, especially today."

The girls in the fields, and ditches, and ravines say that Della is right. That not everyone is coming back. That when a vehicle pulls over next to someone who has fallen through the cracks in society and the driver says "are you lost?" they probably are. Freefalling through a mess of abuse and addiction without a safety net.

Worse still, you can be lost and still go missing. It only depends on who pulls over.

- Broken Roads -

ANIMAL

Before going any further, I really wanted to stress something: this is not a *Making a Murderer* type case. Rhoades is a serial killer, and a particularly vile one at that. He is exactly where he deserves to be. Writing this down, I hoped it would not shatter any illusions, but it is important to be upfront and open about this. The things Rhoades has done are horrific and this process is not about making him a celebrity, by giving him oxygen to protest his innocence or to claim unfairness when he never afforded clemency to any of his victims.

I knew nothing about Rhoades until last year, when AJ at the Foundation introduced me to the case. I guess it gets lost in the big noise which persists around Bundy, BTK, Ed Kemper, and even Jack the Ripper. This devalues suffering, really, because there is no greater value on one victim's life or another and a media fixation does not really reflect the gravity of a killer's actions, just the circulation value of a story. What Rhoades did just didn't have a big enough body count, or quite enough of the gory details released at the time to make it to the twisted hall of infamy. But I know. Boy, do I know what he really is. An animal who may owe a bigger debt than the one he is paying. I tracked down Pamela, who believes she rode in his truck and lived to tell the tale. I poked around in his family history and found his old yearbook, started to fill in the blanks, of which there are many. But two things happened which opened up the case for me. The first was a conversation with Greg and Dean at the Foundation, which I will get to later, and the second started with a thrift store in Seattle and a long wait because of COVID-19.

Internet research is largely dull and often infuriating. Especially since the advent of the all-encompassing disinformation and influence operations - something that I deal with all day, every day, for my regular work. Then there is the mess caused by European GDPR privacy law, which means most

American websites produce 404 errors because no one can work out how to turn off cookies or if that's enough to avoid an eye-watering fine. Once I got into looking at the Rhoades case, the first thing I came across was his old Court of Appeals docket [16] from the Fifth District Appellate Court of Illinois. It provides a good entry point if you have never heard anything about Robert and his murders before. Case number 5-98-0821 was settled on the 13th of July 2001 - Rhoades was contesting his guilty plea for Murder One which led to his life imprisonment on September the 11th 1992. He only pled, he claimed, because the state was seeking the death penalty when it filed back on May 6th that year. His appeal was a long-winded one and followed a pattern of contesting his own guilty plea, accusing his defence of coercion – allegedly pressing him in cahoots with Bond County Sheriff's Office, and aiming to reduce his sentence so that he could be out in the world again. He was dismissed in the end, with Justice Goldenhersh delivering a unanimous decision that, in the Rhoades case, the defendant's right to a trial by jury was not violated. The defendant waived this right, they ruled, saying: "Defendants should not be able to waive a right receive a sentence he subjected himself to and then contend that the right was violated." Basically, they told him to go away. Before he initially pled guilty, you see, Rhoades did get his case heard before a grand jury who returned a seven-count indictment including murder, and that case is summarised in the appeal docket. He was arrested in Arizona and charged with kidnap and sexual assault after a state trooper found his semi pulled over to the side of the road. When the officer shone his torch into the cab, he found a naked woman handcuffed and chained up in the sleeper cab. Rhoades had already been involved in another kidnap and rape case, in which he kept a woman captive for days, taking her from California to Houston, Texas. She, however,

---

16 People v. Rhoades, NO. 5-98-0821, Fifth District Appellate Court of Illinois, Filed 13th July 2001,

https://law.justia.com/cases/illinois/court-of-appeals-fifth-appellate-district/2001/5980821.html managed to escape. When his truck was searched a notebook was found which belonged to missing fourteen-year-old Regina Walters, and a warrant at the Houston address uncovered bondage books, equipment - including a horse bit and a double ended sex toy - assorted women's clothing and nude photographs of Walters in various situations including in a barn. His trucking logs were also seized.

Regina was last seen in February 1990 in Pasadena, Texas, and her badly decomposed body was found in a bond county barn along the I-70. That September, after Rhoades was caught red-handed in Arizona, the girl -and that is all she was - was found strangled with a wire garotte. I found message boards featuring what they call "rare photographs" of Regina Walters' last moments. They show pictures of her in a black dress in the barn, posing for the camera in shocked and scared positions. The internet does not have the full series of pictures which exist, but the Cold Case Foundation does. And I can tell you now, in what the internet can see, Regina thought she was playing a part in a private performance. But there's a moment in the series of photographs which the internet has never seen, in which she realizes is not a performance. I remember the first time I attended a death. It was an old man who lived alone in a prefabricated house. He tripped in his living room and cracked his head on the hearth of the gas fire. It was an accident, and he was only there a few days, so he was not decomposing as it was cold and dry that winter. I remember the silence and the expectation he would somehow stand up at any given second, and that leads me back to the point: humans are full of life, faces animated and in constant motion, eyes sparkling with the essence of the soul behind them. When we die, the animation goes and we lose the very spark of recognisable humanity - becoming a shell which does not quite look real. That picture of Regina in which she realised, the one which is no way near the internet, captures a moment between life and death and that is the reason it haunts you. These photographs came later in the investigation, though. At the beginning of the Rhoades research the appeal summaries were all I knew, which is where the Seattle thrift shop made its appearance.

The book which is most referred to in the Rhoades case is *Roadside Prey* by Alva Busch[17], published in 1996. It turns out it's difficult to get hold of in the middle of a pandemic, but I managed to locate a copy on the other side of the Atlantic and waited patiently for it to be shipped. The biggest delay came at customs, where it sat in a warehouse for several weeks before everyone started to work out how to make things run normally during Lockdown One. When it finally arrived, I quickly flicked through the pages, musing at the phone numbers for Marianne and Lucy scribbled on the first page, before flicking to the black and white photographs in the centre. Fourteen-year-old Regina with her shoulder-length, curly black hair stared back, unrecognisable from the photographs I would later to see. Then there are pictures of Rhoades - one of him alone, one from his wedding to Deborah, one of him in leather bondage gear striking a weak looking muscle pose. Then there's a slide of his trucking route from 1990, a spider scrawl across America. There are some shots of his truck, inside the sleeper, his torture kit and the sex toys. Even the garotte found on Regina's neck. There are women's clothes, an apparent bitemark on his arm, and a couple of shots of investigating officers for good, measure. The book was and was not useful, as is often the case with true crime, but it did help build a picture of what happened in the Rhoades case and exposed the large number of cross-jurisdictional issues which hindered rather than helped the investigation. More than anything, it helped me carry out some more detailed research, starting with the thing which leapt out at me: the bite mark on Rhoades arm and the caption which mentioned the name Shana Holts. I was eventually able to piece together a comprehensive account of what happened by drawing everything together.

---

17 Roadside Prey, Alva Busch, Pinnacle Books, 1996

- Broken Roads -

Shana Holts was approximately eighteen years old, of long term no fixed abode, and a repeat victim of sexual assault. She was highly vulnerable and had been outside of the parental and social care system since she was twelve. A white female, slim built - around eight stone - with red-blond hair, blue eyes, and freckles, in January 1990 - on a date on unknown - she was at the San Bernardino truck stop in California. She been there for several hours, attracting the unwanted attention of waiting staff while trying to attract a ride to Arkansas. A white male truck driver, appearing to be in his forties and wearing glasses, a flannel shirt, and jeans sat down next to her and bought her a cup of coffee. He asked if she needed a ride and, when she gave her destination as Fort Smith, he said he would take her as far as Texas. They left in his white International truck some hours later.

After nightfall, Shana had fallen asleep and stirred as the truck pulled to a stop. She was woken up by the air brakes. As the driver tried to reach into the sleeper, she intuitively felt something was wrong and tried to get out of the passenger door but was punched in the face and found the driver was pointing a gun at her. He forced her to climb into the sleeper cabin. A set of handcuffs on a chain was attached to a metal loop on the ceiling of the compartment and the driver cuffed Shana, pinned her down and removed her lower clothing. He then attached shackles to her ankles, forcing her legs to spread - telling her to be a "good girl" as he carried this out. The driver produced a case from under the bed, withdrew a horse's bit and a leather bridle, and forced it into her mouth, securing the straps behind her head. He then removed his own clothing and tore her upper clothing open. Shana noticed at this stage that he had a US Marine Corps tattoo. Using straight pins from the briefcase, he pierced her nipples and pulled on the pins repeatedly, then placed a long choke chain around her neck and connected it to the set of handcuffs. She was released from the ceiling link and taken outside, naked, where she was chained to the side of the truck while the driver dressed then returned with his briefcase. Using a pair of scissors from the case, the driver cut her hair into a crop, told her he was going to play more games with her, then produced a two-thonged leather whip and proceeded to beat her with it until she urinated involuntarily and passed out.

When Shana came around, it was daylight and she was back in the sleeper compartment. Still naked, covered in red welts across her thighs and back. She was handcuffed to the ceiling loop with her arms overhead, in a stress position, and could smell her own urine. Her legs were not shackled. The truck was stationary and she heard the driver get out and then get back in again. He told her to be quiet and reversed the truck into a new position then stopped again, turning the radio up before leaving the cab and closing the door. She felt vibrations as the bed of the truck was either loaded or unloaded and during this time pulled on the chains, establishing that there was no give in them at all. The curtains between the cab and the sleeper remained closed until the driver climbed back in. He turned the radio down and then they drove away. When the truck reached a steady highway speed, the driver opened the curtains, rubbed her legs, and then pulled over again. As soon as the truck was stationary, he climbed into the sleeper put the bridle and bit on her again, stripped himself, and violently raped her while telling Shana she was worthless. After he ejaculated, he produced an eighteen inch, double-ended sex toy and vaginally and anally sexually assaulted her at the same time before chaining her to the floor and sleeping next to her. When he woke up, he dressed and left the truck, returning with coffee - indicating they had been parked at another truck stop. Shana attracted his attention with a foot and he released her from the bridle and bit. She was asking to relieve herself. As punishment, she was driven for a prolonged period until they reached a deserted piece of road. He put her back in the choke chain, dragged her off the roadside like a dog, and made her relieve herself in the brush. Then he whipped her again.

Several days went by. She counted approximately three before a longer stop when she was left alone and the driver returned. He had clearly showered and brought her a coffee and a sandwich. This was the first food and drink she had been allowed since he first held her at gunpoint. That evening, he chained her to the cab's passenger seat in a kneeling position, facing the rear of the vehicle with a chain running down the back of the seat from a handcuffs underneath it and to her shackled feet. She was whipped again. Over the following days Shana became compliant, learning that obedience earned food and drink. She was never allowed to dress, although she was allowed to have her hands and feet released while the padlocked choke-chain on her neck was fastened to a ring on the floor. She learned from CB radio conversations that his handle was "Dusty" and that he would always use white towels, draping them over her seat if she was in the cab, or using them when cleaning and shaving her pubic region. She also came to know that his demeanour would not change before an assault, but his eyes would. On several occasions she was made to drink her own urine, and Shana believed her humiliation was a source of arousal to the driver.

On February 5th 1990 they arrived in Houston Texas, deposited the trailer at a depot and parked at an apartment complex. Forcing her to wear some of his clothes, he handcuffed her to him, wrist to wrist, held her hand and pulled their sleeves over the cuffs before walking her up the external staircase, leading her to his second-floor apartment which was accessed via a balcony. Shana was led across the apartment, which was strewn with women's clothes, and chained to the bed while the driver ran a bath then made her wash. He made her stand in the bath and shaved her pubic hair again. This was the first time that she had seen herself in a mirror since the kidnap and Shana noticed she resembled a skinny young boy with the cropped hair. She was then chained to the bed and anally raped, during which the driver told her he wanted to get rid of her. After this, he left to get food and supplies, leaving her chained to the bed in the bit and bridle. When he returned, he was openly discussing killing her as they ate. She was given clothes from the apartment to dress in and was placed in the cab of the truck with the choke chain secured to the floor.

The driver stopped at a brewery to pick up a consignment, telling her to "be good" before getting out of the truck. Shana noticed that the handcuff which attached the choke chain to the floor had not been closed. She grabbed the bit and bridle, to use as a weapon if needs be, and ran, eventually reaching a house where the occupant called the police. Officers arrived and she gave an account of a trucker called Dusty in a white International having kidnapped and raped her repeatedly. Officers conducted an area search and located a white truck being driven by Robert Ben Rhoades. They detained him. Shana was taken to the scene to identify him. It was him but she was traumatized at seeing him face to face and told the officers that they had the wrong man, so he was released.

Shana was taken to the hospital for treatment and a rape kit. Then onwards to the central police station where she was interviewed by homicide detectives, her injuries were photographed, and the choke chain removed with bolt croppers - it was booked into evidence along with the bit and bridle. She was taken to a hospital where her records were checked and previous mental health problems were established through a phone call with a family. Sergeant Bromar of the Sex Crimes Unit took the case over, and Shana later confirmed officers had stopped the right truck driver but she was too scared to say anything. She refused to support any further action due to her fears and returned to her family in California. A short while later, Bromar found a record of previous investigations into Rhoades, one which ran between 1985 and 1987. He was never able to find full details of the investigation or what it was about.

The account of Shana Holts should have been the end of it. If the officer had pressed a little harder at the scene, following the suspicion they admitted to feeling when Shana refused to maintain eye contact with Rhoades, it could have been so different. If the officers had searched the truck that night, they would have found the briefcase and the loops in the floor and ceiling. Reasonable suspicion as we call it over here is the same as probable cause for officers in Houston. They would have had legal powers to search the vehicle if they reasonably suspected criminal activity or that the driver was dangerous and in possession of a weapon. But the moment a traumatised Shana said it was the wrong man, it was over. The investigative bias, shown by the focus on Shana's mental health history – checked with the hospital and family members – was clearly on display too. It's the same family of bias which results in the assumptions sex workers only report rape when a client fails to pay.

Things would quite rightly be handled differently now. There was no need for a traumatised victim of kidnapping and repeated rape to be involved in a roadside, one man ID parade - the description of the driver, the truck, and the location would have been more than sufficient for a legal search in the circumstances. This would have minimised the psychological damage and secured more in the way of support for prosecution by Shana. Houston PD Special Victims Division now takes a victim-centric approach to all sexual offences, making sure there is proper aftercare and outreach. You cannot help but wonder if what happened to Shana was part of the reason for that departmental change. Nonetheless, there was nothing Houston PD could do about Rhoades at the time because it was not handled right. Hindsight isn't a time machine and, as a result, Rhoades was left free to continue prowling the highways of America in his mobile torture chamber.

While all this was happening, fourteen-year-old Regina Walters disappeared from her mother's home in Pasadena. She and her boyfriend, Ricky Jones, would meet Dusty the truck driver not long afterwards.

According to Busch's book Regina Walters was born to her mother Carolyn in 1975, the youngest of three siblings in a Texan family. Regina's older sister, Dianna, picked up the tall gene from her father's side of the family and by October 1982 the twelve-year-old was five-ten, a hundred and twenty-five pounds, and was being teased at school which caused her anxiety. Carolyn did her best to help and allowed Dianna to host a slumber party – during which the girls were joined for snacks and drinks in the evening by some local boys, though they were asked to leave before bedtime. Later that night, Carolyn woke to laughter from the girl's room and found Dianna had let the boys back in through the window. As you might expect, Dianna found herself grounded and stayed that way for a few weeks. When Carolyn's niece – the same age as Dianna – came to visit, the young girls spent a long time on the phone giggling with one boy or another and, as supper was served, Dianna asked if she could go roller-skating. This was, of course, declined and, after her cousin left for the evening, Dianna went to her room and Carolyn took a nap on the couch. When she woke up at eight, she decided it was time to talk it out with her oldest daughter but when she checked her room Dianna wasn't on her bed. As the evening drew on, Carolyn assuming Dianna was outside with her brother, an uneasy feeling descended on the mother of three. She went back to the bedroom and looked around once more. The blue and white curtain which covered the entrance to the closet was closed and Carolyn felt drawn to it.

Investigators found a message on the tape recorder near to where Dianna hung herself from the clothes rail. The accompanying note, addressed to her parents, read "hate you forever."

On Thursday February 1st 1990, fourteen-year-old Regina was ready to move back in with Carolyn in Pasadena, having spent time living with her father in Houston. She didn't know her grandfather was dying of cancer and made plans to babysit that weekend instead of joining her mother on a one-hundred-and-fifty-mile trip to Grapeland. Carolyn didn't push it either, she recognised the fragile peace which had brought her daughter home and was herself terribly scarred by Dianna's death. While she was nervous, there had never been a problem at the Pasadena apartment complex and Regina promised to have a friend stay with her. Come Sunday, an apprehensive Carolyn breathed a sigh of relief when she found Regina watching TV with her friend. By around nine pm, Regina's friend had left and the young girl told her mother she needed to return the key where she had babysat. Carolyn agreed it was okay if Regina was home by ten.

"Mom, you know nothing's gonna happen to me," a smiling Regina told her.

Ten came and went. Regina was gone. None of the neighbours had seen her, not even at the place she done the babysitting. He brother knew nothing and her father, over in Houston, had not seen his daughter either.

Regina was reported missing on February 4th and the case landed with Detective Susan Trammel in the juvenile section of Pasadena PD. A day later, Shana Holts fled from Rhoades in Houston. Carolyn and her son, Brian, tirelessly put up missing posters and took shifts on the home phone so they never missed a call, and this paid off. Someone came forwards and this led Susan Trammell to a witness who had seen Regina with two white men about an hour after she left her mother's. With that, Trammel had two names – Casey and Zelda – to work on. With a little help from Auto Crime, she tracked down Casey Cook and Zelda Trent, and this is how Ricky Jones came into the story. Jones met Regina for the first time on the Saturday, hanging out around the apartments and they took an instant shine to each other. Regina had left her mother's to stay with Jones and, as soon as they saw the first flyers, they hid out at Cook's place. Jones had form for auto theft and was already on probation, so when he realised the implications of his relationship with an underage girl he panicked and decided to head for Mexico. Regina refused to let him go alone, so the pair left town together, aiming to hitchhike their way to freedom.

On St Patrick's Day 1990, Regina had been missing for six weeks. At a quarter past one that Saturday afternoon her father's phone rang in Houston. "Mr Walters? Are You Regina Walters' father?" a male caller asked before seeding hope by adding "I know where she is." Her father scrambled for a pen as the stranger's voice continued: "There have been some changes made. I cut her hair. She's got short hair now. She's in a barn, in a loft."

The pen now forgotten, all Regina's dad could say was "is she alive or dead?"

The caller hung up without responding and Regina's father called the police and Carolyn. Ten hours later, Carolyn's phone rang and she switched on a tape recorder, presumably installed by officers. A male voice asked her to meet him at the Stop-N-Go at half six Sunday morning, promising details about Regina's whereabouts. She waited two hours under police surveillance, but no one came. Trammell worked Mr Walters through his phone records and a pattern of reverse-charge calls emerged. March 12th from Jewett, Texas to his business, March 16th from Oklahoma City, and the March 17th the call from Ennis. Two calls placed to Carolyn, on the other hand, came from a payphone in Pasadena – the second leading back to the Stop-N-Go and a potential sighting of a young man in a baseball cap, disrupted by an off-duty cop causing Carolyn to panic.

As the spring of 1990 rolled on, Rhoades was arrested in Arizona, sparking the involvement of the FBI's Behavioural Science Unit in the case. Sue Trammell knew nothing of Arizona or the FBI and carried on working the Walter's missing person investigation. Something about it was sticking. It's more common than it sounds, this copper's instinct. Every now and then you hit a job and all the alarm bells go off and you get this feeling in your gut from the second it comes in. It might sound like exaggeration, but your mouth dries up and you get this feeling, like a stone falling a long way through you to the pit of your stomach. And it's not just some passing thing or related to the tension of the moment on duty. Even years later you'll hear one line on a background radio bulletin or catch a missing person poster flashing past on a social media timeline, and it's there. The stone. I can't explain it any better than that. Sue Trammell must have felt like that with Walters because, despite a heavy workload, she persisted. She gave more. And her instincts were unquestionably good too. Those Pasadena calls to Carolyn Walters didn't fit the pattern of those to Mr Walters in Houston and she suspected it was some local prank arising from the flyers with Carolyn's home number on them. It turned out she was right and, after the young man started asking for sex, Carolyn cradled the phone and the calls stopped. Persistence sometimes isn't enough though. Even though Trammell went as far as she could, acquiring dental records, having them compared against Jane Does, and circulating a bulletin on Regina nationally, she had hit a wall. Even her continued searches for Ricky Jones – almost certain to start offending when ran out of cash, came up empty. Over the coming months, no new leads developed and Carolyn moved out of the apartment.

Out on the I-70 at Greenville, Illinois sat a battered and disused barn, separated from usefulness by the construction of the interstate itself in the sixties. At five pm on Saturday September 29th 1990 the farmer was giving the barn a final once over before the local fire department burned it down in a combined training exercise and plot clearance. He climbed the fence and swept the barn, climbing the wooden shaft to the hayloft.

Bond County was home turf for State Investigator Michael Sheeley and he was on his own farm when the local Sherriff called him in. Sheeley, the Sherriff, and a team of forensics officers gathered around the mummified body in the creaking hayloft, noting the cropped hair and the wire garotte, and removing the body before a storm broke through the broken roof. The ligature had been twisted with a piece of wood sixteen times. It was a brutal death. Forensic examination of the body identified that she was a white female, aged between fourteen and fifteen who had died within the last twelve months, but that was it. Sheeley took the dental records, circulated a bulletin, and began a waiting game which might never end. It did though. On October 16th 1990 when Trammell received Sheeley's bulletin and all but confirmed what they both thought. The call Regina's father had received back on March 17th cemented the conclusion.

Sheeley and Trammell's grunt work met with the FBI's over the months that followed. Rhoades's apartment in Houston was searched after his Arizona arrest, a sequence of photographs of Regina was found among his bondage equipment and clothing. What happened to Ricky Jones was answered, at least partially, by Regina's notebook. The spiralbound was found in Rhoades's possession after the Arizona incident. At first ignored, it was the FBI who examined it more closely after Walters was identified as the body in the barn. The front cover was marked with the word "Regina's."

Her full name, her parents addresses, and their phone numbers were on the inside cover. Another person's handwriting filled other pages. "Exit 99 service road, Fun and Hide, Trees, Water, W301 Water Tank." The code was a roadmap of a sadistic killer's so-called games and the last page featured a drawing of a gun and knife dripping with blood. "Ricky's a dead man" was sketched to reflect blood dripping down the letters. And Ricky was indeed a dead man. His body was found in Lamar County, Mississippi on March 3rd 1991, but it wasn't identified until 2008[18].

In February 1992, two years after Regina left her mother's apartment and a year after Ricky's body was found, Sheeley and FBI Agent Phil Staley flew to Arizona to interview Rhoades, who had been imprisoned for that incident, and to serve him with an Illinois arrest warrant for Regina's murder. As the prosecutors and FBI pressed on with the investigation, dotting the Is and crossing the Ts for a death penalty request as Rhoades's extradition and trial proceeded, a terribly sad witness account emerged. There had been an opportunity to save Regina Walters in March 1990. A depot foreman remembered Rhoades – who reportedly liked to be called Dusty – pulling up for a load with a young girl with boy-length cropped hair. She stared up at him in what he recognised as a silent plea for help, and he did nothing. He cried as they showed him the photograph of Regina.

What happened to Regina during her time as Rhoades's prisoner is an almost exact mirror of what happened to Shana Holts, but he recorded the younger girl's story in a series of photographs. Greg Cooper, the man in charge of the Cold Case Foundation, served his time in the FBI's Behavioural Science Unit and one of the training packages he has delivered time and again is on the Rhoades case. It is absolutely harrowing. Having found the publicly available photographs of Regina in the barn wearing a black dress at an early stage of the research, I originally replied to AJ at the

---

[18] http://www.doenetwork.org/cases/identified9.html, Doe Network – International Center for Unidentified and Missing Persons.

Foundation and told him she was acting in that sequence, because she didn't believe what would happen. After seeing Greg's presentation, I knew that was the case. The photographs Rhoades took are magazine quality but clearly for a private collection. I thought for a long time over what to write about the horror faced by Regina at Rhoades's hands. This traumatic and graphic short-hand account is more than enough, even though I watered it down.

Regina's hair had been cropped short. She was wearing a blue jumper and black cowboy style boots you can see in any of the public crime scene photographs from inside Rhoades's apartment. She looked tired and scared, but compliant. There was a look on her face, one looking for reassurance: *If I do what you say you won't hurt me, will you?* In her innocence, she has been de-sexed. Dehumanised. Next, she was chained to a fallen tree in various states of undress, using sex toys on herself. A silver chain was around her neck and led to handcuffs on her wrists and shackles on her ankles. After this, Regina is in the cab of Rhoades's semi. She was naked, again with the looped chains on - this time they pass through a ring on the side wall. A ginormous double-ended sex toy is being used. She was smiling in one picture. She believed she could get through this if she did what she was told. Rhoades had built up hope. Trained her. Then she was photographed taking a shower in a truck stop, the water is caught in perfect motion by a practiced camera operator. She was wearing jewellery and nail polish. She was being re-sexed, rehumanised. She believed he would let her go. Next, Regina is wearing a black dress and black shoes. Prim and proper and dressed for a funeral. She was standing outside a barn, the one on the I-70 in Illinois. She was performing, being directed. These are storyboard poses, following a script. Inside the barn, she covered her mouth in mock horror. She was still following a script but a doubt had started to grow there. Something was wrong.

Regina was chained to a rafter, her clothes removed one item at a time. At first she poses, they are still playing out a scene and she was in on the production. She had done as she was told at the tree when he rewarded her.

Regina is naked after that. And she knew. She knew she was about to die. She realised it and her soul was dying. Rhoades's captured this on the last photograph. The crime scene photographs fill in what happened next. Regina's naked body was discarded, as if she were trash. Used up. There was no careful placement, the last moments were just his rage. The end of the game. The point of it. She lays on her back looking up, metal wire twisted deep into her neck. I have the strongest instinct he made her watch his face as he did it.

His photographs tell a lot of truth about truth about Rhoades. That the game is the excitement. The build-up. The trickery, the control. His sly little secret. He craved that moment when his victims realised what was happening and their souls died. He was and still is an animal. After that moment of realisation, he got angry with them, because they had served their purpose – in his view ruining it for him. So, he made sure they died knowing he felt it was all their fault and wanting them to believe it. And this is reflected in his trophies too. The black dress, the funeral outfit Regina was wearing that day in the barn, was found among the women's clothing in Rhoades's apartment along with her photographs. He kept her with him after he took her freedom and then her life.

The thing which haunted me about that dress, knowing the pattern of his offending and his long-distance reach, was a simple question. How many other women had worn it?

MONSTERS

The world moves whether we like it or not. Forces of nature and pandemic pulling each of us in multiple directions without let up. But there always comes a point when we are no longer in the storm, when we can look back at it. With a bit of distance, we can see the things we just could not at the time. It doesn't matter if it is looking back at the first or second year of COVID, or a murder spree stretching back decades. Very often, it is also best to get a second opinion too – to make sure you really are seeing things clearly. After the research and review of Regina's case, I turned to my expert colleague Dr. Lawrence J. Simon for exactly that reason. Without having such expertise on hand, making sense of the motivations of serial killer Robert Ben Rhoades would have been much harder.

The case of Robert Ben Rhoades is one of the most disturbing you are ever likely to encounter, but it is rich with lessons too: highlighting the gaps in the system of cross-jurisdictional procedures that any killer could drive a truck through - and did – and, also, how cooperation and good instincts can still bring serious serial offenders to justice. Shana Holts's lucky escape almost handed The Truck stop Killer to police before he murdered fourteen-year-old Regina Walters, but almost is not enough. Was not enough to save Regina and her boyfriend Ricky Jones from horrific deaths at Rhoades hands. If I am honest, I believe a lot of people might think the fact Shana got away just made him angry, made him want the next one more. But that is not the case. His timeline in 1990 just says he was enjoying himself. Doing what he wanted to do. What muddies the water with Rhoades is time, nothing more complex. That same thing which allows us to look back and see things more clearly in most cases just creates confusion around the trucker's actions. And this is probably the reason his case is not up there on the list of constant talking points alongside Ridgway or Jespersen.

Rhoades killed a lot in a short space of time, but the murders were geographically spread out along his trucking routes and the bodies were not located or identified for long periods of time. The upshot, I believe, is the absence of the big man hunt - a gap where the screaming national headlines should be, reducing one of America's most shocking serial cases to a collection of local news items and the odd documentary or book. The other aspect to it, driven partly by this lack of big noise, is that the true crime community have not given the cases a great deal of attention, because it all looks solved. There is no CCTV to endlessly argue about, no salacious gossip about persons of interest to pore over, and no shadow patterns to identify on maps. That does not mean the story is magically finished though. It just means a few cold cases got marked as solved and people stopped looking. Truth is, the Rhoades case is the start of something - just not something you're probably used to, and we will get to that but not yet. Right now, we are looking back and seeing Arizona.

On April 1st 1990, at the city limits of Casa Grande, Arizona a state trooper came across a truck pulled over on the side of the I-10, nose in the direction of Tucson with its hazard lights flashing. It was early morning, it was out of place, and Trooper Mike Miller made a decision which saved the life of a twenty-seven-year-old woman who is often referred to as Katie Ford. She is also often confused with Shana Holts, though she is not the same person at all - it is just Rhoades' pattern which is so consistent. Ford's real name is Lisa Pennal, a fact contained in Greg Cooper's case study published in The Forensic Examiner in 2007.[19]

Bothered by the truck, Miller pulled over and poked around, eventually opening the cab and climbing up on the step for a look when he heard some muffled disturbance. In the torchlight, he was confronted with a terrified naked woman shackled in the sleeper and Robert Ben Rhoades, who casually

---

[19] Murder--One Jurisdiction at a Time: The Case of Robert Ben Rhoades (Case Study), The Forensic Examiner 2007, Winter, 16, 4, Cooper G.

informed the officer he had a gun. Miller did not mess around. Rhoades was handcuffed and strapped into the seatbelt in the back of Miller's cruiser while he attended to the injured woman. She had been whipped and was padlocked into Rhoades' horse bridle and bit. As backup made its way to Miller's location and the trooper tried to release the woman - providing her with something to cover her naked body - Rhoades slipped his cuffed hands under his legs and let himself out of the seatbelt. It was only when Casa Grande colleagues arrived that they were able to search the trucker and find the keys needed to release Lisa. Understandably, she did not even start to relax, not even slightly, until Rhoades was in cells and she was safely at a police station, having her injuries photographed.

Lisa was lucky in so many respects. A pleasant Rhoades had only picked her up earlier that day, allegedly at Rip Griffin's truck stop in Buckeye, on the I-10 east of Phoenix. It has changed hands and name (to TA) since, but comments on an old Wikimapia entry[20] from over ten years ago describe it as: "The Tits and Ass truck stop," adding "this is a good place to stop if you wanna make love to your sister in public." After they left, Pennal fell asleep. He chained her up, and the torture began. As he pulled out his briefcase of needles, chains and sex toys, Rhoades allegedly told Lisa his CB handle, Whips and Chains, and let her know that he had been kidnapping and torturing women for around or over fifteen years. This puts the start date of his offending between 1970 and 1975 and the unsolved death of Judith Pleas in Council Bluffs at his own trail head.

At three in the morning detective Rick Barnhart searched through Rhoades torture kit before his interview with the trucker. He documented the alligator clips, leashes, pins, whips, dildos, and handcuffs. He knew that Rhoades was meticulously organized serial offender before they even met. The tapes began to roll, and the trucker stretched out on the interview room couch, straight away laughing off Lisa as a woman "not playing with a full

---

20 http://wikimapia.org/178554/Rip-Griffin-s-Truck-stop, Wikimapia

deck." He went on to use the colloquial derogatory term *lot lizards* to describe women hitching in truck stops and gave a rich and clearly well-practiced story, then stopped telling it at the point when the truck stopped. He "would not cross that line," as he put it. Rhoades would not dance to the truth, just his own tune. A disturbed Barnhart photographed the bite marks Pennal managed to give Rhoades - on his arm and his flank - and the interview came to an end. The detective did a diligent amount of paperwork and background, and this included a call to Houston PD, where he eventually spoke to Bromar - the investigator in Shana Holts's case which would immediately precede Regina Walters murder. Barnhart called the case in to the FBI at Phoenix and brought agent Bob Lee into the investigation, with the FBI man immediately identifying Rhoades as a sexual sadist. With the help of the truck driver's nosy landlady and the Behavioural Science Unit in Quantico, Lee secured a search warrant for Rhoades' Houston apartment and the evidential avalanche came down on him.

Early on in reviewing the Rhoades case with the Cold Case Foundation team, I spoke with our resident expert in deviant behaviour, Dr. Lawrence J. Simon. We had just sat through the horrifying sequence of Regina's photographs. It was a real privilege to have been able to call in the expert help on this case, joining me from thousands of miles away thanks to the same technology which means cases like Rhoades' get lost in the noise of the internet. Doc Simon, as I call him, authored the book *Murder by Numbers: Perspectives on Serial Sexual Violence*, and its follow up, *Mortal Desire: Origins of Sexual Violence*. Most of his hard-won experience came through the prison system, where he had worked on Death Row and in other maximum-security facilities.

"I've interviewed many folks that have been that convicted of various forms of sexual deviant pathology, and that's what I based the books on," he told me. "You know, certainly on the words that have come out of their mouths, I've constructed some theories behind it. And that's where I've been moving forward ever since, sort of speaking, presenting seminars to law enforcement throughout the country, as well as offering my consult on numerous Cold Case homicides."

Murder By Numbers was written around twenty years ago and it came from a time when Doc Simon first got catapulted into the prison system, specifically examining inmates in federal prisons out in Michigan. He had a unique opportunity to interview individuals with backgrounds in doing what he calls "pretty horrific, horrific things to folks." His work continued after that, moving over to the Broward County Sheriff's Office, in child abuse investigations as a civilian employee.

"I worked with sworn law enforcement but was able to also see some of these things, these crimes against persons - against children - that sort of manifest themselves with motives of sex," he said. "And then, of course, I worked at a violent sex offender facility where they housed sex offenders that were convicted of a sex offence and then were civilly committed to this facility under what we call the sexually violent predator laws. They were housed there indefinitely, so I had the opportunity to work there and conduct treatment with some of these individuals, again, that have done some pretty horrific things."

From there he moved up to what he calls *The Big House* and began the process of writing Mortal Desire in 2015.

"That book was more sort of like, I'm gonna say, I don't know if this is the right term: a memoir. But a lot of the things are from the inmates. The inmates will tell me their stories and, of course, all the names are changed so there's no identifiers or things like that. But they had told me some terrible things that they've done to their victims, mostly murder, and in that process I've constructed - from my psychological expertise - my own theories, if you will: some of the reasoning behind the motivations, why they did what they did, why they kill, why they decided to take someone's body parts and expose them. When I'm interviewing some of these guys in the basement, when they're on death row - at that point most of the time their appeal processes were kind of exhausted - that's the best time for these guys, at least in their minds, to go ahead and just tell all if you ask the right questions. So, for example, I may ask one of the inmates why the person had severed an individual's head and what they did with the head. Sort of like a step-by-step process of the behaviour that they have decided to undertake on their victims, pre and post homicide."

I was recording the conversation, and we both knew it would be available for public consumption at some stage, given the nature of our work, but we were both trying to keep the discussion as PG13 as possible. At the end of the day, we are the ones who must live with the nightmares so everyone else can go about their business without worrying about what is really in the closet. Nobody really needs to know the ins and outs, especially while people are out here to carry the weight of the truth. Even so, the diluted version of what we know is graphic, disturbing, and awful. Doc Simon picked up on this train of thought, which came out as we talked.

"There you go. It's interesting. And that's, that's one of the things I never thought that I would be working on," he told me. "I never thought that I would be working in the prison system, for example, working with death row inmates or in a closed management facility with violent inmates. I never thought I would be doing that. But essentially, these are the monsters because - you said it best, you know - we're the ones that have these dreams and these nightmares, and not to project it or to subject other folks to it. Because these are the monsters underneath our beds. The children, they have their own little monsters - and you see it in their drawings and things like that with the devil horns – but, see, the serial murderers are the adult monsters that are underneath the bed. And that's basically, in a nutshell, what I've been studying for the past twenty years."

When it comes to how Dr. Simon became involved with the Cold Case Foundation, it is a slightly different story to my own - I volunteered out of the blue when I caught The Confessions Killer on Netflix and had never even contemplated doing anything like it before then. It is a true privilege to be able to work with this team and, very recently, I was asked to join to the

Executive Support Team as the Director of Intelligence, having built a trust relationship with Greg and Dean over the last year. Other team members, such as Doc Simon, come with that trust capital built in.

"I was recommended by one of the members and who had gotten in contact with me and I was very willing to give my time to try and solve some of these extraordinarily comp complex cases, you know," Dr. Simon told me. "To be able to work with the experts that we have with the foundation is a privilege, it's an honour. It's very humbling because it's about all sorts of processes of learning – and certainly you learn things as well. You know, about other people, about their expertise, for example the DNA experts, and everybody's got a part to play. It's just fascinating to learn. The goal, for me, one way to solve these cases is to dig together and get to the root of it, like with a puzzle. We dig to find those missing pieces that create the whole picture so there could be some semblance of closure for a family."

It is this ethos which led us straight to one of those complex cases. This case: Rhoades. After we went through the case review and the presentation with Greg, I wanted to know what Dr. Simon's professional assessment of the trucker was, and what led him to do the horrific things that he did.

"Well, I'll tell you this, certainly a troubled childhood was the first the first thing," Dr. Simon said. "That kind of hit me straight away. I mean, there's lots…there's millions and millions of people that have had a troubled childhood and don't end up going down that road. We all know that they've made a choice. We do all know that, but what happens with some of these folks is that the creation of the monster, so to speak, is within the first four to five years of life. What I do believe happened in this case is that there was some anger and there was aggression early on and, at a very early age, that became sexualized. That anger and aggression fused with sex and then we saw the product of it. I would venture to believe that he had some other things going on, maybe some other nuisance type of criminal behaviours that he probably wasn't even caught for. Of course, the motive with all of it was sex. The main crux of what he did was the sexual sadism. Criminal sexual sadism, I would add - I want to be more specific on that, because he's obviously harming others."

Doc Simon believes this would have developed in Rhoades at an early age and been reinforced through his masturbatory fantasies, which were likely going to have been violent, a hypothesis supported by the collection of violent pornography Rhoades was found to own. The collection was extensive, neatly captured in the crime scene photographs from his apartment and the evidence seizures there. Among copies of Hustler and Penthouse, featuring stylised cover images of woman wearing neck chains, Rhoades owned very specific books: *Diane's Lessons of Bondage, Harboring a Fugitive, Slave Daughter in Ropes, Chained Niece, Sadist's Victim, Trained for Lust, Fit to Be Tied, Rachel's Captivity*. The list goes on and on, and many of the covers are a distinctive green, featuring a black and white sketch depicting an act from within the book and a bold white text which reads: "A House of Lords Book." Many of the titles, all coming back to a California company called Oakmore Enterprises LLC, are still listed for sale on so-called vintage porn websites. Many of them were first published between 1982 and 1984. According to a very cursory search, that company incorporated in 1978 and is registered in Van Nuys, CA. They received a Franchise Tax Board suspension in 2000.

Among all Rhoades' amassed publications, a bold yellow page with large white text on a black shadow caught my attention: *L.A. X...Press, Weekly Singles Publication*. Rhoades was actively trawling in California during the height of his offending. I wondered if the publication still existed, imagining it would have died long ago, but found the 1980 established company is still mentioned and kept the same registered address at 1545 N La Brea Ave, Hollywood. The Yelp reviews seemed to come to an end in 2019, with this entry: "Terrific newspaper if you want to meet some of the local working girls as well as great massages and the latest in well freaky things to do in LA. Typically free just pick one up (don't let anyone see you)." The address is visible on Google's Streetview, a grubby looking single storey warehouse with a red "Hollywood Express" sign and some empty newspaper stands outside. I zoomed in on a billboard in the carpark and found the current website, hollywoodpress.com, providing escorts, massage, and classifieds twenty-four-seven. The content is exactly what you would expect. The Oakmore books provided Rhoades and countless people like him with fantasy ammunition and advertisers like LA Xpress provided easy opportunities to play them out. Despite the passage of time, not a huge amount has changed – the trade in these original books continues, with people even entering bidding wars over them, and the Xpress has just moved online, a dark mirror of print media in general. Given that Rhoades' known trucking routes give his passage through California as 1989 and 1990, I opened NaMus and searched for unidentified white females aged under 30 found in California during those years, two cases came up. Neither of them displays the hallmarks of Rhoades, but everywhere you look, there are more women across America who have never been identified. Adjusting the search to missing persons under the same criteria, but giving last contact dates between January 1st 1989 and February 5th 1990, six cases come up. Of those, five are clearly domestic abuse murders where insufficient evidence was ever collected to result in a charge, the other has insufficient detail available to say anything about – other than the victim appears to have disappeared from a university campus, which wouldn't fit Rhoades pattern. I looked at the crime statistics for California in 1989, there were over three thousand murders and almost twelve thousand rapes. In 1989 around thirty percent of the homicides were going unsolved. Even today, this figure rises as high as sixty percent in rape cases. Looking for Rhoades crimes in the California records would be a significant undertaking, but he is somewhere there to be found. Of that I have no doubt.

"He was obsessed with that, and kind of living his life through that pornography," Dr. Simon told me. "He was obsessed with that pornography, even to the point where he would take pictures of women on the road in his truck and they would get angry at him. Understand that dynamic was, for him, that he enjoyed it. Because that was highlighted in the pornographic material - meaning that a woman gets angry at him, okay, and then he gets angry at her, and that's generating that whole fantasy. That's what he was doing with his victims."

Rhoades did take pictures of female drivers while out on runs. I have four of those photographs in a folder alongside his routes and know exactly which picture Doc Simon is referring to - in which the woman driving her beige, boxy looking saloon waves her hand at him in a "what the…" gesture through the windshield. She is wearing a drop-shoulder, black top and there is a blue child seat in the back of her car. It appears empty. In another, the target is a red saloon with the sunroof open and Rhoades had tried and failed to get a picture of the brunette driver but messed up his angle. Another is a white two-door coupe with leopard print seats, being driven by a brunette in a brown blouse. She seems oblivious. The last one, a black GT with a part open sunroof showing an auburn-haired woman in sunglasses stopped me in my tracks. I noticed something I had not seen before. The black car was moving at speed, so Rhoades was not constraining himself to traffic jams to use his camera, but the reflection in the window showed his white truck imprinted over the blonde-brunette passenger with the bare legs who was covering her face. It was not the same white truck shown in a warehouse being processed by forensics investigators, which means there is another crime scene out there somewhere - possibly in that 1985 gap when Rhoades worked out of Georgia. The signwriting is different, though I cannot make it out in these old scans of old photos – it could be AGAF but may not be - and the truck has trim covering the fuel tanks, whereas the International he was arrested in does not. I trawled through photographs for a while, looking at galleries of all the big trucks from the seventies and eighties, searching a high-position rear handle at the very back of the driver's side and a progressively slanted trim over the fuel tank. As a lot of things do, this led to nowhere but a headache. Thankfully, not everything goes that way.

"The truck driving is very easy to figure out," the Doc said. "That's a great job for someone like a serial killer - for someone like him to be more specific - because, the driving, the isolation on the road, allows the violent fantasies to become reinforced. He has this violent pornography, he's on the road by himself initially, okay? And he's observing this violent pornography. So, he's becoming obsessed with it. And he knows he's not going to be able to get anybody unless, really, he pays for it. Ted Bundy was known for neutralizing his threat, he was very good at doing that. This guy? He was more for opportunity. For example, people hitchhiking, but keep in mind the decision to go ahead and commit these crimes he was already obsessed with, through the pornography. Being a long-haul trucker, this whole fantasy takes shape, it formulates into this story plot that goes hey, I'm gonna go ahead and do the real thing. Hence the taking of the women for a long period of time, so he can go ahead and do what's in those books he's reading."

Rhoades was not just a reader. When in prison after his capture in Arizona, he wrote letters to his wife, Debra. In one passage, manipulating her by explicitly stating he had never manipulated her, he wrote: "I always told you there were three things you could do. Play, pass, or run. And tried to show you what other people's games were so that you'd know that these games weren't being run on you." The mantra of games was one Rhoades obsessed over, referring to 1960s book Games People Play[21] by psychiatrist Eric Berne. The core theories behind it were perverted into a behavioural regime by the trucker – the first being his almost entirely transactional existence and the second his mastery of "mind games." If you've never read this book, my personal advice is do not bother. It was rejected by Berne's community at the time it was written and deserves to be left in the past. The attitudes of the author, displayed through the sexual games chapters alone show that it has little merit – due to its focus on woman as the creators of the games which men, such as incestuous fathers and rejected lovers, must

---

[21] Games People Play: The Psychology Of Human Relationships, Eric Berne, Ballantine Books, 1973

play to their own eventual detriment through punishment. If I can sum it up – and sum up why it was dangerous in the hands of someone like Rhoades – it is a long-winded excuse, written for every occasion that a man engages in violence, fraud, rape, or murder. And it also helps set the narrative which leads to those outcomes. Pages and pages of "she made me do it" in the language of science which I have no intention of quoting directly. It reminded me of one of the first stated cases we ever looked over during my police training – the 1985 murder of Erika Corlett by her husband Thomas in their London home[22]. A civil servant, Thomas Corlett strangled Erika because, in his words, "I always placed my newspaper on one side of my plate, the mustard on the other. But she moved my paper and put the mustard in its place instead." He prefixed this explanation with: "It was her fault." He was not convicted of murder, receiving only three years in prison for manslaughter, and his case eventually led to changes in the way "provocation" is handled in the UK. Until then, the system would have suited Berne and his games perfectly. At first, faced only with internet research on a limited amount of background on Rhoades, it is easy to believe that "Play, Pass, or Run" was a catchphrase he used, a spoken calling card. But that is not the case. It was simply part of a twisted psychology built on childhood experience, ego, and the material he chose to read which narrowed his worldview further. The phrase is purely his own personal absolution because nothing could ever be his own fault. Rather than waste time on Berne and his own games, I asked an actual expert why some women got away from Rhoades without incident and why others died at his hands. The answer is exactly what an expert would tell you: the triggers are complicated.

"Well, I think it could be really anything but, usually, trauma. You've got to remember trauma is perceptual. This is why it's a difficult question," Dr. Simon told me. "In my experience, when I've interviewed these individuals,

---

[22] https://apnews.com/article/d11d294fddd5139dad32f68512bce7be, Man Accused of Killing Wife in Dispute Over Mustard, Associated Press, July 9 1987

whether in death row or close to and standing trial, anyone that's had this type of sexual deviant theology, things have happened in their lives that may not be traumatic for us. It's almost like, as an example, police involved shootings - sometimes it may affect someone a little bit differently. But certainly there is something in this individual's life." This is the truth, as scary as it may be: we may never know what specific thing sets a killer off, making the difference between walking away and not. And the reason we may never know is because they are always the last one standing, so there are almost never testimonies which explain the exact circumstances which flipped the switch. Only their stories remain as a tainted monument where the truth should stand. "I'm a stats guy, so I tend to go with statistical probabilities," Doc Simon continued. "In my experience, what I what I find with these individuals is that they compensate for very low self-esteem and they compensate with narcissism. An overblown sense of self-worth. And Rhoades is able to live in his world of omnipotence - greatness through the kidnapping, the abductions, and the sexually tormenting his victims. That's where he feels the illusion of power, the illusion of greatness. These guys don't feel that with their girlfriends or wives."

You can see Rhoades sense of power genuinely was projected onto his victims. As we sat through the presentation in the case review, specifically the sequence of Regina's photographs, both Dr. Simon and I recognised this desperately sad shift between the spark of hope in her eyes at one stage and the understanding that the truck driver was going to kill her towards the end. During my time in policing, I have been through life threatening situations and could literally feel the emotional memories coming up as the slides went by, but that gives my view a personal taint, I guess, which means it is not entirely trustworthy. I asked Dr. Simon for his thoughts on the evidence.

"I think instinctively we're usually operating out of the fight or flight - really the biological need to survive," he told me. "So, in theory, I think she saw the death of her boyfriend that she was hitchhiking with and then she figured that: look, I need to do whatever the hell this guy tells me to do and, if I don't, then I'm going to end up dead. Here's part of the sadistic mindset, and this is what I think in my opinion that probably was going on in that interaction, what he wanted to do is make her feel safe and then change the tune a little bit to get her to be scared. And that's part of the attraction for him. It's like, they're calm, and then they need that sexual excitement, they need that fear. Probably he had promised her that: hey, you do what you need to do and you're going to get out of here alive. When you're dealing with this type of predator, especially the criminal sexual status that's harming others, it's all a pathological continuum. You're really dealing with somebody quite rare, which is a very good, but somebody that really needs to take it to the limit of their script. I believe that from all the porn that was recovered that he was trying to live out that story plot. The entire process there was arousal. So, you know, I think at the very end she knew and I think that likely was the most sexually arousing for him."

The transition afterwards, from the carefully stage-managed lead up to Regina's murder, to the way she was brutally executed is what we saw in the crime scene photographs when she was eventually found. I saw rage there, along with final insults, but Dr. Simon is an expert in this field with a long history of examining these offenders first-hand. I wanted to know what he saw at the end of the fantasy.

"Well, I don't know if it was so much an explosive crescendo," he told me. "He had enough. I mean, he wanted to go and get a different victim. And it just hallmarks the nature of what is the whole story plot and theme with regards to the criminal's sexual sadistic pathology. He left her there as he had enjoyed the way he killed her, and then that was it. And he relived that experience, and would continue to really relive these experiences, through the photos. But again, you know, he's gonna end up trying to get someone else. There's no doubt in my mind whatsoever because there was no other way this individual would feel omnipotence unless it's through the torture and the killing. You're looking at God awful situations with these type of predators - a need for control, the need for greatness and omnipotence -

because they live through that illusion. Reality is too tough for these individuals. There are other aspects that are going on that we don't see, for example biology. We're not sitting in front of a functional MRI looking inside his brain, but certainly you can almost surmise that there's some things that are going on internally with them, whether they're neurotransmitter imbalances, structural brain issues, whatever it is. And then of course, you have the other fifty percent would be the environmental issues."

I remembered reading about this a couple of years ago and looked it up again. The study, Aberrant Brain Gray Matter in Murderers[23] was published in July 2019 – a team effort between universities in Chicago, New Mexico, and Wisconsin. They used brain scans of a study group of over eight hundred prisoners and found those convicted of homicide and attempted homicide offences had less grey matter than other types of offenders. The areas of the brain most affected were those which control "emotional processing, behavioural control, and social cognition" – the anterior temporal lobes and the orbitofrontal cortex. It was the first study which set aside offenders with psychiatric disorders, giving as clean a view as possible of criminal minds. It is not complete work, of course, so you cannot say that reduced grey matter means the subject is a murderer, but it was the biggest study to date, so we are a step closer to understanding this area. It sits alongside the ongoing research and meta-studies on the links between serial killings and either autism spectrum disorder (ASD) or head injury – the latter of which has become a true crime favourite these days. There was a good study on this very subject completed by the University of Glasgow in 2014[24] which gives

---

23 Aberrant brain gray matter in murderers, Brain Imaging and Behavior volume 14, pages2050–2061 (2020), Ashly Sajous-Turner, Nathaniel E. Anderson, Matthew Widdows, Prashanth Nyalakanti, Keith Harenski, Carla Harenski, Michael Koenigs, Jean Decety & Kent A. Kiehl

24 Neurodevelopmental and psychosocial risk factors in serial killers and mass murderers, Aggression and Violent Behaviour Volume 19, Issue 3, May–June 2014, Pages 288-301, Clare S. Allely, Helen Minnis, Lucy Thompson, Philip Wilson & Christopher Gillberg

a deeper insight into environmental factors, as Dr. Simon calls them: of the one hundred and six serial killers with either ASD or a head injury, fifty-five percent experienced significant traumatic events in their childhood. These "psychological stressors" included abuse and family member deaths. Rhoades background in Council Bluffs is never far away, no matter where you look.

"He kind of became this well-rounded predator - and I say well-rounded because he needs that control, but that needs to be manifested through the violent sexual torture and torment of a victim," Dr. Simon continued. "It cannot be a compliant victim, by the way, and that's where it goes back to you thinking to yourself: why couldn't his wife or his girlfriend do this? It wouldn't satisfy him. These individuals need to go beyond that. And the pornography would kind of take these people to the point where they're okay with doing it. Thank God, lots of people look at violent porn and don't go on like this - they have certain systems in their brain, or they're able to navigate through life, through the traumas that they've experienced - because we generally have the tools, whether it's internally or externally, to be able to stop. In the end, it's all a choice. This individual would fall into our category of adult monsters. This individual made a choice. The porn only went so far, and he decided to take it to the next level. And once he took it to the next level, in his case specifically, there's really no turning back."

I mulled over Rhoades' appeal case. His desperation to get back out of prison. I asked what would have happened if the truck driver had succeeded and obtained his freedom.

"If this guy was able to ever to get out…I mean, he would go on and go right back to doing it," Dr. Simon said bluntly. "This is what he is. He's lived this life for how long? I mean, we don't even when his first kill was, but certainly, whenever it was, he was living his life through those obsessions. That's why the truck driving because, oh brother, it set him on that path. That doesn't mean if you're a truck driver, you're a killer, I just want to make that clear! What I'm saying is, in this specific case is that it allowed that retreat into being what, specifically, he was. If you interviewed him, he would probably be able to pinpoint the first time he had set in his mind to go ahead and do this. He would remember that."

There is a part of me that did want to interview Rhoades, but I always came back to why? So that he could try and spin out thirty years of pent-up Berne psychology or repeat the lies he told Debra in his letters - such as: "I am not guilty of what I've been charged with, either here or in Arizona. A set of very bizarre circumstances, yes, but I did not do any of what is being said about me." Fuck him, I often think, speaking frankly. I have seen Regina's last photograph and don't want to listen to his version of "she moved the mustard." I think more about this case in terms of what we can learn from the facts and what went wrong. About what is still there to find after everyone stopped looking. I had thought for a long time about the way people are probably used to the concepts of staging and signatures when we talk about serial killers and their crime scenes, so I asked Dr. Simon if there was more to it than anger at a finished game.

"The only thing is that it would have lent to the humiliation and degradation," he told me. "She wasn't covered up so, keeping in mind that his whole theme from beginning to end with this particular victim was to torment her and to humiliate her, that is exactly what he did. Serial killers do all sorts of things. I've interviewed one guy where he took her out into the woods and buried her, and he put up rocks in the form of a cross. I've seen a victim photos where they were completely dressed. So, this level of humiliation - where he could have put her clothes on, he could have covered her up…he didn't have to put her out there to where the world can see. He just left her where she lay. He could have done something more as signature but, for the most part, it's fantasy. The remaining fantasy here is: okay, I did what I did with her and I'll continue to humiliate her, even beyond. He had already captivated what he wanted. He took the photos of that."

Decades before my conversation with Doc Simon - back on April 6th 1990, days after Lisa's life was saved by Mike Miller on an Arizona interstate - Special Agents entered Rhoades' apartment and removed all his bondage material, women's clothing, and his favourite white towels - one of which was soaked in blood. The towels mattered because, in the testimonies of both survivors Shauna and Lisa, Rhoades had placed one underneath them before commencing his established pattern of torture.

Amongst all this evidence, the agents found the heart-breaking sequence of Regina photographs I would later be discussing. They haunt everyone who sees them, no matter what storms we have walked through.

FORENSICS

The accounts of the Rhoades case which exist are not what you would call forensics focused. In 1990, DNA was still in its infancy, having first been used to crack a murder in England in 1986 – the offender, Colin Pitchfork, has just been released after serving a thirty-three-year sentence for the rape and murder of two fifteen-year-old girls, causing disgust across the country. The uncle of victim Dawn Ashworth nailed public sentiment in mid-July 2021 when he told the BBC[25]: "It sends the message that child rapists, killers, murderers can at some point in time resume their lives when they themselves have deprived their victims of their lives." He would be recalled to prison two months after walking free.

In America, the first outing for this new technology occurred in 1987, securing the conviction of rapist Tommie Lee Andrews in Florida[26]. It was prompted when Assistant District Attorney Jeffrey Ashton saw a magazine advert for paternity testing and wondered if it could be used to catch the man who raped a woman at knifepoint in her own home. Andrews covered his face and largely kept his fingerprints out of crime scenes, leaving the police flummoxed while twenty-two similar offences went on to take place between May 1986 and March 1987. It was not actually DNA alone which led to his capture though. He was careless at one scene, leaving two fingerprints on a window screen which could not be matched to any known records, but he eventually got caught by officers after a terrified woman reported a prowler. They ran his prints and matched him to the crime, then used DNA to reinforce the prosecution case. We would still be in a much more chaotic

---

25 https://www.bbc.co.uk/news/uk-england-leicestershire-57737050, Colin Pitchfork: Double child killer's release confirmed, BBC Local News, July 13 2021

26 https://www.police1.com/police-products/investigation/dna-forensics/articles/police-history-how-a-magazine-ad-helped-convict-a-rapist-wEnPKjpf6S3brBpF/, Police history: How a magazine ad helped convict a rapist, Police 1, August 28 2018

situation now if the judge had bowed to the defence's argument to exclude the DNA as it was "untested profiteering" by Lifecodes Corp in New York. History was written in Florida that day in court and Andrews was tried repeatedly for other crimes as new evidence was tested. His eventual sentence stretched to one hundred years.

At the very beginning, the sample sizes needed to perform DNA tests were much larger than today and the tests were less sensitive, using what is called restriction fragment length polymorphism (RFLP). Over the years things have changed significantly and the way crime scenes and individual items of evidence are processed has evolved – the cheaper and easier polymerase chain reaction (PCR) testing being one example. New methods and technologies are being developed constantly, which led to me to a conversation with my Cold Case Foundation colleague Francine Bardole. Her background is fascinating.

"I attended the 10th set session at the body farm. I was very lucky to have Patricia Cornwell help pay for my attendance there, which was a ten-week training," Francine told me. "It hit every area, and it was the most phenomenal training. I learned so much from that. Experts were all there and I keep in touch with a lot of them. It was a wonderful, wonderful opportunity for me."

Francine has worked in criminal justice for over twenty-five years, carefully taking steps at every stage not to advance herself but to advance forensic analysis and the way victims are treated.

"I began working with pre-sentence investigation reports for defendants out of prison or on looking at probation prior to their sentencing," Francine told me. "This is where I became really involved with looking into crimes and what was going on. After I had done this for approximately five years, working with people that were going to be sentenced, some of them some very heinous crimes, I wanted to know what victims went through. Because, in doing the pre-sentence reports, there's a place where we discuss what the victims have gone through, if they want to address the courts, and if there's any restitution. I found it interesting that the victims were very upset and angry because they felt that they had more to say, and they felt ignored. I didn't quite understand what they were meaning, so I took a job working as a crime scene technician with a local police department - Western City Police Department - but I did that part time, so I could understand what victims had gone through."

Francine genuinely cares, and that warmth and passion radiates whenever you speak to her. She made a conscious decision to step beyond the sterile review process of pre-sentencing and put herself into the horror and chaos of active crime scene investigation. There is an obvious and stark contrast between her psychology and Rhoades's, referring to the active choices he made - as highlighted by Dr. Simon.

"And it was certainly not like what the common person would understand," she said. "We see what we get from the news or from television shows or from the media. But when I was able to see what victims have gone through, it was even more touching and heart-wrenching. To be there at the scene to see how many people are affected. And I decided to go ahead and take this job as full time. From that time, I continue to work as a crime scene technician until I got really good at crime scene investigation. And I became a crime scene investigator."

Francine is modest. She did not just become a CSI, she became an exceptional one and has spent her entire career looking for ways to improve the quality of the work and do it more efficiently.

"For several years where I would go out to the crime scenes, I'd photograph, I'd collect evidence and, in the process, I would have to make the determination of what evidence was the most probative. Some of the evidence isn't what we would think would be normally probative," she said. "I was introduced, after a while of doing this, to a method of getting DNA off clothing- the M-Vac, which is a wet vacuum device that is made here in Utah. I had heard about it from a friend of mine who worked at a laboratory,

Carol Raleigh, and she was one of my mentors while I was learning about DNA."

Carol is the Forensic Account Manager at Sorenson Forensics in Salt Lake City. Sorenson has been focused on helping state crime labs clear processing backlogs in rape kits for several years, but this doesn't come without controversy, as volume processing of DNA evidence almost always will. Kentucky State picked up an error in results from Sorenson – who were handling a forty-year backlog of over four-and-half-thousand kits for them – relating to misidentified black male suspect in a crime committed by a white offender. Fewer than ten cases were impacted[27]. Despite a change in procedures and a second inquiry by the Texas Forensic Science Commission, the volume of testing continued to grow as state labs pushed out their workloads and a further dispute arose with the Illinois lab in 2019. The Innocence Project prompted an investigation into Sorenson[28] which delayed the Texas report's publication, due to the alleged combination of a sample which saw a man named Kevin Bailey sentenced to eighty years in prison. Sorenson dispute what happened, claiming that it was The Innocence Project who requested a combined sampling process. The arguments are bitter, and Sorenson's CEO Kent Harman has been quick to point out that seven errors in five years of work is miniscule compared with errors made at public laboratories – which appears to be a valid point based on assorted research papers over the years. It is not just unique to America as an issue either. The case of the "Phantom of Heilbronn" is a well-known anecdote these days, relating to investigators across Germany, Austria, and France pursuing a non-existent female serial killer and international shed burglar

---

[27] https://eu.courier-journal.com/story/news/crime/2018/12/20/contamination-triggers-delay-kentucky-rape-kits-backlog/2310035002/, Lab contamination slows progress on Kentucky's rape kit backlog, Courier Journal, December 20 2018, Matthew Glowicki

[28] https://www.kuer.org/justice/2019-05-07/private-utah-dna-lab-faces-scrutiny-after-crime-evidence-said-to-be-mishandled, Private Utah DNA Lab Faces Scrutiny After Crime Evidence Said To Be Mishandled, Kuer 90.1, May 7 2019, Rebecca Ellis

between 1993 and 2009, only to find the DNA was coming from the same factory worker, a woman producing sterile but not forensically clean cotton swabs which should never have been used in DNA testing across Europe to begin with. None of this tarnishes the evidential value of DNA, it just means the processes for handling this vital material need to be constantly monitored and enhanced.

The M-Vac mentioned by Francine is an advancement in collection rather than testing, so it sits at the very front of the examination process, in the hands of CSIs. It facilitates the collection of tiny samples which may never have been viable in years gone by and, now that DNA testing has caught up, can provide vital information from the smallest evidence.

"It was really interesting, because this was such a unique technology," Francine told me. "It was like a little carpet cleaner that you could use on an item of evidence, say clothing saturated with a clear clean blood buffer solution, and it would suck up that solution. Along with sucking up that solution, it would loosen the DNA that was embedded in the fibres and get those skin cells that contain the DNA into that solution and into a bottle. After which I would pour it through a filter that would trap the skin cells. Once this filter is dried, I can ship it to a laboratory and they can tell me how much DNA is on the filter. And then we will know what our next step is, which would be DNA testing. I believe Western City Police Department was the first police department to obtain this system. The results are wonderful, even the FBI has put out a report that these results go far beyond what traditional methods of swabbing can do. And what's really interesting is since that time and me acquiring this, it can get mixtures but now we have software that can unmix those mixtures."

This is genuinely exciting. A mixture occurs when the DNA profiles of multiple people are present and finding them is more common since the sensitivity of testing improved, allowing profiles to generated from just a few cells. I looked for the FBI report Francine mentioned and found a more recent study in the Journal of Forensic Sciences[29]. The report recommends further development in the technology and cites expense of set up as a barrier to its wider use, but does highlight the advantages of wet-vacuum where the material to be collected is on a porous or difficult substrate – such as cinderblock, which breaks swabs. In those use cases, M-vac makes a lot of sense. As the study found, it not only retrieved more material than traditional swabbing, but also extracted material from previously swabbed surfaces. M-Vac Systems have gone out of their way to work on validation, asking public agencies such as the Washington State Patrol, Richmond County Sherriff's Department, Philadelphia PD to test and feedback on the product. It seems to be a friendly company, well intentioned, and came from the investigative community, so it does deserve the credibility it is building. Of course, once you have the material – whether it comes from swabs or a wet-vacuum – you may get those mixtures. The question has always circled around what to do with them.

"Well, that that was an argument by a lot of laboratories for a long time," Francine said. "It was: oh yeah, we've got a lot of DNA but there's a lot of mixtures. There's STRmix, the software's have been around for a while, but not a lot of laboratories have it - private laboratories will have software and now some of the state laboratories, a lot of them are getting it, but back in the day, they really didn't. What do you have? Too much DNA, not enough DNA? As if you're really thinking you're going to get the perfect amount. So, we must learn to work within the boundaries that we have. And that's what this software can do."

STRmix, which is Star Mix to Francine and others, was developed by the New Zealand Crown Research Institute working with Forensic Science South Australia. It sorts DNA samples, even mixed ones, and can run its

---

[29] https://doi.org/10.1111/1556-4029.14508, Comparison of the M-Vac® Wet-Vacuum-Based Collection Method to a Wet-Swabbing Method for DNA Recovery on Diluted Bloodstained Substrates, Journal of Forensic Sciences Volume 65, Issue 6, Pages 1828-1834, November 2020, Jessica M, McLamb M.S, Lara D, Adams M.S & Mark F. Kavlick Ph.D

own internal database for comparisons. I spend a lot of time tinkering with practical software, making it do useful things as opposed to needful things, and this is one of those developments which makes you sit back and say "wow." All this costs money though, whether it be the software or the vacuum, and I wondered if this had an impact on whether it was put into use in the US.

"Oh, yes, yes, it did," Francine said. "Typically, the state labs are reliant on the legislature and their state funding to get the equipment they need, the manpower they need, the buildings they need. Anything they need, they have to rely on the legislature. And, sometimes, the legislature just doesn't understand that there are new technologies or there are new things that happen and they need to put these in place. But if they get a technology one year, they'll say: okay, this is good for a few years, and they probably won't look into giving any more money for a while. The state labs are kind of at a handicap depending on what is going to be given to them as far as money and, don't forget, the state labs are run on taxpayer money - so the taxpayers are also carrying that burden as well." This structural defect creates a number of conflicts and reinforces the cross-jurisdictional issues which run rampant across America, creating the environment which lets people like Rhoades offending become serialised. Outwardly, this always boils down to reputation and public perception, often producing knee-jerk reactions and spending which is more tuned into political capital of public officials. The most common outcome, however, is that nothing happens at all, leaving agencies constantly behind developments and running to catch up.

"When we're not getting cases solved, and we're not getting things done, it makes things look bad," Francine continued. "Not because the state labs are bad, but because they might not have access to the technologies and funding they need. Private labs, number one, have the technologies. They have the newest technologies and they have the most updated ways of doing things. The problem is they charge a lot of money and state labs, the police departments, or the agencies - through the taxpayers - must come up with the funding, and they are not a bottomless source of money. It's very difficult for law enforcement to provide the money and the funding for every case that happens. They've got to be very careful about where they're putting their money so they can get these cases solved. Plus, a lot of law enforcement agencies are not aware of what technologies are out there, or what can be done."

These issues are circular and self-feeding, leading to situations like the backlog in rape kit testing and the eventual conflicts between state and private providers like Sorenson.

"Another factor," Francine sighed, "state laboratories have a huge backlog. And so typically, for me, in order to get DNA test results from my state laboratory, it would take between a year to a year and a half to get anything back. Private labs usually have six-to-eight-week turnaround time, so there's a big difference there. If you want to solve crime, don't let the perpetrator go around for a year and a half, two years. Better six or eight weeks."

I remember the waiting for results from the Forensic Science Service, back when it existed, being much shorter and have watched in horror as forensic analysis in the UK descended into chaos when it was abolished in 2012 under the post 2008 austerity measures which stripped public services to the bones. By 2019, the House of Lords Science and Technology Committee[30] was loudly ringing the alarm, with Chairman Lord Patel stating: "a forensic science market which, unless properly regulated, will soon suffer the shocks of major forensic science providers going out of business and putting justice in jeopardy." They cited a lack of leadership, lack of funding, and insufficient research setting the stage for a future littered with "wrongful arrests and unsolved major crimes." The move to private providers from a state system has always proved problematic in the UK, where regulation is always left wanting, and the forensic transition has already led to scandals and collapses. Syntec was de-accredited for passing mobile phones seized for analysis to

---

30 https://www.labnews.co.uk/article/2029976/forensics-in-crisis, Forensics In Crisis, Laboratory News, September 2 2019

consumer phone shops, Key Forensic Services couldn't handle the workload and went bust, and Randox Testing Services were suspended from police contracts after they were found manipulating data and forty convictions were overturned. A once secure and reliable public service was replaced by a badly organised rabble, opening new backlogs, and creating a much larger cyber-attack surface than ever existed previously.

Francine recognises the problems only too well but, rather than get bogged down in what is broken, she pushed forwards to make things better. Over the years, she invented and refined a processing method all her own. She is rightly proud of the achievement. It is called the Bardole method.

"There were many times I would, or other agencies would, submit shell casings or smaller items of evidence to their laboratories and only afterwards they'd process the shell casings for fingerprints for DNA," she explained. "Rarely did we get anything off them and this went on for years. Finally, I sat down and I thought: why would I keep sending these shell casings in only to get the same results – it was the definition of insanity, doing the same thing over and over and getting the same results, and I thought I'm tired of this. So, I did some research and studying on shell casings. I looked at them under microscope, at skin cells, looked at what other agencies were doing, other countries that were working on doing things. And I was able to come up with the Bardole method, which is able to get DNA off of spent shell casings."

Francine was highlighting the problem which arises from the need to carry out multiple processes to secure evidence, often causing the erosion of another piece of evidence due to the chemicals and physical techniques involved. It is a very real dilemma faced by investigators, sacrificing one avenue in the hope another is viable. With the Bardole method, Francine found a way through this maze.

"It is quite simple method, there are no chemicals involved," she told me. "It's clean and it's a method that just about any police department could use. I am finishing up my research on this but have worked with different agencies to help solve cases, Broward County being one where they have solved a case. And there was also a case solved out of Fort Lauderdale using my method on a necklace chain, something very small. So it works on very small things and shell cases."

Non-destructive testing which can fidget valuable evidence from small items as well as shell casings is a priceless innovation. To put this in a practical context, if you applied the Bardole method to a famous case such as that of six-year-old JonBenét Ramsey, in which a garotte was twisted with a paintbrush, it would work well compared to standard swabs. This little girl was murdered in the basement of her family home in Boulder, Colorado on Christmas Day 1996. The tiny beauty queen was found by her father, seven hours after she was first reported missing. She had been hit on the head, fracturing her skull, and was asphyxiated with the garotte. For years the family faced suspicion, which circled around a ransom note seized upon as staged by them to protect someone in the family. The case rumbles on to this day, ownership of it shifting between Boulder Police and the District Attorney's office.

"That would be a very difficult thing to swab and get anything," Francine explained. "Because if it's a wooden handle there are little ridges on it. The only way you can get into that is to use my method. Those skin cells can go deep down into the grains of the wood." Francine's work is truly extraordinary, and also works on rocks – which are notoriously difficult to get useful evidence from. "Yes, yes, it works. If they're smaller than tiny stones, or if there's, you know, bolts and screws or little things like that, then my method will work. But I have used my method garottes, which is what JonBenét had, and I'm getting DNA off of them. And this is DNA that you know, should be, you know, perpetrator DNA. And it seems to be working well."

If I think about my time in policing, if we had even had the opportunity to deploy this technique in burglaries or other serious crimes, we would have caught many more serial offenders. I am still blown away by the possibilities of what she has done to advance practical forensic analysis. The reason the Ramsey case came to mind is a simple one: with Rhoades and the murder of Regina Walters, we found ourselves looking at a murder which has a very similar conclusion to it, in terms of in terms of the use of a garotte device made from wire and wood. Much as I had asked Dr. Simon for his professional opinion on the case review, I wanted Francine's thoughts too, on both the case and how she might have approached the evidence collection process.

"I want to say first of all that Rhoades preyed on people he thought were forgotten or were social throwaways," she said. "And I believe that everybody deserves to live their life and not have it taken from them through a predator like this. That's from my personal view and it makes me very sad. It's almost heart-breaking to think that his victims were mostly very young and their lives hadn't really begun to take shape. It just it sickens me, you know, that somebody can do this sort of thing. From a professional viewpoint, as I looked at some of the evidence - aside from the fact he's a very sick individual, for whatever reason, I know his background was difficult - I do believe he is not just one or two time killer. I do believe he is a serial rapist, and I believe he has many more victims than we understand or realise. I think there is some wonderful probative evidence to be worked on - all the evidence that was found whether it was in the truck, or whether it was in his apartment. I think there's some real good stuff. So we would know exactly how far and wide he did things and took victims."

I wanted to know which items she would focus on, thinking back over Greg's presentation. I asked Francine where she would start and how she would proceed if we were able to run that job from fresh today.

"Well, first of all," she began, "Regina Walters was located in a barn in Illinois. Around her neck was baling wire. Now what would be interesting to know is how that baling wire was twisted around her neck and more about the garotte that was used to twist it. I would like to see that - I think I could get something even off the baling wire, depending on how it was made and how was twisted. The other would be the piece of wood. I could use the M-Vac and I could also use my method on that, so I could get as much DNA as possible using both those techniques. Also, from what we looked at, in his apartment there was a plethora of great evidence. I mean, there was women's clothing. Who did this clothing belong to? There were towels, bloody towels, one of them was similar to the cotton fibre that was found with Regina's body. There was jewellery and torture devices and there were leather straps - probably all sorts of things that we can use M-Vac or my method on. I believe there was the black dress that was identified as similar to the one that Regina had on, that would be great. I looked at all the stuff he had the briefcase - I guess they would call it his rape kit…I would love to get my hands on it. I'd like to go through it. I could sit down and look at each piece of evidence and I could tell you, what would be the best method for each item. That's what I do with cases: I go over them in detail and I look at all the photos, I look at the evidence, and make that determination of what would be the best to work with. They had great evidence there."

I pressed her a little more, asking what she would have zoomed in if she were the lead crime scene examiner at the apartment. Being able to do this properly comes from experience, and experience comes from learning on the job – often including hard lessons about collecting too much evidence, which most of us go through early in law enforcement careers, before we understand how to prioritise. I wanted the practical step-by-step, not the movie version of what we all do, which people are so used to.

"I think this is what a lot of crime scene investigators learn as time goes on: you don't collect everything because not everything is going to be as probative," she told me. "So, as you look through his residence, Rhoades took a lot of photos of his victims. And having those photos would really help determine the evidence that we're going to go after. The clothing items, why would he have women's clothing there? I mean, he wasn't married anymore. A profiler would probably tell you that these are souvenirs that he takes from his victims. And that's not unusual. Always collect anything that is dissimilar to this person, stuff that shouldn't be there. There's always reason for it being there. I believe he told one of his victims who escaped that his name was Whips and Chains, so he likes to use those whips. And I could probably get stuff off those so easily. The chains, depending on what they look like - on how the ends are and how they were used - if you could look at the photographs or see them at the scene, I would definitely collect those. And I would collect them not only as evidence but evidence to be processed."

This is a genuinely important distinction, as Francine went on to explain.

"Sometimes you can take evidence to just show that they match this or they look like this. Or we are going to process these for fingerprints or DNA. Also, the jewellery. I've run into a lot of older cases where they will give the jewellery back to the victim's family. And then you know, nothing is ever done with that. Then there's the towels – something I see a lot of in cases of homicides is, oftentimes, you'll probably see an item that's been used to clean up blood or to wipe up blood regardless whether it's a towel, or tissue or handkerchief or whatever it is."

The horse bit is not something either of us overlooked and, set in the context of the availability of software like STRmix, it takes on a much more important meaning than it might have in 1990.

"If there's mixtures, we've got that unmixing. I mean, it's gotten really good. It certainly wouldn't be something you wouldn't want to try to process because think of the saliva, the skin cells, the stuff that's on there. Now, there could be quite a bit but there might be something that really stands out that we can include, or we can exclude."

The changes in the way DNA evidence is handled does not stop at PCR, STRmix, or any of the collection developments already mentioned. Francine has been working at the forefront of a new DNA technique which is dramatically changing investigative practice and allowing those working these cases to step beyond the confines of the central Combined DNA Index System (CODIS).

"CODIS is what law enforcement the FBI and agencies use to try to make matches," Francine said. "You enter a profile, and you get someone's DNA profile from an item of evidence, and you don't know who this person is so, you'll put it into CODIS to see if it hits on anybody. I can tell you from my own experience, there have been some killers that have gone under the wire. There are those that never get in the database because, remember, we didn't start really doing a lot of entering until later on, say early '90s and mid-90s. Also there were a lot of prisoners and people in prisons and jails that their DNA was not taken to put into that CODIS database. What we now have is genealogical profiling."

I knew where she was headed and had used some of these services to fill in Rhoades' background in Council Bluffs.

"If you think about Ancestry, Family Tree, and 23andme," Francine continued. "There's different genealogical databases that people want to know who they are related to. There's a lot of this information. Now that isn't the same. That isn't the same part of the DNA that we use to put in the CODIS database, the genealogical database uses what is called SNP or snips. You can't reformat what's in the CODIS database into a snip, it has to be done from the start, so snips are what they use in order to get your genealogical profiling - for example phenotyping. And what a phenotype is, it will tell you the hair colour, the eye colour, the skin colour. According to these snips are the probabilities of you having blue eyes - say it comes up with: this person has a ninety-six percent chance of having blue eyes, and brown hair, maybe eighty-five percent. We can get an idea of physical characteristics from this phenotyping, which can really help if you're getting the person in as soon as possible."

The question which dances around new developments like this, is always: does it have a practical use? The answer is yes, in this case. And it has already landed big fish in the under the radar serial killer world.

"One would be the Golden State killer, out of California," Francine said. The Golden State Killer, Joseph James Dangelo – a former police officer –

committed thirteen confirmed murders, fifty rapes, and one-hundred-and-twenty burglaries from 1973 to 1986. He was only identified and finally captured in 2018, in his seventies. The genealogy records of a relative were tied to DNA collected from his crimes – which had, until then, sat unmatched in CODIS for years. "He started out raping, then he ended up killing and he went free for a long time, until they were able to put it into GEDmatch. That matches the genealogical databases where they were able to find out closest relative so you can move into the direction of where this person would probably be and who they're related to. This is very valuable. I know there's a lot of kickback with people not wanting their DNA in a database or being able to be searched but, in my estimation, if you're not guilty, there really shouldn't be an issue with it. I would rather see a killer off the road or off the street or out of my community than attack somebody I care about or love. A child, a parent, a brother, whoever. This will really help in that situation. I do believe, in the future this is the direction things are going to go."

Thinking about an expanded DNA database, I imagined how different the story of the girl in the pasture would be. She would never have become an anonymous kid - an unidentified body scattered by animals and left incomplete. Who she was would not be a mystery, her family would be known. More than likely her killer would be known. The sheer volume of cold cases would be reduced in a stroke by eliminating one of the greatest opportunities which exists in America: the ability to cross state and county lines and be unknown. One little pin prick at birth could change the shape of crime in America forever and change the destiny of little children who never even grow old enough to appreciate the concept that some people regard human life as disposable. This is a huge issue, though. Well beyond my personal capacity to even know where to start, so I let the thought burn down and poked the embers of the rest of my conversation with Francine.

Sat in an evidence locker somewhere, unless it has been thrown away or destroyed, or rusting in a junk yard, inside an old International truck or the alternative rig, sits the evidence she could use to light up Rhoades' true offending history. But, without the political knee-jerk required to open purse strings across multiple states already struggling to comes to terms with backlogs and competing budgetary demands, it may never happen. The barriers to justice are, sadly, as big as the potential for its delivery.

DESERET

Far from Council Bluffs and its golden spike, at the far end of the Mormon Trail and almost one thousand miles away on foot, Salt Lake City nestles in an ancient basin. The Oquirrh Mountains flank the city to the West, Traverse Mountains lay south, and the majestic Wasatch Range and its canyons impose from the East[31]. The Jordan River flows through the city to the North-West, where it drains into the Great Salt Lake. Marshlands and mudflats separate the city from the water, kicking up what is known as "lake stink" a couple of times a year as bacteria does what it does. Pollution connects both ends of the historic trail between Council Bluffs and Salt Lake City, the latter suffering from air quality rather than water quality issues, arising from the geography of the basin and winter temperature variations trapping gunk. Legislators have acted on this, responding to protests with free public transport for seven months a year and compulsory responses when air quality falls below safe levels.

Despite the problems of a growing city and the beauty of the mountains which phalanx around it, Salt Lake City may one day cease to be. The Wasatch Fault[32] runs at the base of the mountains, flexing its brutal strength every thousand years or so. Scientists say an earthquake at six or greater on the Richter Scale is probable in the next fifty years. To make matters worse, the sleeping seismic line is not alone, joined by the West Valley Fault beneath the basin. Scientists now believe the two move together[33] and say the soft clay beneath the city – the product of the prehistoric submersion by Lake Bonneville – would liquidate. The result would be landslides from the

---

[31] https://en.wikipedia.org/wiki/Salt_Lake_City, Salt Lake City, Wikipedia, CC BY-SA 3.0

[32] https://en.wikipedia.org/wiki/Wasatch_Fault, Wasatch Fault, Wikipedia, CC BY-SA 3.0

[33] https://www.livescience.com/28782-utah-bigger-earthquakes-wasatch-fault.html, Salt Lake City Could See Bigger Earthquakes, Live Science, April 17 2013, Becky Oskin

Wasatch range and inbound waves from the Great Salt Lake. A biblical event, you could say, which would kill thousands, flatten buildings, disrupt utilities and transportation, and take out around half of the city's hospital beds. The shadow of Twin Peaks looms deadlier knowing this.

As pioneers of the late 1840s arrived in the valley described in the vision of Brigham Young, many days since the Missouri river crossing, the indigenous population once again faced the trials brought by the relentless explorations of American settlers. In 1847 they brought Measles and, according to local history[34], thirty-six of the natives were buried in one grave alone. But this was how the Latter-day Saints came to settle, wasting no time in getting started on building the Salt Lake Temple – a forty-year labour, eventually dedicated in the spring of 1893. The intervening years saw great change. In 1849, the State of Deseret was petitioned for and refused, with Congress as it was then establishing the Utah territory a year later. Slavery came and went, the Utah War – a conflict over polygamy – began and ended, and the Transcontinental Railroad arrived. Salt Lake City and Council Bluffs are, forever it seems, tied together.

Deseret is a curiosity, something I first learned about while studying secondary school history – because the curriculum still did everything in its power to evade Britain's past, with good reason, from the State's perspective, when I was a child. Deseret comes from the Jaredite word for "honeybee", at least according to the Book of Mormon, which was first published in the 1830s but claims to be much older in origin. It remains subject to some criticism, but those conversations and concerns are not mine to argue or repeat. The State of Deseret, as it was proposed, would have been huge – stretching across Utah and Nevada, and bringing parts or California,

---

[34] https://www.deseret.com/2007/1/5/19993469/tidbits-of-history-151-unusual-highlights-of-salt-lake-county#part-of-downtown-salt-lake-city-will-soon-be-redeveloped-by-the-lds-church-for-decades-the-salt-lake-temple-stood-out-as-the-areas-most-prominent-structure, Tidbits of history — Unusual highlights of Salt Lake County, Deseret News, January 5 2007, Lynn Arave

Arizona, Colorado, New Mexico, Wyoming, Idaho, and even Oregon within its bounds. Those who drew it were allegedly trying to prevent disputes with other European settlers and they nearly managed it, unbelievably. At least in part, as then President Zachary Taylor proposed combining Deseret with California to reduce the number of Senate seats and preserve power. But this was all eventually set aside and the Territory of Utah came to be, with Brigham Young as the first governor. It was only when the railroad came and the golden spike was driven at Promontory Summit that the idea of the State of Deseret began to lose its hold and the shadow government of Mormon elders, led by Young, began to give up the proverbial ghost. Still, that old honeybee persists and Deseret News, originally founded in 1850, is Utah's oldest operating business – at least according to its website[35]. It appears to be a subsidiary of a company owned directly by The Church of Jesus Christ of Latter-day Saints, but you don't really need to look much farther than the state symbols. Almost everything features a beehive.

Dr. Todd Grey took the long way round to Utah, years before he joined the Cold Case Foundation and eventually ended up speaking to me over the internet in 2020. He was invited onto the team by Dean Jackson, the Foundation's Deputy Executive Director, who had worked as a coroner in Wyoming and met Dr. Grey several times as he delivered training to law enforcement.

"My background," Dr. Grey told me, "Is that I received an undergraduate degree from Yale University in anthropology - it was actually social-cultural anthropology, not physical anthropology - and decided late in my university career that I thought pursuing a career in medicine would probably be better than an academic career as an anthropologist. So, I applied to medical school and was accepted at Dartmouth Medical School for the class of 1980."

---

35 https://www.deseret.com/pages/about-us, Deseret News, About Us

Like many of us, youth brings with it decisions which need to be rectified, and Dr. Grey did not leave it nearly as late to fix as most of us unfortunately do. Choices, as the other Doctor, Doc Simon, might point out with a smile on his face.

"In medical school I was not exposed to forensics really," Dr. Grey said. "I was not given that much of an idea of what a career in pathology would be like and chose to start a residency in paediatrics." He did start an internship in that field, at the University of California in San Diego, but very quickly decided it was not for him. "Fortunately," he continued, "The pathology department at the University of California in San Diego had an opening for another resident. I did what was essentially a lateral transfer from paediatrics into pathology and was having a much nicer and more interesting time. At UCSD, I was mentored by a forensic pathologist named Frank Rosch, and he invited me down to the medical examiner's office and said: You know, I think you might enjoy this. I was hooked literally from the word go. I just found it fast-paced and interesting, and almost immediately decided that I wanted to do a forensic fellowship and become a forensic pathologist."

Social-cultural anthropology is quite interesting, a form of practical study of humanity to understand what makes us all philosophically similar or, indeed, different. But I fully understand Dr. Grey's instant addiction to the sharp end of things. Rather than the study of culture and society, forensic pathology is the close-up examination of a person to establish how and why they died. People who train in this field are experts in both the human body, in collecting and interpreting evidence, and in the mechanisms of death. It is a multi-disciplined role, requiring at least working – and often expert – knowledge of toxicology, ballistics, trace evidence, and bloodwork including DNA. They co-ordinate, the supervise, they inform. They show and tell. Across the jurisdictions where you find a medical examiner, you will normally find a forensic pathologist carrying out the autopsies. The concept of the Medical Examiner does not exist everywhere, for example over in the

UK it is only being more broadly rolled out in 2021 to 2022, expanding from a non-statutory establishment over the last few years which focused on Acute Hospital Trusts. In the coming years, it will become statutory[36], and all non-coronial deaths will fall within the remit of the role. The system based on Coroners, effectively a Victorian-era legacy in America, gave rise to the Medical Examiners - eventually being replaced by them, or mixed with them in a hybrid model, in all but eleven states. I have good memories of coroners. They were always keen to get to the root of events which led to a death and equally open to taking extraordinary steps to protect grieving families but those closed-door conversations stay where they are. I also had positive experiences with forensic pathologists, having always had the uncanny ability to attract the really strange sudden deaths, but the concept of a medical examiner is a recent change. There was always a dividing line between the two.

"My wife had an obligation to pay back scholarship time to the Public Health Service," Dr. Grey said, starting to explain his path to the Medical Examiner's Office. "So, when she completed her residency in internal medicine, we moved to Gallup, New Mexico. She had a staff position at the Indian Health Service hospital there. I, again, sort of lucked out and found a part time position in the local non-Indian Health Service hospital, working as a surgical pathologist. We spent three years in New Mexico doing that. I also had contacted the New Mexico medical investigators office and offered my services as a part time pathologist out in the community - to do forensic cases there in New Mexico, even though I had not undergone formal forensic training. When my wife's obligation had been paid off, we, well I, decided that I wanted to do a forensic fellowship and was accepted into the training

---

36 https://www.england.nhs.uk/establishing-medical-examiner-system-nhs/#:~:text=The%20purpose%20of%20the%20medical,of%20deaths%20to%20the%20coroner, The national medical examiner system, National Health Service

program at the Dade County Medical Examiner's Office in Miami, Florida. We spent a year there while I was trained in forensic pathology."

The geography and weather immediately sprang to mind. Heat and humidity. Bodies of water. Autopsies are not compulsory attendance for police officers, at least not on my side of the Atlantic, but they perhaps should be. I was a probationer working one of my odd circumstance sudden deaths when I volunteered to attend my first one - auto-erotic asphyxiation is supposed to be a once in a career event, though that's not how things went. I had already seen multiple bodies, in multiple states of decay, by that point so figured I could cope with it. And I could, mostly. I was fine with the body cavity being opened, with the weighing of the organs - even the removal of the face, despite the inverted moustache which has painted numerous dreams over the years. The problem came out of the freezer and onto the next table, and that is when I reached for the bucket. I nearly used it, but for the mortuary assistant handing me a pair of earplugs and telling me to shove them up my nose. It worked, in preventing an involuntary physical response at least, but the smell emanating from the poor soul found floating in the river impregnated everything. My clothing, my hair. My tastebuds. The only thing which helped was lemons, using the squeezed fruits to scrub your skin and the juice to wash your hair and gargle with. The process is a series of discomforts, from the stinging in any open cuts or scrapes you happen to have on your – frequent companions for any response officer - to the weird agony of gargling with pure lemon juice. There's also the unfortunate blonde-red tinge to the hair if you happen to be summertime mousey, as I am. The lemon suggestion did not come from the mortuary assistant, as it happens. I remembered one of the characters mentioning it on the original series of CSI. The human brain files information in strange ways. That is a fact. By the time I was fishing a body out of one of the lakes on Hampstead Heath, which had been called in by a woman walking her dog as a "dead badger in the pond," several years had gone by and I was able to walk the inexperienced officers under my supervision through the process, without them having to learn things the hard way.

As Dr. Grey pointed out, though, the challenges in Florida weren't just the weather and the water.

"We used to joke around that there were only two kinds of cases that we would see in Miami, and that was regular and unleaded," he told me. The early 1980s was a dark time in Florida's history. In 1981 most of America's cocaine, marijuana, and even fake Quaaludes were being trafficked via Miami. There were so many bodies in the city the morgue, they overspilled into a refrigerator truck which was kept until 1988. "When I was there, it was sort of toward the end of the cocaine wars, so there were an awful lot of homicides related to drug trafficking. In that vein of business, I completed my fellowship."

This made me think of Mexico. I have been out there twice. The first time as a guest of Assuntos Internos of the Policia Federal, funded by the US Embassy. I spoke at an assembly meeting of police chiefs and ambassadors from across Latin America, giving them a speech on the importance of accurately recorded crime figures in designing complex law enforcement strategies. Along with other dignitaries, we spent a day being taken on a tour of various facilities. Our bus was flanked with Federales in pickup trucks, machine gunners standing in the beds in case we were targeted and made examples of. It was a more likely outcome than my hosts originally let on. I vividly remember sitting in the security services bunker as part of our privileged excursion. The central table, complete with the President's place at the head of it, was surrounded by darked windows. They lit the rooms behind up for us, exposing banks of huge screens and busy staff monitoring everything from air traffic to military deployments. I watched with curiosity, then coughed quietly as they explained the screen showing police and military deployments in response to reports of violence. The group quietened as my chaperone translated.

"Imagine what would happen if the air traffic data was wrong and was used to guide planes across Mexico…it would be a disaster. Imagine if the crime data was wrong, and that was used to guide policing and resource deployments across Mexico…" When I delivered my speech later that day, all the attendees listened that little bit harder as I repeated this. That is also the only speech I have ever finished with an Irvine Welsh quote. It was 2014, and I was lucky enough to be in Mexico City for the Day of The Dead. I returned home just in time to deliver a speech at a special screening of Serpico for a whistleblowing charity in London.

Two years later I was back in Mexico again, once more in time to see the beauty of Coyoacán on Día de los Muertos. This time a think-tank had flown me over to work on a report about crime rates in Mexico. I was bolder that visit, not being a guest of Internal Affairs, so I walked each day from my hotel to the office – a stone's throw from the Leon Trotsky Museum and just on the rim of the Land of The Wolf itself. I helped them reverse engineer the sexual offence figures, to give a probability of true rape levels in Mexico – a terrifying number – and worked something else out too. Using recorded crime alongside other elements of public data – such as accidental death rates, which "mysteriously" increased when homicides reduced – you could identify local government corruption through the changes in crime patterns. By the time I had finished, I was able to pinpoint transition dates in the data and later confirm them with election timelines and inbound or outbound public figures. This is a scary technique because it provides attribution to something often thought of as intangible. I was offered the opportunity to go and visit some of these areas, to talk with these administrations about the findings. For reasons which I still think are quite clear, I was happy to decline and flew home after the press interviews were done. I completely understand why Dr. Grey needed a change.

"The next step was: where do you want to be?" he told me. "My wife had lots of contacts and good employment opportunities in New Mexico. I also could have easily gotten a job with the Medical Examiner's office in

Albuquerque, but that office was going through some political turmoil at the time, and I decided that maybe that wasn't where I wanted to be. And so looked around elsewhere in the West. It turned out that one that the chief medical examiner in Utah at that time, was somebody I had worked with before, when I was in Gallup as a part time pathologist, and he was quite happy to recruit me and bring me out there."

Dr. Grey took the position as an Associate Medical Examiner for the state of Utah in 1986. His chief at the time decided it was time to move on two years later so, in August 1988, he was appointed Chief Medical Examiner. He had no idea he would end up involved in the case of Robert Ben Rhoades in the years which followed the completion of his own two-and-a-half-thousand-mile trail to Deseret.

"I'm relying on you know, fuzzy memory. This was back in the 90s after all," he told me. "So, it's been a while since I've had an opportunity to actually look at photographs and review the autopsy and all the information - what it is in the medical examiner's file about this case. My recollection is the report of death was made in the early afternoon. And, since it was a slow day, my chief investigator and I decided that we'd both drive out to the scene to see what was going on. The information we had at that time was scant, it was that there was a body of what appeared to be a young female in a moderate to severe state of decomposition found in a rural area. Scrub pinyon trees and typical Utah desert climate wilderness, just off a major north-south freeway in Millard County."

Public records and stories from the Deseret News[37] pinpoint the location as just over twenty miles south of Fillmore, in Millard County. Out on the Western edge of Utah, bordering Nevada, Millard County is bordered to the West by several peaks, including Mine Camp and Pioneer. The I-15 tracks the edge of the mountains north to south, joining the I-70 at the county's

---

37 https://www.deseret.com/2005/2/25/19879187/illinois-killer-is-sought-for-trial-in-1990-utah-slaying, Illinois killer is sought for trial in 1990 Utah slaying, Deseret News, February 25 2005, Pat Reavy

south-western edge. From there, you can head North to Salt Lake City, West to Denver, or South to Las Vegas without leaving major roads. Perfect for a killer such as Rhoades. I tracked the twenty miles south from Fillmore on the map and found the flat scrubland around Black Rock Volcano and Fishlake National Forest. It is wild out there, bleakly so. The expanse of it intimidating even in images viewed from a distance. If you exit the interstate at Meadow, heading for Kanosh, it is possible to reconnect with I-15 on County Road 1, only adding two miles or so to the route. The road is quiet, less open. Pinyon and scrub within easy access of a truck driver, should they pull over. Dirt roads and unpaved lanes criss-cross the area.

"We drove out there and came to the scene with investigators from the Sheriff's Office," Dr. Grey said. "My recollection is that we had an unclad decomposed female body that, if I remember right, was lying face down in the dirt - in the scrubs and weeds with what appeared to be at the time multiple gunshot wounds on the body. The scene was otherwise not very helpful or enlightening as to how this body got there. Clearly, as it was a side road adjacent to the freeway, any tracks or prints that might have been in the area had been obscured by whatever additional passers-by and people driving on that dirt road might have done to it. When we brought the body back to the medical examiner's office in Salt Lake, I did the examination and confirmed that she was indeed the victim of multiple gunshot wounds. The degree of decomposition meant that we could not obtain useful or comparable fingerprints. So, she remained as an unidentified female for literally at least a decade if not longer."

I checked the timeline against my file. It was thirteen years.

"Her DNA was submitted to the lab in North Texas and, eventually, that is how, if I remember correctly, her body was identified," he told me, sometimes straining through thirty years of lapsed time and without paperwork to hand. "I'm not that up on the specifics of how the investigators tied her to Rhoades. I do remember that one of my investigators was very, very interested in this case and worked really hard trying to tie him to this particular homicide. He did a lot of comparison between Rhoades' travel logs, and when he might have been in the area where the body was found and when, based on that, the young woman could have been murdered. My recollection is there were multiple torso wounds. I do not recall if there were any head wounds. I believe we did recover projectiles, so there was something that might be able to connect the victim to any weapon that was in the possession of or tied to Mr. Rhoades."

I asked Dr. Grey what the standard practice for identifying a Jane Doe was at the time the body was discovered, knowing just how far DNA has come and thinking of my conversation with Francine.

"The practice would have been to look at any local missing persons reports," he said. "And that would mean anyone within the state of Utah. If there was a report of someone who might be a possible match to our victim, we would then attempt to find dental records - or any medical records - that might show specific pathologies this individual had or any implantable devices such as, you know, artificial joints, things like that." The girl in the pasture came to me again, with her missing front teeth, the only implants to go on in her case are the fillings in the remaining teeth of the upper jaw. "Identification would basically depend upon having somebody report a potential victim that we could then match with findings from the actual victim."

This is one of the incontrovertible truths when it comes to dealing with unidentified body cases. A recent one, for me at least, surfaced while I was recording a training session on how to use NaMus in missing person research. Randomly selecting a missing person case, I found myself looking at the face of a young woman named Stefanie Stroh, who went missing on her way home to California after calling her parents from a truck stop in Wells, Nevada, in 1987. Rhoades sprang to mind, of course, but his routes in 1987 kept him in the Texas to Alabama loop. Research, however, did turn up an admission from a convicted killer, Tommy Lynn Sells. He claimed to have picked her up, taken LSD with her, and killed her before dumping her body in a hot spring. I switched to unidentified person searches and found a potential match – a female skeleton found near the hot springs in Elko, Nevada, in 2018. There was no obvious witness testimony or other evidence, but there was now this potential match, only fifty miles from the last place Stroh was seen, loosely matching the disposal site description offered by Sells which had not previously been linked. While no charges were brought and his admission was apparently waved away as exaggeration by his investigators, the Elko body was discovered four years after the serial offender was put to death in Texas. The only available course of action was contacting the case owner for Stroh, passing them the details of the unidentified person case, and advising a request for DNA analysis if a sample was retrievable. That process may never start – depending entirely on the will of the investigating agency – and, even if it does progress as a viable option, could take years. Point being: the process described by Dr. Grey is still the procedure. There is no magic spell, investigation is a process not an outcome. But times have changed, and this got me wondering if DNA could be retrieved from the remains of the girl in the pasture. GEDMatch may now hold the answer to her identify or, at least, open the door to her family.

At the time Dr. Grey and his team recovered and examined the body in Millard County, DNA was still in its infancy. Hence his mention of fingerprints. I wanted to probe this a little, for the sake of clarity.

"A lot of people don't have experience of forensic pathology," I said. "I'm guessing by what you've said the body was decomposing but not skeletal, and that got me thinking about an arcane practice we still use now in London. Say for example a body is recovered from the Thames, they still put calls out for police officers to volunteer to help in fingerprinting. You know, where the skin is removed, and the volunteer effectively wears it as a glove to run the prints. They pay cops twenty-five or fifty pounds for doing this, you know?"

When I talk about things like this, it feels almost backwards, but this is a legitimate practice – and one which Dr. Grey recognised.

"Due to the deterioration with we couldn't pull a glove of epidermis off the hands and roll any prints," he said. "Essentially, it was just sort of awful goop and there was no recognizable print material."

One of the most common types of body we come across in the UK, at least in my experience of countless sudden deaths, is people shut indoors with their central heating on, who have died and their absence has not been noticed. The result is a state of decomposition which is halfway between solid and liquid. I remember a particularly unusual one, in the home of a hoarder, where I eventually found the body in the bathroom. Probationers had assured me no people were in the flat but the smell I knew so well by that point said otherwise, so I started the search again and led them through the peculiar passageways and crawlspaces formed of stacked newspapers and magazines. When we reached the bathroom, the collapsed stacks drew my eye straight to a protruding lock of human hair. The conclusion was obvious, the victim had been sat on the toilet when one of her newspaper walls caved in. She had been there for a few weeks before anyone noticed she was missing – a sad fact of London and all its scale is that people become invisible too quickly. The body was carefully excavated and the unique nature of it was revealed. The top half, crushed by compacted papers, was dry. Mummified. The lower half, sat on the toilet and exposed the water, created a humid heat trap. What remained was jelly-like and disintegrated. It was the first time I shared my hard learned knowledge of lemons with others. None of this is said to shock. That, perhaps, cannot be adequately stressed enough. It is simply the reality of the unseen work which is done every day by normal people with an extraordinary role in society.

While the very mention of Florida was enough to invoke memories of bodies found in or near water, Dr. Grey's mention of the decomposition which had taken place out in the Utah scrublands prompted me to ask about the local climate and its effect on the woman found in Millard County.

"It's hot in the summertime – that blistering, really hot and dry," he told me. "In the wintertime it is snow, you know, lovely snow and ice on the ground. The vegetation is things like juniper trees, sagebrush. Tumbleweeds. If you think about, you know, sort of a John Ford Western, that's it. In this environment, or at least in the outdoors in Utah, we tend to get mummification and skeletonization pretty quickly. In addition to just the putrefactive changes, the bugs and animals out in the environment will tend to break down a body pretty quickly. If I remember, right, her fingers and toes certainly had evidence of small animal, post-mortem feeding on them, which also made the recovery of any prints less than likely."

The body was found in October of 1990 and is thought to have been there since January the same year. The last weather discussion I had with Dr. Grey was the first time I met with him, during a case conference for the Foundation. That case was far away from Utah, in Russia, and the much colder weather played a big role in both the manner of death and the discovery. I looked again at Rhoades trucking logs, tracing a line from the north-western corner of Texas to Utah. By the look of it, Rhoades route into Deseret would have cut upwards from the I-40 somewhere near Flagstaff, Arizona, following Route 89 as it skirts the Grand Canyon, Grand Staircase-Escalante, eventually slicing up the Eastern side of Fishlake National Forest before joining the I-70, just south of Fillmore. His direct route south-west, on the I-15 from Utah, leads straight to San Bernardino, where Shana Holts was picked up that same January. Rhoades left no gap in his offending. While there may have been no fingerprints left on the woman Dr. Grey examined, Rhoades had left his own prints all over the map.

"How common are unidentified bodies like that in Utah?" I asked, more out of the professional curiosity fed by the sheer volume of such cases across America.

"We would generally have, I would say, a half a dozen to, at most, a dozen cases of unidentified human remains every year," he told me. "The majority of those would be skeletal remains from ancient Native American graves. And not ones which, you know, had any sort of hint of modernity, or the need for further investigation and identification. So, you might find, you know, somebody might be digging in their yard and turn up a Native American burial site or a pioneer burial site. The number of unidentified bodies where we suspected that they were the victims of the homicide or some other unnatural event? Actually, we do not have that many. I would say no more than three or four a year."

I quizzed him, thinking out loud really, about the juxtaposition between these tiny numbers and the huge number of cold cases in America – some one hundred and eighty-five thousand accumulated since the 1980s. That, combined with tens of thousands of open missing persons cases and unidentified persons, produces an almost overwhelming scale.

"One of the other problems," he started. "I've noticed in my career the fragmentation of police and investigative agencies throughout the country. You have all these little fiefdoms, with Sheriff's offices and local Constabulary. The ability for people to share information really impedes the process of trying to match up remains and victims with ongoing criminal investigations. That's frustrating on a national scale. It's frustrating on a local scale. I mean, Utah, even though we don't have a very large population, we have probably at least one or two hundred individual law enforcement agencies or investigative units. Even with something as simple as a case which starts in one county and ends in a second County, that fragmentation of investigative coordination can make it an unsolved case for quite a while." There have been efforts to bridge some of this, from uniform crime recording to ViCAP – which Greg Cooper headed up for a time. But none of it seems to have done enough. "The limitation of ViCAP is it's only as good as the information that's put into it. The diligence of agencies to make sure that their entries are as complete and accurate as possible is, to me, one of its more important limiting factors."

I use a simple expression to describe this problem: shit in, shit out.

"Yeah," Dr. Grey chuckled. "Garbage in garbage out. My experience has been: yes, we've had successes with ViCAP, then we've also had cases where, ultimately, we see how the process broke down. Even though there was an entry, it was not complete or thorough enough to really allow matching and comparison."

This rings true of NaMus too, again leaving me thinking about the girl in the pasture and that mention of cut hair which was not quite a reflection of the facts. I asked Dr. Grey what he thought the prospects were for the introduction of nationally standardised processes and crime recording databases, designed to eliminate this problem. His answer was honest. Depressing, but honest.

"I think that the issue is one of turf protection," he said. "Unfortunately, it is a not uncommon problem with law enforcement agencies throughout the country, you know: this is my case, I'm going to solve it. I don't want nobody else messing with my case. You get that that proprietary. Feeling like that can make collaboration and cooperation more difficult. Segmentation and fragmentation." Even referring to the *Roadside Prey* book, the inter-agency wrangling was clear.

While I could have talked to Dr. Grey for days, I steered the conversation back to Rhoades and asked him what he took away from the case review.

"I thought it was a very succinct and powerful presentation," he said. "His geographic spread across the country was just amazing. As I said, one of my investigators really, sort of got a hard-on for Mr. Rhoades, and was trying to track him. When those pictures came up, I said: wait a minute, I know this case, I'm involved in this case. So that to me, that was sort of an aha, oh, my gosh, moment. You clearly - I mean: clearly - saw the whole story. This must have been a horribly terrifying event for this unfortunate young woman. That's one of the hardest things about the medical examiner work, when you realize just how awful what happened was and how the person must have suffered both psychologically as well as physically. That's one of those sorts of things you do bring home with you. You have to learn how to deal with those demons."

You do. You must learn. And, somehow, you have to retain your own humanity and the ability to keep doing it too. There is no training course which can help. Nobody even tries to hold your hand. The truth is not everyone can do it. Some simply leave. Others wind up broken. The rest of us find a way and deal with the dreams. They might fade over time, but they never go away.

I asked Dr. Grey for his expert view on Regina's final crime scene, probing what he would have done had he been the medical examiner on the case.

"We would have thought that this was going to be a case which required comparison to known exemplars," he said. "That means: if we had dental records from a suspected identity or, if we had DNA, we could compare DNA to parents or siblings. I sort of thought that was where we were going with this case. I was highly doubtful that her identity was going to be established in any straightforward simple way." He was right, luck played its significant role in establishing who Regina was, alongside comparison.

The manner of death, that wire garotte, was something else I wanted his view on. Given Dr. Grey's wealth of experience, I wanted to know how recurrent a method it was. Given how common the understanding of it is in the public at large, the answer surprised me a little.

"I have rarely seen it in my career. Ligature strangulation is quite common in terms of homicidal strangulation modalities, but a garotte is…I can only think of maybe two or three other cases in my career where we saw something which looked like that kind of mechanical constriction to the neck."

This led to me to vastly different causes of death between Regina and the woman found in Utah. I asked why he thought there was such a substantial change in Rhoades' behaviour.

"It's: whatever gets you off," he said. "You're dealing with the psychology of someone who likes to kill. Oftentimes, there's a particular way that they like to kill they repeat over and over and over again. And in other cases I've seen of serial killers, they are not limited to one MO. Why some of them will do that and some of them won't is beyond my capabilities as a pathologist to understand." We talked briefly about Doc Simon, then he carried on. "I've been involved with at least three separate serial killers who have operated in my area of jurisdiction. The most upsetting and difficult aspect of those cases to me is the anonymity of victims in so many cases, and the perpetrators skill at throwing off the scent. One of the serial killers series that I was involved in…I mean, he killed at least three people before anybody knew that they were homicide victims."

This is the crux of what is haunting me more and more, as I pick through this case and discover all those others surrounding it. Unknown victims, or the simple fact that they can remain unknown, is feeding serial killers a staple diet of opportunity to carry on without being captured. Part of this – a big part of it – stems directly from the cross-jurisdictional gaps in processes and standards.

"His MO," Dr. Grey continued, "Was he would go after frail little ladies and lay them out in their residence in a way that made it look like they had, you know, just collapsed in bed and died of their myriad of natural disease problems. What finally allowed investigators to recognize what was going on was an astute family member going through the scene after the body was gone. They said: this is wrong, she would never have left a crumpled nightgown on the bathroom floor the way that it was, with a stain. It turned out that's what the perpetrator used to wipe up semen after he masturbated on the body. It's always, always the little details."

This is why gathering witness testimony is an important art. Statements are not just about the big details, or the obvious ones. Police officers walk through people's lives daily, but the important thing is we walk straight back out again. We might not notice the one figurine pointing the wrong way on a shelf – and that may be where the fingerprint is. Once the evidence is collected and preserved, there is only a potential gain to be made by walking through the scene with someone who knows what those details look like. My experience of working both a smaller force in Derbyshire and the largest one, in London, taught me that there's a higher quality of investigation where there is less resource, and it's carried out more efficiently because there is less time to correct mistakes. Appreciating my perspective is a UK one, I asked Dr. Grey what he saw among the hundreds of Utah agencies.

"Sometimes you will get a better investigation from a small agency that realizes they're dealing with something that's over their heads," he said. "So, they try extra hard to dot all the Is and cross all the Ts, compared to a larger agency that sort of thinks: well, we know what we're doing, we don't have to do it this way. We don't have to do that. It's a national phenomenon. Sort of the hubris of a little knowledge."

There are, of course, regional variations in the UK. But Sheffield and Birmingham are not going to be vastly different. Different form numbers, different IT systems, shift-patterns, sure. But the way that we are taught the law, procedure, investigation is a national standard, all designed from a central point. Uniformity across the uniform. You can walk into any police force, any custody suite, and you can guarantee that the procedure for getting the prisoner out into interview is going to be the same because of the Police and Criminal Evidence Act – which came in 1984. If you work with an officer from another force, they are going to be asking the same questions for the same reasons as you well. The one fascinating thing, at least from an American perspective I would presume, is that we do not use the pantomime approach to staged interviews. We do not set up props or go at people for hours and hours until a confession materialises. We do not polygraph. We go into interview with the evidence that we have got and follow that evidence, there's no predefinition of the outcome and very little reliance on gut feelings, which sometimes come across as primary across the ocean. The difference always strikes me.

"Unfortunately, the reliance upon intuition sometimes becomes a handicap as opposed to, you know, a breakthrough," Dr. Grey told me. "I've never been trained as a police officer, so I don't know what happens to you as you go from, you know, dumb idealistic rookie to a more jaded and hardened, experienced investigator. I don't know."

We wrapped up and I sat for a while, reflecting on our conversation. He may not have had his thirty-year-old notes to hand, but his recall was accurate and I understood the full horror of Rhoades 1990 spree of murders.

Patricia Candace Walsh was born in December 1966, in Seattle, Washington. By the age of twenty-three she was a newlywed, married to Douglas Zyskowski, three years her senior. In November of 1989, the pair hitchhiked together to Georgia to attend a religious workshop. They called their families from San Antonio, Texas on the return journey, letting them know they were on their way. The couple were dropped at Six Flags in Atlanta[38] at the beginning of January and made their way to Tuscaloosa, Alabama to stay with acquaintance before continuing. They never made it home.

In January 1990, they accepted a ride from Robert Ben Rhoades somewhere on the I-10 between San Antonio and El Paso, Texas. This was on his straight-line route across the state, according to the truck logs. Douglas's body was found on January 21st, about thirty miles east of Ozona. Drawing the line on a map, this leads to the desolate scrubland just outside of Sonora, on from the Safety Rest Stop around the Caverns Road exit. The terrain and vegetation are eerily similar to that in Utah, out by Fishlake. Douglas was not identified until 1992. Reports are not detailed, but the general theme is that Rhoades killed him almost immediately after picking them up, much in the same way he did Ricky Jones. Patricia was held captive by Rhoades for what is believed to be a week, subjecting her to the same torture and sexual violence as Shana, Regina, and Lisa. She was finally identified in 2003 and a formal request to extradite Rhoades from prison in Illinois to Millard County was placed. Dr. Grey, who examined the young woman's body, and carries the memories with him despite the passage of time, finally knew her name.

---

38 https://news.google.com/newspapers?id=T3UjAAAAIBAJ&sjid=G6YEAAAAIBAJ&dq=patricia-candace-walsh&pg=6270%2C5909430, The Tuscaloosa News, 22nd April 1993, Wendy Reeves

There is a strange force which connects Council Bluffs to Deseret. That old trail between the two places seems to have stayed open in some dark way. And, while the State of Deseret once had those ill-fated designs of sprawling reach, boundaries stretching from the Sierra Nevada to the Rockies, in the end it was Robert Ben Rhoades who achieved a perverse version of the same.

- Broken Roads -

PREDATOR

Rhoades lost control of his situation when he was arrested. The very fabric of the reality he had carefully constructed for himself, the rule of his stage-managed domain, came crashing to the ground. He could not charm his way out of trial any more than he could successfully escape from Officer Miller on the side of the Arizona highway. It was over.

The Arizona charges were brought but he never faced trial, instead bargaining his way to a paltry six-year sentence with the chance to be out in half that with good behaviour. At the time, according to Alva Busch, the rule was a day-for-a-day and he could have gained other advantages too – work release or becoming a trustee both got you beyond the walls, despite the fact he had offered no such respite to Lisa. Keeping him away from the opportunity to offend again became a race against time for the investigators dealing with Regina's murder in Bond County, Illinois. But the wheels of justice turn slowly. The state attorney, John Knight, finally secured the barn in which Regina had been found in October 1991, preserving it for an eventual tour by jurors. Or so the intention was. Then, in February 1992 the prosecution team finally secured Rhoades' arrest warrant – issued without geographical limitation, meaning the fact he was out of state was no barrier to bringing him in. Sheeley, who had stayed as the principal investigator, was joined once again by the FBI, flying to Arizona with agent Phil Staley to interview the trucker. On arrival, they found a weak and pathetic man had swallowed the monster Rhoades became when alone on the road. He was in seclusion – effective protective custody – which he had sought out himself after being attacked by inmates and, when interviewed, he sat quietly, indicating he might want to talk further in future.

The legal process played out. Rhoades accepted the interstate agreement of detainers on Valentine's Day 1992, triggering a time sensitive pre-trial period for Knight and the Bond County team. The grand jury was convened

- 125 -

to start on March 27th 1992 but a key piece of evidence was missing: Regina's sequence of photographs seized from the Houston apartment. And, with that, the cross-jurisdiction, inter-agency stink began to kick up. The FBI in Texas dragged their heels on releasing the images and, even after the intervention of Assistant U.S. District Attorney Norman Smith, a personal dispute between Sheeley and Agent Bob Young had simmered and bubbled over. Busch puts this politely in his book, but it's quite clear what happened: touchdown envy. Thankfully, the two men settled whatever their grievances were and focused on putting Rhoades away. Lee presented the photographs, discussed the items of clothing, and set the calls which had been made to Regina's father against Rhoades's trucking logs. The grand jury barely hesitated, returning a seven-count indictment against the truck driver and Knight made the arrangements to transfer custody of Rhoades from Arizona to Illinois within days. With the dispute settled, the FBI stepped in to provide Sheeley with a plane when the Illinois State Police could not. They bounced across the country in a Cessna and retrieved Rhoades from the state prison in Florence, before making the return trip with an overnight in Oklahoma City. Along the way, Sheeley watched a shackled Rhoades run a charming routine on young waitresses, gaining some insight into how easy it must have been for him to lure victims in. For good measure, they stopped near the barn where Regina was found and asked Rhoades if he saw anything familiar. I've no doubt they reminded him Illinois was a death penalty state too, even before the prosecution had outlined the intention to seek it in court.

Rhoades was well defended, all the costs covered, but resisted any discussions of sexual abuse in Council Bluffs when he was a child. They tested him with mock questioning, gave him accounts of the state's last execution, and stripped down his belligerence until, eventually, Rhoades asked them to make a plea deal. He opted for life without parole and was sent to serve out his time at the Menard Correctional Centre in Chester, Illinois. After his extradition from Arizona, when the case hit the Houston news, the suspected link between Rhoades and the killing of Douglas Zyskowski was first made but it wasn't formally pursued until 2003, after Patricia was identified in Utah. DNA belonging to Walsh was subsequently found on items seized from Rhoades after Lisa was rescued in Arizona. This led everyone straight back down the cross-jurisdiction rabbit hole when, in 2005, Rhoades was to be extradited to Utah in a capital murder case but this was swiftly set aside in favour of a Texas trial - as he had also been charged with the murder of both Patricia and Douglas in that jurisdiction. Finally, however, it appears that someone took the views of the families into account and this formed a large part of the agreement to run one trial in one place. Eventually, in March 2012, when the trucker had already passed sixty-five, he pled guilty once again. He was sentenced to two more life sentences for the murders of Douglas and Patricia[39], likely done to continue avoiding the death penalty. Rhoades was returned to Menard, never expected to have to serve time in a Texas prison. A slow death by ticking clock, rather than the instant impact of a lethal injection.

I looked at Menard, first finding myself staring at a Captcha form on an inmate search page. It was asking me to identify images of trucks, an algorithmic quirk too close for comfort. Then I found Robert Rhoades' inmate number, B24683. His home at Menard is an old prison, doors first opened in 1878, which can accommodate just over two-and-a-half-thousand inmates but currently holds about three hundred less than that. It is the largest maximum-security facility in the state of Illinois[40], with well over a hundred buildings enclosed in a forty-one-acre perimeter on a sprawling two-thousand-six-hundred-acre estate. They process meat, produce cleaning supplies, and provide recycling, and got their first female governor – Kim Butler - in 2014. News reports covering the facility are a mixed bag,

---

39 https://www.deseret.com/2012/3/29/20500547/serial-killer-with-utah-ties-gets-2-more-life-sentences-in-texas, Serial killer with Utah ties gets 2 more life sentences in Texas, Deseret News, March 29 2012, Pat Reavy.

40 https://www2.illinois.gov/idoc/facilities/Pages/menardcorrectionalcenter.aspx, Illinois.gov

with everything from high profile arrivals to inhumane cell sizes mentioned. Standard prison stuff, you could say, without stepping into the politics which encircle the prison system.

Given Rhoades sadistic, sexually motivated offending, Illinois is a suitable place for him to eventually expire. It is one of the twenty states which have adopted Civil Commitment for Sex Offenders, meaning he probably would never have been free to roam America's interstates again in any case.

Back in 2006, Congress enacted what is often referred to as the Walsh Act, introducing United States Code 4248[41]. This allows federal government to commit those defined as "sexually dangerous persons" to detention under civil, rather than criminal, law. There is no cap on the duration of confinement, unlike prison sentences. The definitions are broad, covering mental health disorders, difficulty in refraining from further offending, and even duplication of the language associated with criminal offences: "engaged or attempted to engage in sexually violent conduct or child molestation." Alongside the Walsh Act and Code 4248, a growing number of states had adopted local legislation as early as 1990, often called "Sexually Violent Predator" laws, allowing non-federal action to be taken along the same lines. Illinois introduced the legislation in 1998 and strengthened the provisions in 2006. This has caused (and continues to cause) legal debate and challenge[42]. Cases all the way up to the Supreme Court have decided that these state adaptations do not violate due process, double jeopardy, or even constitutional rights, and that Congress had not gone beyond its authority by introducing the federal legislation. It is complex though. On the one hand it protects the population from harm and serial offending while, on the other, it changes the fabric of crime, punishment, and rehabilitation. It is also a

---

[41] Civil commitment of a sexually dangerous person, 18-U.S.C. 4248, Last Effect Date January 24 2020

https://www.govinfo.gov/app/details/USCODE-2019-title18/USCODE-2019-title18-partIII-chap313-sec4248

[42] https://www.apa.org/monitor/2010/01/jn, Can the government civilly commit sex offenders?, American Psychological Association Judicial Notebook, January 2010, Marc W. Pearce, JD, PhD, and Leah C. Skovran

high value business, which brings with it ethical and moral questions around who really benefits – the Illinois facility at Rushville was authorised for a two wing (two hundred resident) expansion[43] in March 2020, to the tune of some thirty million dollars. Rushville was originally built for the Illinois Department of Corrections as a prison but never opened its doors as intended. Rather, in 2006, the Department of Human Services cut the ribbon on it as a Treatment and Detention Facility for the state's Sexually Violent Predator program, closing the units at Sheridan and Joliet and transferring the residents in. It had already been expanded once by 2013 and, once the next expansion concludes, it will house over eight hundred civilly committed individuals.

Rushville has been subject to a deal of scrutiny, described in one article published by In These Times[44] as "the endless nightmare of indefinite detention." The journalists started with the story of one man, Otis Arrington, who had served a twenty-nine-year sentence for an aggravated rape in 1989 and was committed to indefinite definition immediately on his release date. The state law says that offenders committed this way, such as Arrington, should be subject to "control, care and treatment until such time as the person is no longer a sexually violent person." On plain reading, that means indefinite detention but seems to be tempered by the provision of treatment to eventually achieve a release. However, there are some warning signs that this never materialises. Around half of the residents have been at Rushville for a decade, and a fifth for twenty years. The "treatment" is operated on a for profit basis by a private corporation – Liberty Health Care - whose interests are clearly better served by residents staying inside the facility. A string of complaints has emerged about conditions, including

---

[43] https://www.tspr.org/post/expansion-coming-rushville-treatment-and-detention-facility, Expansion Coming to Rushville Treatment and Detention Facility, Tri State Public Radio, March 11 2020, Rich Egger

[44] https://inthesetimes.com/article/civil-commitment-rushville-treatment-detention-facility-prison-indefinite-detention, Inside the Endless Nightmare of Indefinite Detention Under "Civil Commitment", In These Times, August 19 2020, Sarah Lazare

troublesome claims that much of the therapy is inmate-led group therapy in which sex offenders talk about their sexual preferences and acts. It is not hard to deduce this will have little therapeutic value and is likely to be a close equivalent to pornography for some residents. The American Psychiatric Association have spoken out against civil commitment too[45], writing: "sexual predator commitment laws represent a serious assault on the integrity of psychiatry, particularly with regard to defining mental illness and the clinical conditions for compulsory treatment. Moreover, by bending civil commitment to serve essentially non-medical purposes, sexual predator commitment statues threaten to undermine the legitimacy of the medical model." Across NGOs and civil rights groups, the consensus does not generally shift far from this view - the system is seen as one of punishment rather than treatment.

All of this is balanced by the harsh reality which led to the introduction of the laws in the first place: some offenders will go straight back to committing horrific crimes the moment they leave prison. Offenders just like Rhoades would not hesitate. The issues could be well addressed by defining national standards and procedures, but this runs head long into the same cross-jurisdiction problems which allow offenders such as the truck driver to commit serial crimes in the first place. There is never an easy answer to be found, it seems.

Given how alien a concept this area was to me, I called upon the expertise of my Foundation colleague Dr. Allison Schechter, seeking background on the practical aspects of the Sexually Violent Predator field and to discuss the more insights into the Rhoades case from her perspective. She is part of a new cadre of experts who will influence how offenders are dealt with for many years to come.

---

[45] http://jaapl.org/content/38/3/386, Normative Versus Consequential Ethics in Sexually Violent Predator Laws: An Ethics Conundrum for Psychiatry, The Journal of American Academy Psychiatry and the Law, September 2010, Shoba Sreenivasan, Allen Frances, and Linda E. Weinberger

"I received my doctorate in clinical psychology in 2007," Dr. Schechter told me. "Prior to receiving my doctorate, I had completed various practicums and internships at psychiatric hospitals, forensic facilities and sex offender treatment programs. I got a job with a company that contracted with the Illinois Department of Corrections to complete Sexually Violent Persons evaluations for the Illinois Attorney General's office. I worked with that company for about five and a half years and then, after I left them, the Illinois Attorney General's Office offered me a private contract to continue my work. I continue to have that contract today."

A practicum, a strange sounding academic word to many of us, is simply a practical course of study. This is explained is much simpler terms within training centred on investigative doctrine, a course which I have also written for the online academy at Cold Case Live, one of the Foundation's projects. Investigative knowledge can be trained in an educational environment, using courses, reading materials, and even academic study. However, investigators require practical experience of dealing with crimes and criminals for theoretical knowledge to realise a real-world value. The inverse is also true, in that investigators can learn entirely "on the job," from colleagues and in live cases, but without studied knowledge of theory and procedure, the quality of investigations is likely to be lower. Academic studies and workplace application thereof have identified that the best solution is the combination of theoretical and practical learning.

Know-how is acquired in different ways and at different paces, depending on the individual, but a key psychological aspect which defines whether it can be acquired (and how successfully) relates to the desire of that person. Effectively, to learn something you must be interested in it. The best investigators are interested in acquiring knowledge, and this does not just apply to the cases they are involved in, but also to improving their skills and broadening their knowledge base. Conversely, if an investigator is not interested in working cases or lacks the motivation to acquire knowledge, they will typically perform poorly and the quality of investigations is highly likely to be significantly lower due to a lack of effort and applied skill.

Dr. Schechter has achieved the best possible balance between theoretical knowledge and practical experience. Her role exposes her to both the prison environment and some of the most dangerous people in it. She explained the SVP program evaluation process to me, with the benefit of genuine know-how.

"Essentially, my own person's evaluation is completed on sex offenders prior to their release on parole, when their parole date is coming up," she told me. "Sex offenders are screened to see if they have what is called a qualifying sex offence - dictated by the SVP statute in the state of Illinois."

Those offences, according to the Illinois General Assembly's compiled statutes[46], include rape, sexual assault, sexual activity with children, sexually motivated first-degree murder, and any solicitation or conspiracy to commit such crimes.

"If an offender has what is determined to be a qualifying sex offense, they're screened," Dr. Schechter continued. "And, if the screener determines that they may be a sexually violent person, they then have an evaluator complete a full evaluation. The evaluator then renders an opinion if the individual meets statutory criteria to be found a Sexually Violent Person - or if they don't - and those findings are given to the Illinois Attorney General's office to proceed as they will."

The evaluation process itself falls within some of the controversy around civil commitment, but much of the writing on the topic is from the offender perspective, or covers the purely administrative and dry legal aspects. Dr. Schechter provided me with a rare glimpse into the evaluator's point of view.

"The Illinois Sexually Violent Persons evaluation is similar to the other twenty or so states and the District of Columbia," she said. "In order for an

---

46 https://www.ilga.gov/legislation/ilcs/ilcs3.asp?ActID=1990&ChapterID=54, Illinois General Assembly, Illinois Compiled Statues, (725 ILCS 207/) Sexually Violent Persons Commitment Act.

individual to be found to be a Sexually Violent Person, they need to meet the three prongs of the statute. They first have to have the qualifying sex offence which I talked about earlier. You also have to have a qualifying mental disorder that affects their emotional or volitional capacity - essentially, the way they think they feel they act they behave. And the third prong is, as a result of that mental disorder, they have to be what is called 'substantially probable' to commit future acts of sexual violence. Substantially probable is defined as 'much more likely than not.' So, in order to complete one of those evaluations, we're given a full file on all of the sexual offenses that the individual has committed, any previous evaluations that have been completed, court records, and police documents. We read through the file and then we do a full clinical interview of the offender - if they're willing to participate - and we complete risk assessment measures. Ultimately, based on all of that information, we then render an opinion to the court."

The process is detailed, has built in steps and safeguards, and bears similarities to several elements of criminal procedure. The substantial difference is that the deciding standard is not reasonable doubt. Rather, it is the balance of probabilities which does the heavy lifting. In terms of decision-making, this is a much lower threshold and tends to involve a lot more human instinct. Ultimately, it is the source of much of the conflict around whether indefinite detention can safely be determined this way. Again, I can see how difficult this is to balance – with risk on one side of the scale and established norms of crime and punishment on the other.

We talked briefly about high profile cases and the ones which tend to follow you home and haunt your dreams. This led us to chatting about how we came to the Foundation and, it transpires, Allison's route was the same as my own: Netflix.

"By chance, I had watched the documentary that was done on Henry Lee Lucas and I was fascinated by it," she told me. "That's where I learned of the foundation and I just decided to reach out. I was lucky enough to be asked to join."

We both became part of the team at around the same time, my experience initially seeing me placed on the investigative team, while Dr. Schechter joined the mind experts. She is both a clinical and forensic psychologist. I asked her to put that distinction into easy terms almost anyone could understand.

"Forensic psychology is essentially the intersection of human behaviour and the law," she told me. "My degree is in clinical psychology, so I'm a clinical psychologist, but I'm also a forensic psychologist because I have specialised my work in that area. A clinical psychologist is probably what most people think of when they think of a psychologist, you know: clinicians that are in private practice, that do therapy, that maybe teach at a university, that work in various types of hospital psychiatric hospitals. A forensic psychologist focuses on work that is done with individuals who have some type of a criminal or court involvement. So forensic in the world of forensic psychology, just literally means 'of the court.' I had worked previously in a in a forensic psychiatric facility, where individuals were in the hospital, deemed not guilty by reason of insanity or, pre-trial, when they were not found competent to stand trial. Essentially anything that has to do with evaluating human behaviour of individuals that come in to contact with the law."

Our attention turned to one such individual, Rhoades. Dr. Schechter had sat on the case review with me and the others on the team. Her assessment, from the perspective of an experienced professional dealing with Sexually Violent Predators in Illinois itself, would be invaluable.

"Unfortunately, he strikes me as a pretty clear individual who would be diagnosed with sexual sadism disorder." She told me. "In the DSM, the Diagnostic and Statistical Manual of Mental Disorders, there's different sections and one of the sections is what is called the paraphilic disorders. Within the umbrella of the paraphilic disorders, there's about eight or nine different paraphilias. One of them is called sexual sadism disorder. Essentially, to be diagnosed with sexual sadism disorder, the individual has to have recurrent and intense sexual arousal from the physical or psychological suffering of another person."

There is little doubt the truck driver sits comfortably within the terms of the diagnosis. The DSM-5[47], which has a text revision coming out in 2022, is interesting. It defines the persistent period over which sexual arousal from the suffering of another must manifest and specifies the absence of consent of the victim. There also useful insight into how this diagnosis might be applied in a Sexually Violent Predator assessment. It gives instructions to specify in the diagnosis whether the offender simply has their access to opportunity restricted (being in prison, for example), or if they have gone into remission – being at liberty but not acting on their urges for at least five years. In many ways, this does beg a question: can you ever specify remission if the subject is always detained in an institutional setting, such as the Rushville facility?

Broader societal questions aside, Rhoades is a textbook subject in the very literal sense. He would be classified as an admitted individual, given his conversations with Debra and his acting on his impulses, but could also fall into the category of a subject denying interest, given his responses when caught. He also fits the description of a "recurrent" sexual sadist, having acted on more than three victims on multiple occasions, and displays associated features – namely the extensive use of sadism related pornography. He falls within a small sub-population of sex offenders, with only ten percent of civilly committed residents across the board having this disorder on their file. According to studies, sexual sadism disorder generally manifests at the age of nineteen and, while sexual sadism is described as a "lifelong characteristic" the full disorder may come and go, depending on stress and distress, or many never develop at all.

---

[47] https://www.psychiatry.org/psychiatrists/practice/dsm, Diagnostic and Statistical Manual of Mental Disorders (DSM–5), American Psychiatric Association

"It's manifested by urges behaviours or fantasies, and that the urges fantasies or behaviours need to persist for a period of at least six months," Dr. Schechter said. "The second part of that diagnosis is that the individual has acted on these sexual urges with a non-consenting person. So, you know, when we were shown all the erotic materials that were found in his possessions, you can get a great idea of a person's sexual fantasies by looking. The type of pornography that he was drawn to had some type of a sadistic nature to it. Binding individuals, torturing them, somehow tying people up, hurting them, whipping them, cutting them. For sexual pleasure, essentially. That's typically how a paraphilic disorder starts. They start looking at pornography on whatever their area of interest sexual interest is and then the fantasies turn into urges, and the urges then turn into behaviours. As the person starts acting out one of the fantasies that they've had, and they see that they can get away with them, then it just sort of reinforces the fantasy and actually increases the urge - because now they've played it out, and they've experienced it. Now they can fantasize about the actual memory of what they've done and that just perpetuates the ongoing urges and fantasies. Ultimately they continue to act out."

She described Rhoades as a master of his craft. I saw him more as a casting, poured into the mould of a DSM-5 sexual sadist. We talked through his pornography and the books, setting them against the sequence of Regina's photographs and the accounts of Shana and Lisa. It was like laying two matching puzzles in a stack. The conversation followed its north and we ended back at the observation Dr. Schechter had made during the case review, about Rhoades' demeanour and attitude when confronted with the authorities.

"When I do a sexually violent person's evaluation, one of the instruments that we often administer is called the hare psychopathy checklist," she told me. "It's a personality instrument and Robert Hare, who's a very famous psychologist, had invented this concept of a tool to measure the traits of psychopathy - of being a psychopath. His instrument is now very well-known and when the Hare psychopathy checklist, which we call the PCL-R for short, is administered to an individual there are about twenty areas that are assessed. That's done by clinical interview, mostly meeting with an offender, and making observations, reading through their Department of Corrections records to see how they've interacted with others, and their criminal history...you know, anything that we have to be able to administer this psychological instrument. After it's scored, it's divided into two primary areas. One is antisocial qualities and traits. You know, an individual who lives in antisocial lifestyle - meaning, unstable, impulsive, criminal type behaviour. The other side is more ingrained in their personality, as far as having sort of a selfish, callous, remorseless use of other people."

The Hare test really is famous. Personally, I score a little higher than average for psychopathic traits but well below the psychopathy threshold. I've met people well above it and one of my commendations for bravery arose from meeting one of them on a dark winter's night in 2009. Online clickbait outlets are constantly offering people the opportunity to find out if they are Patrick Bateman, the lead character in *American Psycho*[48]. Society reduces the truly scary things to harmless fun for a variety of reasons, displacing rational fear being one of them, but the side effects are a behavioural escape mutation - leaving many fixated with psychopathy and elevating its portrayal to celebrity.

"They're often narcissistic. They often think that they're grandiose and, sometimes, like the Ted Bundy's of the world - who clearly was a psychopath, they can fit in quite well with society," Dr. Schechter started to explain. "My suspicion is that Mr. Rhoades would have scored high on the other part of the instrument - an individual who, similar to Ted Bundy, functions quite well. They are able to hide under the guise of being a normal guy, like BTK - again, for example, somebody who just sort of fits into the world, to society, but then they have this secret life that they live. That is

---

[48] American Psycho, Picador, 1991, Brett Easton Ellis

what becomes so arousing and fulfilling to them: the secretiveness of having this other part to their personality or life that that nobody else gets to see. Rhoades probably fit in quite well - he was married several times; he was charming enough to have three women want to marry him."

This rings true, because of the observations of his interactions with waitresses made during his transport from Arizona to Illinois. Even in handcuffs and a prison jump suit, he could turn the charm on with strangers.

"In the limited reading that I did, I learned that he probably had gotten away with this for over ten or fifteen years," she continued. "Again, the reason for that is because not only did he become a master of his craft but he also, outside of his torture chamber, probably just sort of fit right back into society as regular type of guy."

He preyed deliberately on those less likely to report him, or simply ensured they could not, to preserve the separation between his two worlds and preserve both. The girls like Shana and Lisa, those he called Lot Lizards and derided in interview, he had clearly assessed as less likely to engage with law enforcement or be believed by officers. Those like Regina and Patricia, Douglas, and Ricky, he likely decided were a greater risk, so were destined for a single outcome from the moment he met them. This presents a deeper challenge in identifying his further offending patterns. Based on statistical probabilities, there may well be a higher number of victims who survived but never reported their ordeals than there will be unidentified person cases on NaMus or elsewhere. Thinking on this, my mind drifted back to Regina and the change we had all noticed in her expression and body language as the sequence of photographs progressed.

"Throughout the days it did seem initially she was disgusted, terrified, afraid, fearful. All of those things," Dr. Schechter said, carefully assembling her thoughts. "And then it seems as if, as the days wore on - I don't think that she certainly was happy to be there or was enjoying herself by any stretch of the imagination - but I think that she just sort of resolved herself that this was where she was and who she was with. And, while I'm certain that she was fearful of him the entire time, it did seem like she probably just became less terrified of him."

I already believed part of Rhoades method was to make Regina believe she would be released or treated better if she complied, so this made sense to me. With my layman's understanding of Stockholm Syndrome – an emotional response to kidnap or hostage-taking which can see bonds or feelings develop between captive and captor over weeks or months of close contact - I recognised it could potentially be used to describe some of the things which happened with Regina, but was not quite the right explanation. I am not a psychologist or psychiatrist after all, so I asked Dr. Schechter what the clinical reason might be.

"I don't claim at all to be an expert by any stretch of the imagination, in Stockholm Syndrome, but I don't think she would have been with him long enough for that to fully have set in." she told me. "I think that perhaps there were elements of it, that maybe had started to set in for her. I'm sure that Stockholm Syndrome is sort of on a continuum, as far as victims who just sort of become - I don't want to say comfortable - but just sort of resolved to where they are, all the way to the other end of the extreme where they form a strong bond or attachment to their offender. And I certainly don't think that she was at that end of the spectrum."

Logically, we turned our attention to the final crime scene and the way Regina was discovered. I asked Dr. Schechter for her observations on the scene and the manner of death.

"I found it interesting that, on the final day of her life, he had had her dressed up, almost as if she looked like an adult in his mind," she said. "He had her fingernails painted, and he had high heels on her, and a black dress. And makeup. Which is why I don't think that he had any type of paedophilic interest. I think he was drawn to a certain body type, which was in line with at least the one wife that we saw pictures of. And I think that he was trying to make her look older than she really was. I almost got the sense that he took her to this barn and maybe told her that they were going to play out some type of a scene. Film a movie or take pictures. He was telling her to pose in certain positions or have her arms a certain way, or to have a certain look on her face. Then, as the pictures progressed and he was undressing her, it became apparent that the fear had really set in for her. One of the things about sexual sadism disorder, is that what they are really aroused by is the fear of the victim. The psychological fear of the victim can be very, very arousing to them and so it's certainly possible he told her that he was about to kill her. And he wanted to capture her reaction to that on film, so that he could have that pornographic material for himself later."

I asked if this fell within the broader definition of "trophies," which we often think of serial killers amassing over their offending histories.

"Certainly, yes," Dr. Schechter told me. "I mean, the, you know, the fact that he had several items of her clothing in his possession, he probably used that, ultimately, to masturbate with and to relive the fantasies. To get a better mental picture of exactly what he had done. The fact that he, it seemed at least from the photograph, he killed her by wrapping some type of metal or a wire around her neck with the plywood and twisting it, That's very personal. That's a very personal way of killing somebody, versus shooting them from a distance, for example. I'm sure he was probably sitting on top of her as he was twisting that wood and as she was experiencing those final, extremely horrific final moments of her life, he probably was very aroused."

The way Rhoades had, for want of a better term, curated Regina's appearance from her kidnap until her murder remains one of the most disturbing elements of Rhoades' offending behaviour. The dehumanisation secured compliance and the re-humanisation – the shower, the make-up, the nail varnish, and the dress – secured his final prize: that moment captured on film in which her soul died. I felt there had to be clinical explanation for it and asked Dr. Schechter what she thought.

"I think the detailing was all part of his fantasy," she told me. "He had created a fantasy, a picture. A script in his mind. And he needed to play that out with her. They showed his briefcase. I guess it was what, in the SVP world, we call a rape kit. It's the real sure-fire way of diagnosing somebody with a paraphilic disorder. When they have some type of a rape kit, and they have materials that, clearly, they have obtained over time, and used over time, they figure out what works and what doesn't work. It appears that he probably had done this type of thing before - found a younger teenage girl and wanted to get her dressed up. I believe that that was all part of, of the script that he had in his mind.

I pressed her on the switch in his behaviour, from the carefully stage-managed sequence to the final violent act and the discarding of the poor girl afterwards. I was attempting to get further into his decision-making process.

"Well, my guess is that if he truly had been doing this for many years, as is suspected, I think that probably initially when he would kill somebody, he probably took greater effort to try to dispose of the body secretly," Dr. Schechter told me. "Over time, as he learned that he was able to get away with it, I think that he used to her to live out his fantasy up until her very last moments and then he was done with her. She was in a barn in southern, rural Bond County, Illinois…there's not much out there. You can leave someone's body in a barn on the side of the road and know that it's probably not going to be discovered very easily. That's more the sense that I got: that he was just done with her. She was in a barn, and he just had no more use for her."

We talked some more and came back around to the hair cutting.

"I think that it probably most likely had to do with trying to disguise her," she said. "I think that was probably the primary reason that he cut her hair so short. If anybody came looking for her or posted, you know, pictures of her in the media, she would look much different than she did prior to coming into contact with him. I also think that maybe more of a secondary element of it, as I mentioned earlier, is that I think that he was trying to make her appear older than she was. He was in his mid-forties at the time and if he was taking her to showers at rest stops, I think that if people saw a forty-four-year-old man with a fourteen-year-old girl that looked young, perhaps that would be noticed more than him with somebody who maybe appeared older. That would be my guess."

I have thought about the haircutting often. I do not doubt changing a victim's appearance did play its role, and that this folds into disguising age too, but I get the impression from the survivor accounts that the haircutting was part of the fantasy. The internet is awash with violent bondage portraying this as an act of control, punishment, and immediate dominance. The deeper you read, the more you discover, and depilation does recur across a range of fantasies – though it appears to be practical in certain cases. Shaving of pubic hair, for example, is often linked to either the prevention of lice or simply to make genital piercing more visible. This is something Rhoades did, and he depilated his victims too. This made me wonder about the haircuts too and I have come to believe a secondary purpose to humiliation was the simple visibility of and easy access to the padlocked neck chain. But this is still guesswork, just my own and not Dr. Schechter's.

Thinking about the photographs of the evidence found in and taken from Rhoades' apartment, I wondered if secondary and even tertiary purpose was a theme in any other areas of the truck driver's behaviour. I asked what Dr. Schechter made of the clothing and its repeat use.

"I think that keeping clothing which smelled like her would make sense," she told me. "The olfactory sense is our only one that actually goes straight to the memory area of our brain. He might have put her in perfume or had her smell a certain way, or just her natural body scent. He was probably smelling them as he was masturbating or fantasizing to evoke stronger memory."

One of the common suppositions about Rhoades which comes up is that he was paedophile and the evidence base for this appears to go back to the haircutting and intimate shaving. I have never felt that Rhoades was inclined to child sex offences and something about this theory had stuck in Dr. Schechter's mind too.

"Somebody had said that maybe he had cut her hair, made her look a certain way, to make her appear younger," she told me. "I disagree with that because I think that there's really no evidence to suggest that he was into that he was into prepubescent children. What essentially differentiates a prepubescent child from a post-pubescent child is the development of secondary sex characteristics and Regina clearly had developed secondary sex characteristics. He was more interested in young girls who were developed, so I don't think that he was a paedophile. I would be surprised - usually there's not a crossover like that."

As we came to the end of our conversation, I asked if she had been surprised to hear that Patricia had been identified as a Rhoades victim. The answer was not unexpected.

"Not at all," she told me. "By the point he got caught he had done this probably many times and knew what he was doing by that point, so I wasn't at all surprised that, unfortunately, there's probably many other victims that are unknown."

Another call across the ocean came to its end, bringing with it more insight into Rhoades and what drove him. What was still missing was Rhoades' own confirmations or denials. Throughout this process, I have been resistant to the idea of speaking to him, keen to avoid giving him oxygen, but his own account of his actions has never really been documented - largely due to the guilty pleas ensuring he avoided trial everywhere he was put before the court. Alva Busch recounts a series of exchanges between Rhoades and investigators like Sheeley but, to be blunt, these all have the hallmarks of law enforcement legend and do not tell anyone a lot about the truck driver. Meanwhile, Rhoades sits there in Menard, silent in the ruins of that terrifying kingdom he once built to reign over. No matter how much time has gone by, certain aspects of his personality are never likely to change.

Wanting to know the truth and wrestling with how to get to it, I opened a Pigeonly account and searched for him by the prisoner number. I clicked the "write a letter" icon and sat watching the blinking cursor in the text box for a longer time than I intended. In my mind, I replayed the conversations with my Foundation colleagues and the pages of research on Rhoades case. With my right hand I moved the mouse pointer to the "back" button, then stopped before clicking it. I knew Rhoades by then - understood enough of his psychology to pull levers. There was a way to get something out of him beyond a personal propaganda broadcast. Maybe. Confronting him with emotional pleas about victims and justice would not work. It may even have aroused him in some way. Showing myself to be more intelligent than him would throw up defensive walls around that fragile ego. Focusing on his primary drivers, control and power, and rubbing salt in the wound of creeping mortality was the best approach, as far as I could see. The former a lure. Bait. The latter a trigger. A provocation. Ego has a fascinating psychological impact on the ability of a person to deal with the inevitability of their own death - studies have shown that those with low humility and a high sense of entitlement are more likely to bite[49].

I moved my hand back to the keyboard and started to type.

"I am currently writing and researching a book on your case. I will keep this brief as that will serve both of us better. I am not interested in questions of guilt or innocence, nor in personal attacks. And I'm not a headshrinker, rest assured. Our time on this planet is fleeting but all our personal truths can make an impact. That may be one which helps us others find peace, or which helps anyone of us take charge of the way history sees us. That's real power and something we can each have absolute control over. No pass, no run. I simply wish to know, in your own words, why? What drove you to that offending spree in 1990? How many were there before that? You're sat in an environment which is controlled for you, where your power is limited. Where your agency has been removed, absent since 1990. You're seventy-five or so now, the freedom you once relied upon isn't coming back. So, take

---

[49] https://pubmed.ncbi.nlm.nih.gov/24660992/, A quiet ego quiets death anxiety: humility as an existential anxiety buffer, Pub Med / University of Colorado, April 2014, Pelin Kesebir

this chance to take control. Whatever you decide to say won't open the prison gates, the life sentences are stacked up. But your final truth is something you can own and control."

Twenty-nine years and few days after Robert Ben Rhoades was first sentenced to life in prison I clicked send on the letter. I never expect a reply.

- Broken Roads -

FOUNDATIONS

The Rhoades case was instrumental in the creation of the Cold Case Foundation itself.

There are a growing number of cold case not-for-profits, but the Foundation is one of the real heavyweights, though its profile may not present with the flashing lights and sirens you seem to find across the True Crime community by and large. Based in Utah, the Foundation quietly goes about its business of working through its growing caseload, and the team spend a lot of their time travelling America to deliver training and case support to agencies. Heavyweight is not a term used lightly either. John Douglas served as the first Chairman of the Board and now sits as the Chairman Emeritus, a steady hand and a guiding light who helped put the organisation together. Douglas is a legendary figure in the investigative world. If you have seen the series Mindhunter, you will have seen the fictional embodiment of him based on his book by the same name.

The FBI formed the Behavioural Science Unit in 1972, responding to growing numbers of murders and sexual offences and, in 1974, Special Agent Robert Ressler coined the phrase "serial killer." It stuck and still resonates across the world – it describes what Doc Simon referred to as the monsters under the beds of adults. Douglas joined Ressler and Dr. Ann Burgess in the late seventies, and this is where they embarked upon the creation of a database of serial offenders. This work saw them travel the country, interviewing shy of forty convicted serial killers and rapists to extract what drove them, how they planned, the specifics of their offences, and how they disposed of the physical evidence and victims. It was ground-breaking and put them in the history books, though whether profiling really works in practice remains a subject of debate and academic back and forth. The initial research led to the creation of the sister department, the Behavioural Science Investigative Support Unit (BSISU), which eventually became the National

Centre for the Analysis of Violent Crime. In turn, this saw the creation of the Violent Criminal Apprehension Program (ViCAP) and the formalisation of profiling as Criminal Investigative Analysis, used by the FBI's current Behavioural Analysis Unit today.

The work of the BSU can be found across America, from the fictional worlds of Criminal Minds and Hannibal Lecter or the X Files[50], to the all too true cases which fill the media and feed the True Crime ecosystem. From Wayne Williams (the Atlanta child murderer) to Robert Hansen (the "Butcher Baker"), John Douglas has played an integral role in the capture of serial killers and the development of the tools, techniques, and tactics which give American law enforcement a fighting chance against them. But the work does cut two ways and has led to rightful exonerations - the West Memphis Three being just one example.

Gregory M. Cooper – or Greg, as I know him – is the Executive Director of the Cold Case Foundation, and the driving force behind everything we do. He had been in the law enforcement game for forty years by the time I saw him on the Confessions Killer documentary and sent that first tentative email, asking what I could do to help. He started out as a police officer in Provo, Utah, then served as Police Chief in Delta before joining the FBI. We speak regularly but I booked some time to focus a conversation on him, the Foundation, and the Rhoades case.

"I joined the FBI back in 1985," he told me, line dipping in and out as it tends to with Greg. "I was with the FBI for 10 years, my whole primary focus of going into the FBI was to become a criminal profiler. After having served in Seattle, Washington in what's referred to as a resident agency - it was a two-man resident agency - I was assigned to the Olympia area, which incorporated about four different counties and five different Indian reservations. While serving in that capacity with one other agent, I was at

---

[50] https://en.wikipedia.org/wiki/Behavioral_Science_Unit#cite_note-:3-5, Behavioural Science Unit, Wikipedia, CC BY-SA 3.0

least one year by myself and worked very, very closely with local law enforcement."

A resident agency is, for want of a better term, a satellite of a major field office. A small, local facility facing a broad range of challenges with a heavily restricted resource.

"With a number of different types of cases, when you're in a resident agency, you cover all federal cases within that area," Greg explained. "Unlike being out of headquarters - in Seattle you are assigned to a desk which specializes in one particular area. So, I served there for about five years and then we went to Los Angeles division the Santa Ana resident agency. Then, finally, I had the opportunity to be selected to go back to the Behavioural Science Unit, or what was called at that time the BSISU which housed the Violent Criminal Apprehension Program and the Criminal Investigative Analysis program. I was assigned as a profiler in the Northwest Territory of the United States and, for whatever reason, it included Hawaii. I did not debate or argue that, I was happy to receive an assignment which had the opportunity to go to Hawaii."

Greg was recognised for his ability to teach others and, while serving as a profiler, taught at the National Academy in Quantico for around four years. His class list included criminal psychology, community policing, and his own take on Criminal Investigative Analysis – something the Foundation teaches across the country today.

"I ended up serving as the program manager for ViCAP and then, ultimately, as the Acting Unit Chief for the BSISU after john Douglas retired. I served there for about a year before I left," he told me. "I was really, really fortunate. You know, I have no regrets. None whatsoever. And I would say that all my expectations were not only met, but generally were exceeded. It was just a tremendous experience having been mentored by John Douglas and characters like Roy Hazelwood and Ken Lanning. Those guys are what we would refer to as probably the first generation of profilers as we know them today and I would be probably incorporated as the second generation of profilers."

I try and fail to contain my professional excitement every time Greg and I discuss this. Ken Lanning served twenty years across the BSU and National Centre for the Analysis of Violent Crime, longer than anyone else in the field of work. His research on child molesters is second to none. Roy Hazelwood was responsible for the distinction between organised and disorganised offenders and is often credited with development of the six categories of rapists.

By 2010, Ken Lanning's book *Child Molesters: A Behavioural Analysis*[51] was already in its fifth edition – a joint publication of the National Centre for Missing and Exploited Children and the Office of Juvenile Justice and Delinquency Protection, supported by the FBI. It is an operational manual for investigators whose efforts are concentrated on the sexual exploitation of children. It covers everything from incest to ritual abuse and draws several important distinctions between offender profiles. I find it particularly useful as it starts with something regarded as crucial in UK policing: definitions. Law enforcement works best and less speculatively when definitions are created and operationally used. Additionally, while the concept of grooming often appears to be new to some people, it has been well-defined and explained by Lanning for years. Grooming is how offenders attract the attention of and maintain relationships with child victims. It might be something as simple as showing simple kindness to a troubled kid or buying treats but has come to include purchase of the latest trainers, hardware and software, and is now also used to recruit children into drug trafficking and violent extremism.

I have already mentioned Roy Hazelwood's book, *The Evil That Men Do*, but a mention alone does not do justice to his theories and their impact on

---

51 https://www.missingkids.org/content/dam/missingkids/pdfs/publications/nc70.pdf, Child Molesters: A Behavioural Analysis, National Center for Missing and Exploited Children, 2010, Kenneth V. Lanning

investigative practice. Disorganised offenders tend not to plan their offending and may be under the influence of controlled substances or suffering from a mental health crisis. They also tend to offend closer to home and are more likely to commit frenzied attacks, leaving the victims wherever the offence takes place. I have that bravery commendation for apprehending one of these offenders on a dark London street - a night I often wish I could forget. Organised offenders are different. They meticulously plan their offending, their victim selection. They carry kits, they travel more broadly. They focus on controlling every aspect of their offending and on managing the evidence they leave behind. Dennis Rader, or BTK as he is commonly known, is one example. Another case, which is very recent and particularly challenging to discuss due to the issues it raises, is that of Wayne Couzens.

Couzens was a serving police officer in the armed, Diplomatic Protection Group (DGP) of the Metropolitan Police in London. He had previously served in other forces before transferring in. In March 2021, he hired a car, surveyed an area of London, and used his warrant card and handcuffs to falsely detain an innocent young woman, Sarah Everard, who had been walking home. He cited COVID restrictions as a reason to place her in handcuffs and in the back of the car. She was then driven across county lines to Kent, where she was subjected to a horrific rape and strangled to death with his police utility belt. In the following days, Couzens burned her body and placed her in a rubble sack on woodland he privately owned, even visiting the site with his children as she lay there undiscovered. He disposed of her telephone in a local river. He was caught through the assembly of CCTV, made up of doorbells, buses, and dashcams – which captured the heartbreaking moment he stopped and handcuffed her by the roadside.

A number of warning signs were missed through inadequacies in the vetting system. A vehicle registered to him was involved in indecent exposure offences in Kent in 2015 – while he was serving - but no action was taken and, by their own admission, Scotland Yard would have probably waved him through vetting in any case, due to a recruitment problem with experienced firearms officers. He was also linked to other exposure offences, including in the days before Sarah was murdered, and it has since emerged he was named as the suspect on the crime reports.

Couzens - who planned the offence in its entirety and wrongly believed he was forensically aware enough to get away with it - has now received a rare, whole of life prison sentence. He will die in jail but that does not repair the loss he caused and the relationship of the police with public has been severely damaged. Complex questions on double-crewing of all officers and restricting the deployment of plain clothes teams are now ongoing, and women fear being stopped by the very people charged with protecting them. From my perspective, he clearly displayed the characteristics of a serial offender and I would suggest he is likely to have committed other offences more serious than flashing, potentially against sex workers as they are less likely to have been reported. Before, however, such a likelihood becomes a probability, there would need to be an extensive investigation

Returning to Roy Hazelwood, the categorisation of rapists was not, in fact, solely his work. He openly credits Dr. A. Nicholas Groth whose 1979 study, entitled *Men Who Rape*[52], defined three types of offenders. Power, Anger, and Sadistic rapists. Power rapists, the most prevalent type, tend to be compensating for personal inadequacy and use only enough force or threat to subdue their victims and exert control for the purpose of the sexual act. Anger rapists use sex as a weapon to humiliate and debase their victims, acting violently and deliberately. Sadistic rapists are calculating, using restraint, ritual, and items to gain their own sexual gratification through a process of inflicting pain. The latter are the most likely to kill their victims. Hazelwood approached these groups with additional data from the unique BSU interviews and expanded on the typologies. He introduced power-reassurance (constructed fantasy of consent), power-assertive (entitlement), anger-retaliatory (motivated by personal grievances), anger-excitation

---

[52] Men Who Rape: The Psychology Of The Offender, Springer, 1979, A. Nichloas Growth and H. Jean Birnbaum

(sexual sadists), opportunistic, and gang (three or more offenders) categories. Perhaps instrumental in the growing use of Sexually Violent Predator laws and civil commitment, Hazelwood's well-respected and often repeated view is that adult criminal sex offenders, in particular sadists, cannot be changed[53] or reformed.

Robert Ben Rhoades was (and is) a sadistic or anger-excitement rapist who sits somewhere in a grey area between organised and disorganised offending. He was controlled and controlling but, as he fragmented during his spree in 1990, he became more frenzied and frenetic in his approach. This led to the recklessness which saw him captured. I propose there is a psychological phenomenon which descends on serial killers, not dissimilar to the red mist. Leading them to narrow their focus to the excitement of the act itself - creating a form of tunnel vision which prevents them from continuing to see the broader needs of organisation as they did when their offending began.

The work of the BSU, of Douglas, Lanning, Ressler, and Hazelwood took the FBI directly to the creation of ViCAP, the prevention program which aims to stop offenders such as Rhoades or Couzens. Having led it, Greg's insight is invaluable.

"It contains a database of unsolved homicides for the United States, missing persons, and unidentified bodies," he told me. "Also, more recently, they've added sexual assault with serial characteristics. When I say sexual assault, primarily, we're talking about rapes. The whole concept behind it is to build a national database that allows individual police departments to submit their information on those cases that fit the requirements of the database, and then compare their case with other cases in the system -and representation of those cases around the country - and make a determination if there are patterns of behaviour which may suggest a common offender."

---

53 http://www.crimelibrary.org/criminal_mind/profiling/hazelwood/2.html, Crime Library, Roy Hazelwood: Profiler of Sexual Crimes, Katherine Ramsland

A ViCAP submission is a lengthy form which needs to be manually completed and submitted by the local police department or the investigating officer. It is incredibly detailed, breaking the elements of every aspect of the offence down for immediate statistical analysis from the point of data entry – this is also, partly, the basis of my concept for a computer system. While originally my intention was that THEMIS, would be designed to bridge the cross-jurisdiction recording gap in America, I have swiftly come to recognise that it has potential global purpose – in particular when combined with another system I built earlier this year, which automates the risk assessment in personnel vetting and can scour multiple sources for publicly available electronic information (PAEI). Unexpectedly, in the wake of Couzens conviction, I also see a potential use case for it in the UK – a country often regarded as advanced in unified police systems.

ViCAP itself does have a rather significant problem built in, too. Something Greg was quick to highlight.

"It is a volunteer system, meaning that law enforcement agencies voluntarily participate," he told me. "They're not required by law to participate. And I think that there's an argument to require it. As in any database, the output is only as good as the amount and the quality of information that goes into it. Unfortunately, our program still only has probably a fraction of the actual number of cases that otherwise would be available if we had all agencies participating and committed to it."

Across international fibre lines, there was a brief interruption to my conversation with Greg as Dean Jackson, the Foundation's Deputy Executive Director joined us. His background is just as fascinating as Greg's: he has debriefed first responders after numerous fatal critical incidents, suicides, officer-involved shootings, homicides, and sexual assaults. He juggles his Cold Case Foundation role with also being an active member of the Utah Critical Incident Management Team and a Chaplain for the Provo Police Department.

"I grew up in Japan and was actually the son of a missionary over there," he told me. "My father was in the military, so that's kind of his connection to Japan and, when I was seven years old, we moved. I spent all my childhood there and then came back to go to college. Probably the most interesting thing about my background and relationship to what I do today is that I didn't want anything to do with death."

He has personally performed hundreds of death notifications and recently finished work on his first book, *Death Notifications: Delivering an Offensive Message in the least Offensive Manner.*

"I didn't like to go around mortuaries. I didn't want anything to do with any of it. The whole idea really bothered me," he said. "In 1984, I was doing an internship in Japan and, while there, I had gone out to the car to get some items. A gentleman had the decided to commit suicide that day and the building I was outside was a high-rise. He jumped off and landed not too far from where I was, after going through an awning. It was a horrific scene. Dismemberment. Just every one of my worst-case scenario fears and imaginations were right there in front of me and I was the first person to him."

Suicide remains a major societal issue in Japan[54]. By 2019 the suicide rate was the second highest in the G7, behind only America. Jisatsu, as suicide is called in Japanese, has grown to become the leading cause of death in men aged between twenty and forty-four. Health issues and financial problems are major drivers. This kind of event is a recognisable trauma in and of itself, and far from usual or every day. We each carry our first witnessed death around with us and this one could have crushed Dean, but it had a different effect.

"I tried to process that in the, first, just seconds, then minutes, days, hours, of moving on," Dean explained. "I came to grips with a reality about me that I didn't know. I think we have those moments in life where we kind of

---

54 https://en.wikipedia.org/wiki/Suicide_in_Japan, Suicide in Japan, Wikipedia, CC BY-SA 3.0

assume we know what we can handle what we can't handle, and what bothers us and what doesn't bother us. My takeaway was that it was horrible, it was awful, but it didn't affect me the way I had anticipated that it would. I felt just horrible that another human being could be that desperate and hopeless to do something like but the gore part of it didn't do to me what I thought. The reason that's important is because, less than about a year and a half later, through a whole series of events, I was invited by a Deputy Coroner to go to a training. I'd been friends with him, he had paid for this training and had a deputy that was supposed to go but was unable to. He said: Dean, would you like to go check this out? Had I not had the experience in Japan, I would have just said there is no way. But I'm kind of a sucker for free education. And I thought, well, I'm gonna go see him and see if I can learn something."

"I went to the training," Dean continued. "The trainer was the Chief Medical Examiner for Belfast, Northern Ireland and the entire training was on bombings and reconstruction. I was fascinated by what they could do. I was twenty-one years old, kind of thrust into that for a moment, so that's really how I kind of got my start in the field. And, since then, it's just taken a lot of different twists and turns. I got heavily involved about thirty years ago with critical incident stress management, debriefing first responders on all types of various incidents, and met Greg back around 1998. He was, at that time, the new chief for Provo, and I had been doing some work with the department but also wanted to do some chaplaincy work for them as well. So, we met and talked about whether or not that would be possible and, within a year, Greg brought me on board. We've had a lot of adventures together since and we quickly became friends. So, when Greg got ready to launch this foundation, one of the things that he was looking for was somebody who could really help him understand the whole non-profit world which I've been involved in for years - I'm a Rotarian - and now we're going into seven years, and I always tell people every day is school."

We talked about the Confessions Killer documentary – the thing which brought and Dr. Schechter and I to the Foundation - then turned our attention from Henry Lee Lucas to Robert Ben Rhoades as Greg's internet returned.

"When I was first assigned to the profiling unit, the investigative support unit as it was called the time, I had to go through this first year of training," Greg told me. "We were on probation, basically, for that first year, before being certified as criminal profilers. We had to go through the training, pass the collective performance evaluation, and - if you were fortunate enough to qualify - then at the end of that timeframe, which was a full year, then you were certified. Before that, everything that we did had to be passed through a committee or supervisor to ensure that we weren't going to get anybody in trouble. One of my instructors was a gentleman by the name of Roy Hazelwood, and Roy was among those individuals who would be considered as that first generation of profilers as we know them today."

I am genuinely in awe of this. It is the law enforcement equivalent of training at Hogwarts.

"Having been trained by Roy, well, there's one particular class that I took from him that was called Interpersonal Violence and he reviewed the Robert Ben Rhoades case as a model example of what we refer to as a serial killer. Also, he was a serial rapist. I told Roy, within a couple of years, that I wanted to start teaching this class I was putting together for the National Academy students - law enforcement representatives from Lieutenant and above, within an organisation that applied to go to the FBI National Academy. It's international and generally takes at least three to five years to be accepted, and they go through a twelve-week program. They study anything from behavioural sciences to investigations, to firearms, training, physical training, etc. And they get credit, through the University of Virginia, for attending those courses – which are all taught by FBI agents with at least a master's degree or above. So anyway, I had the opportunity, I was asked to put a course together on profiling and I told Roy I needed some material. He offered the opportunity to use the case of Rhoades – he actually had worked it and had all that material - and gave me permission to make copies of it.

So that was my first introduction to the case, just simply as a model as an example of what a serial killer is."

"But what makes a serial killer, from the perspective of a trained profiler?" I asked.

"Well, you're looking for patterns and behaviour," Greg replied. "You're looking for mobility oftentimes, not always. We certainly have had serial killers that are locals if you will, and live in the area but, more often than not, we find that serial killers are quite mobile. Even though they may be living in a particular area, they'll go out and commit their crimes and come back to that area within a loop."

This is not restricted to serial killers. Many times over the years I have mapped the routes of burglars, robbers, and other criminals so efficiently that I am now able to create predictive maps which often fair better than many of the other more technical methods – whether they be based on radius and recurrence theories or adapted earthquake algorithms. My 2008 commendation for Operation Gloucester would not have come at all, had I not invested the time in mapping the connection between violent street crime, burglary, and the proximity of a several handlers to one particular crack house which occupied a whole block of flats.

"There may be a representation of what we call a signature aspect of the crime," Greg continued. "Which is a projection of the personality of the offender into the crime scene. I go through a process that I developed back there when I was teaching, a concept I refer to as the Ten Filters of Profiling. It's through this filtering, as a metaphor, that we identify the behaviours that are engaged in between the victim and the offender. It's difficult to just tell you: well, here's three specific behaviours. You have to engage analysis in many, many different areas before you can make that determination."

We talked a little more about the importance of taking your time to create a profile, to make sure it was based in available fact and not speculation, then returned our focus to Rhoades.

"I utilised the case for that purpose in teaching and instruction, then I came to Provo, Utah as Police Chief," Greg explained. "I wanted to get in touch with Robert Ben Rhoades and tried to set up an interview with him - because we would go out and interview serial offenders. So, I made a phone call, made arrangements to talk with him over the phone while he was in prison in Illinois, and they set it up in the little room. He had phone access and I explained who I was, and what my interest was in talking with him, particularly about the Regina Walters case. And I'm sitting there in my office, he's on the other end, I introduce myself telling what I'm interested in. Then we start talking back and forth. Of course, this guy has a very peculiar personality – he's belligerent, denies everything. He starts to discredit, if you will, and disrespect Regina Walters and I became quite incensed about his blaming her demise on herself and her boyfriend. It got to the point where he and I were, you might say, a little bit in conflict with one another, so I let him know what I thought of him. I let him know that I would do anything I could to make his life as miserable as possible if I had the opportunity. He took the phone and threw it across the room."

Though Greg did not know it at the time of the call, he was going to get the opportunity to make Rhoades very miserable indeed.

"Within six months of arriving as Police Chief, I was invited to a convention in St. George, Utah, and they asked me to give a presentation on what I did in the FBI," Greg continued. "So, I presented the Robert Ben Rhoades case. There were about probably one hundred people in the audience and, among the people attending that course, was the Sheriff of Millard County, a guy by the name of Ted Phillips. His Lieutenant was also present, as was the sheriff that I had worked with very closely in Delta before I joined the FBI. So, anyway, I'm going through the photographs of Regina Walters, and the various poses that Rhoades had taken of her out in a very rural jungle and Ted raises his hand, and he says: you know, Greg, in some of those photographs the area environment is similar to some of our area here. I showed them the truck logs, the map of his travels in 1990, and guess who had travelled through Utah? Ted raises his hand again, and he says: we have an unsolved case in the county, in 1990. So, I said, well, let's talk after class."

They did talk and eventually a bloody rag from Rhoades' cab was DNA matched to the unidentified body – a woman we now know to be Patricia Walsh.

"I told him I'd make his life as miserable as I possibly could," Greg said. "And, by fortune, I had the opportunity to present his case and, as fate would have it, we identified another case he was responsible for. So that's how I got involved."

Greg's internet line dropped out for a short time again.

"When we started putting the Cold Case Foundation together," Dean said. "We kept trying to say: well, how do we describe to people what it is we do, is there a case that we can kind of point to that says how we can be a resource, particularly where you're talking about older cases. I think, early on, the idea was that here's a case that Greg had for such a long period of time that he was just sharing with people and helping them to understand what serial offenders are doing and how they're functioning. It's so often you hear about cases that somebody starts saying the real key moment was kind of a break was to investigators who happened to show up at the same conference together. When you get a whole group of investigators looking at a case, it's different than when you have just one investigator looking at it."

Old-fashioned common sense teaches us that two heads are better than one, and there is something in this. There is also a clear parallel with the red mist or tunnel vision which I believe impacts organised offenders the more they offend. A single investigator may well focus on one angle or one person who has angered or irritated them, to the detriment of the investigation. This can – and has – led to wrongful convictions, whether you look at the case of Steven Lybarger from Council Bluffs or the West Memphis Three. The problem, of course, is that for every time the wrong suspect becomes the centre of attention, the right one escapes justice.

The story of the West Memphis Three[55] is a dark episode in tunnel vision. In May 1993, the bodies of three eight-year-old boys, Chris Byers, Stevie Branch, and Michael Moore, were found beaten and hogtied in a Robin Hood Hills ditch. Chris Byers had been castrated. They had been reported missing less than twenty-four hours before the discovery. Investigators fixated on a satanic cult theory, driven largely by a probation officer, and three teenagers - Damien Echols, Jason Baldwin, and Jessie Misskelley Junior - became the targets. Misskelley was interviewed, with only thirty minutes being recorded and, after several hours, he came up with a confession which didn't match the crime scene. There are similarities with the Lybarger cases, despite the passage of twenty years since his conviction was overturned.

The police pressed ahead, even though Misskelley immediately recanted his coerced confession, and chose to ignore Chris Byer's blood being found on a knife his stepfather, John Mark Byers, had disposed of. Prosecutors separated the trials out, fighting the submission of inconvenient defence evidence at both and the teenagers were convicted. Misskelley and Baldwin received life sentences, whereas Echols faced the death penalty. After the conviction, one prosecution witness admitted perjury, the jury foreman admitted misconduct by discussing the case with his own attorney, and new DNA was found in crime scene samples which matched one Terry Hobbs – Stevie Branch's stepfather. The appeals process was a mess, but eventually the three were released having lost their early adulthoods. To rub salt in the wound, they were never found not guilty. Instead, an Alford plea was used to secure their release – meaning they pled guilty to lesser offences to nullify the murder convictions. Eleven years after that, as Echols still fought to secure the crime scene evidence for independent analysis, it was announced

---

55 https://encyclopediaofarkansas.net/entries/west-memphis-three-3039/, West Memphis Three, Encyclopedia Of Arkansas

that everything had either been lost or destroyed by fire. The lost samples included blood found in a local restaurant, left by a mud and bloodstained man who had burst in on the night the victims went missing, another lead the police had never pursued as it did not fit with their narrative.

"We should all accept the fact that many law enforcement agencies are interdependent with each other and that we should be approaching our jobs collectively, not exclusively," Greg said, as his internet line came back to life. "Because, generally, even though you've got two federal agencies who have their jurisdiction, and you've got the local agencies that have their state-wide jurisdiction, typically when you get involved in a case you need to rely upon each other, to satisfactorily identify and apprehend an offender. I have three Cs. They are Communication, Cooperation and Coordination between agencies throughout the country. If we communicate, cooperate, and coordinate with one another as law enforcement agencies, sharing critical information, we can both identify and apprehend offenders, thereby extracting them out of society and enhancing the safety of the public at large."

As well as training and connecting the agencies which investigate offences, the Foundation is designed to connect directly with the public, teaching individuals how to spot suspicious activity and how to reduce their own risk footprint.

"When Robert Ben Rhoades was initially arrested, they executed search warrants," Dean said. "They found a lot of things clothing and shoes. So, I think the first point for the general public, is if they see a relative or somebody they know or boyfriend who has a stash of, say clothing that doesn't make sense, it could be a red flag. There's a difference between, you know, being full of fear and being paranoid of everything, and being situationally aware of what's going on around you. As human beings we want to give everybody the benefit of the doubt but if things are making you uncomfortable, move away from that point, get somewhere else. Make a note, get some details, because it may not be that relevant right now, but it could be extremely relevant later on, as law enforcement comes in."

I thought back to the workshop foreman, who had seen Regina with Rhoades. There is a version of this story which has entered law enforcement folklore, in which Regina was holding a handwritten help sign to the truck window, and the location had become a Truck stop.

Greg has heard this from training participants over the years but the core problem always comes back to the same thing, no matter whether it is the true version or the fairy tale. "Unfortunately, he didn't take the opportunity to report it," he said. "While we as members of society don't want to get in people's business and we prefer to allow people to maintain their own privacy, when we see something that just doesn't look right or feel right to us, we should be looking out for one another. Call authorities if need be and let them figure out if there's a problem. Had that happened, Regina Walters would probably be here today. So, you know, it's necessary that good members of society take the initiative to do something if they see or feel that something isn't right. Get the authorities involved and let them worry about what materialises. That's their job and they're happy to do it."

This is a truth society misses a lot of the time. Perhaps because we are taught not to be weak – or be seen as weak – or because we are taught not to be a burden. But the truth is simply that public services are there to protect us and pick us up when we need help, and there is never harm in calling on them, even just to make sure of something. Or that is how it is supposed to be. There are aberrations, sadly, which challenge this and threaten to collapse the concept entirely. Wayne Couzens is one - the very person put in a position to help used that power to facilitate a horrific offence.

By nature, what he did moves the contract of trust with the public and policing in the UK has struggled to grasp how to repair the damage, or even begin to. One Police and Crime Commissioner suggested Sarah Everard should not have "submitted" to her arrest – a level of blame transference to the victim with is badly-informed and morally repugnant, resulting, rightly, in calls for a resignation – while Scotland Yard spent days suggesting that women should ask officers for their radios, so they can speak with control room staff and verify officer identities, or even flag down buses if they are stopped by police. None of these proposals are practical or realistic and they do not get to the heart of the problem.

Reinstituting trust after a breach like that is a long road, which may well lead to dark and complex places. Vetting throughout the employment lifecycle is essential, but that alone is not the answer. Better crime recording and enhanced protections for police whistle-blowers were put in place in 2014 after the select committee inquiry into police recorded crime I sparked, but there is still a clear need for cultural change and better cooperation between forces. Operationally, a decision will need to be made to deploy only double-crewed officers - a matter of basic safety for everyone, including officers and the public - and this requires proper investment in policing, namely a significant recruitment campaign and public spending. As immediate investment is unlikely, given global economic issues, an immediate tactical decision would be the reversion of plain clothes policing to surveillance only, with any arrest and detention carried out by double-crewed uniform officers only. Mixed gender pairing of officers may also have to be mandated.

These are interim measures and will not fix the problems raised by the brutal murder of Sarah Everard and the reality is there are no easy answers. Policing, in the UK at least, is going to face a whole range of new issues on the streets, which may see a reduction in public and officer safety develop. Legitimate criminals will actively resist arrest and detention, abusing the safety advice, while other criminals may develop new impersonation tactics to use in offences. Either circumstance poses a genuine risk to the public and officers alike. Whatever the solution, it is going to require a whole of society response and authoritative leadership. It could take years.

All this ties back into situational awareness, too. The way in which we each risk assess the world around us and make decisions as to what or what not to do. I'm currently at the start of a piece of professional-life work focused on what's broadly known as Active Bystander Theory, largely about exactly this.

"People need to ask themselves three questions," Greg continued. "What am I doing? Where am I? Who am I with? If it's low risk, they're familiar with where they are, what they're doing, and who they're with. If they can say, I'm not comfortable with where I am, or what I'm doing, or with an individual, they need to take action, regardless of what the other individual may think. If they're legitimate, they're not going to be offended by it. I just want the public at large to realise that they have the control and it's quite simple to make a determination as to whether or not they're in a low, medium or high-risk situation."

"People think that they've got a lot of time to process and check a little more," Dean added. "The problem is that if you're in reach of a predator, you don't have that kind of time. So, you're better to get to a safe place and try to evaluate from there. It's kind of like that moment in the movies where the person thinks something weird is in the other room. We've all been to the movie, where we're sitting there saying: don't go in the room, don't go in the room, and they walk in there knowing something's wrong. It comes out a lot in Greg's book about predators, this idea that we're dealing with two different kinds of individuals out here. We're dealing sometimes with people who just make us uncomfortable - they're a little strange or a little bit of a weirdo - and then you have predators. And these people, they're hunters. That's what they do. And when you cross paths with them, you don't have a lot of time."

Through the work of the BSU, almost all of us recognise there is a well-defined link between serial killers and their application for, or success in entering, law enforcement roles. Ed Kemper was only rejected because he was too tall at six feet nine inches, for example. Rhoades was interested, Dennis Rader too – though he eventually became a dogcatcher. The Golden State Killer was a cop, Couzens too. Even as I write, a new case has come to light[56]. This time in France, where fifty-nine-year-old François Vérove, a retired Gendarme, committed suicide in his apartment after being called in for interview. His DNA was matched to series of rapes and murders committed in Paris between 1986 and 1994 in which the offender, known as the "Pockmarked Man", used a police warrant card, handcuffs, and restraint techniques to capture young women and girls. His youngest victim was just eleven. These offenders, the ones in uniform, present the greatest challenge to everyone. Because they significantly shift the parameters of predatory victim acquisition and seriously damage the mitigation measures which make society safe. In many ways they attack and destroy the premise of situational awareness and personal risk management by introducing elements of value conflict which are near insurmountable.

While the Rhoades case itself exposed the challenges of geography and jurisdiction and affirmed the need for collective expertise – such as that provided by the Cold Case Foundation - the elements of it are echoing down the decades, across the whole of society, and even across continents. There is more need than ever for cohesion, multi-agency working, data collection, analysis, and training. This is how the hunters will become the hunted, in the end.

The solutions we build to ensure this happens matter. They must provide real protection and be able to weather storms for many years. I take some heart in the fact the foundation is solid.

---

56 https://www.theguardian.com/world/2021/oct/01/paris-serial-killer-of-80s-and-90s-was-ex-police-officer-dna-shows, Paris serial killer of 80s and 90s was ex-police officer, DNA shows, The Guardian, October 1st 2021, Angelique Chrisafis

DRIVERS

From the moment I started to talk about the Rhoades case publicly through Cold Case Live, a steady stream of new cases started to be referred. Curious retired detectives wondering if a case which had followed them through their career was an offence committed by the truck driver were among those who reached out. David Hornung approached me with one such investigation he had worked cold in Arizona: the rape and murder of Marsha Wilson.

Twenty-year-old Marsha was blonde-haired with blue eyes. She stood approximately five-foot-six tall and weighed just over a hundred pounds. In early July 1979 she moved to North 29th Place, Phoenix from Chula Vista, California, to help care for her grandmother. On July 28th 1979 Marsha told her grandmother she had met someone from the local area, at the park near the home address, and set out her plans to meet them at the Verde River the following day. A neighbour collected Marsha on July 29th and dropped her off at the Thomas Mall. At around two in the afternoon on July 30th, a local Public Safety Officer was flagged down by a motorist near Milepost 244.5, seven or so miles south of Payson on the Beeline Highway. The officer was asked if he had "come for the body."

Marsha was found deceased near the guardrail, at the side of the rural two-lane. The driver who had flagged down the passing officer claimed to have been travelling along the road when he noticed a "mannequin" and stopped to take a closer look. The young woman he saw was wearing only a bathing suit. A medical examination found the cause of death to be strangulation and she had numerous additional injuries indicative of a serious, violent assault. Semen was found when intimate samples were taken. Approximately one week after Marsha's body was discovered, an anonymous letter was sent to Gila County Sheriff's Office, stating the author had seen Marsha being picked up over fifty miles south on the highway by an unknown man, having tried himself to offer her a lift - which she declined. The case has been reopened twice, once in 1988 and again in 2016, but remains unsolved. David believed the case may be connected to Rhoades as the anonymous witness letter described a "truck driver with a lazy eye" being the one to pick Marsha up on the Beeline. The lazy eye description stood out to him as, in later prison pictures, one of Rhoades' eyes had developed a pronounced squint. I agreed to take a look and probed the evidence, going through the documents which David had neatly assembled.

She was discovered alongside a highway which runs through remote scrub with long views of oncoming traffic, almost seventy miles from her grandmother's home and over fifty miles from the place she was allegedly seen by the anonymous witness. To summarise that person's statement, not that the length of it requires much shortening down: "Heading north from the Salt River Reservation back to Payson late evening. Saw the girl on Highway. We were going to stop and give her a lift, but we were drunk and she refused to get in with us. Saw a black Chevy pickup with Texas plates and white wheels – 1976 or newer - talking to her. Driver six feet to six-three with a funny looking eyelid. Went to Mogollon Rim to finish drinks by the river. Staying anonymous because I don't want my wife to find out." It was sent to local law enforcement on August 10th. I describe that as an illogical statement and one which is suggestive of involvement. The original note and envelope need to be tested for fingerprints and DNA for comparison, but these actions have never taken as far as the file suggests. What I do not doubt, though, is that Marsha was in a pickup truck, not a truck, and that Rhoades had nothing to do with it – not least because the eye problem did not fit with his photographs at the time. It felt to me, if I am blunt, as though the local officers suspected someone they knew well and took a good old boy's approach to putting the matter bed for reasons of local convenience.

The evidence relating to the discovery of Marsha's body is, at best, irregular too. The public safety officer's incident report has been purged from local records and subsequent reinvestigations mention that the driver present when the body was located gave false details. Because of this, I will not print the alleged name - we live in an age of wild internet behaviour and do not want a potentially unconnected person to become the subject of harassment. I do, however, want to outline the bizarre account given. The twenty-three-year-old man stated he was driving along the Beeline at twenty-five miles per hour and saw an arm protruding from beneath the guard rail and stopped, believing it was a mannequin. He then sat there until a cop drove past by chance. Clearly, this was a long time before mobile telephones, but it is definitely odd. From the records, it is clear than no elimination samples were taken. The crime scene photographs are as grim as you would expect, and as limited in number. On the one hand they appear to negate the idea Marsha's hand was protruding the guard rail, leading to a logical suspicion the young driver was stopped by the officer only seconds after dumping the body. On the other hand, they show physical evidence which cancels this suspicion if you know what to look for.

Marsha is shown on her back in the scrub, feet towards the bottom of the embankment. Her head lay to one side. The lividity – the pooling of the blood with gravity - was extensive, showing she had been resting on her side. The blanching marks confirmed this was her resting position - tiny white marks in the lividity where the skin had pressed against hard surfaces, displacing the pooling. The blanching matched exactly with stones which would have been under her before she was rolled over. She had lain there in just her red and white striped bathing suit, in that lonely spot at the side of the Beeline Highway, for hours.

Hornung had found the paper file in a disused filing cabinet, out in the Gila County repair yard, when he picked up the case. There was not much to it but, alongside the scant number of crime scene photographs, were a handful from the autopsy and the medical examiner's report itself.

The examination was carried out at ten in the morning on July 31st. The photographs show the beating Marsha received was focused on her face.

Pressed in bruise marks on her legs, where they were held, were visible, as were others around her groin. These latter marks followed the hem of the bathing suit where it was pushed aside. The strangulation marks, clear human fingers, were visible, as was the bruise around her left wrist showing her arm had been pinned down. Damage to the fingernails on her right hand indicated that she fought. Toxicology revealed her blood alcohol was 0.14% which, in a young woman of her size and weight, would suggest she was suffering a loss of physical control, blurred vision, and would have been on the edge of dysphoria – the medical term for feeling unwell. Given where the file was found, the state and location of the physical evidence is not known. If the intimate swabs are still in existence, they need to be tested, as do the victim's fingernail clippings. The other investigative opportunities are limited: two of the witnesses may still be alive, but one was anonymous and the other appears to have given false details. There is no CCTV and no ALPR from the Beeline.

From what limited information there was, I drew out a hypothesis containing different probability options on the sexual assault element, based on the geographical, photographic, and autopsy evidence. I wrote the case up and sent it to the Foundation for a full review and formal investigation by the team. Marsha was not killed by Rhoades, no matter how neat a conclusion that might be. On the balance of probabilities, the person who raped and murdered her has lived their life in on or near Payson. And somebody in the town knows who did it, or least suspects another local and always has.

This was a different case to that of the girl in the Texas pasture, in that what I call a Digital Canvas was an available option. This technique is something I have developed, first as a possibility and then as a refined activity, thanks to the portion of my company's work which focuses on ethically identifying, accessing, and communicating with small audiences. Digital canvassing in the law enforcement context provides the capability to knock on thousands of virtual doors at a fraction of the resource commitment and expenditure which a physical exercise would take. For cold cases this is a near-perfect solution. I used the method to create a specific audience - men and women aged fifty and over, living in the tightly confined geography of Payson itself and around 29th North Place in Phoenix – and the trusted digital platforms used by people in these areas were used as an access point. A single infographic was designed using some psychological principles. "Somebody in Payson knows what happened to Marsha," it read. "PAYSON KNOWS WHAT HAPPENED," it said. People are deeply connected to their communities, and this simple message was designed to provoke community interest and challenge it to be the best it can be. Psychology opens doors and it can be used positively. Beneficially. Though mostly it is used to sell us something we do not need.

Using the digital canvas technique, I reduced a total geographical audience of over one-and-a-half million people to just over twenty thousand digital doors in a single trust network and knocked on nine thousand of them individually. Marsha's face and that simple text has already started its work, prompting a conversation which will ripple outwards and may eventually lead to new information after forty years. The connected world of interwoven technology we live in may have caused a significant number of problems and raised growing concerns over privacy, but it can be a tremendous force for good, if used properly and with good intent. I did with fifty pounds what would have cost a local police force thousands of dollars. But not all cases are the same as Marsha's and Rhoades was not a lone abnormality. Truck drivers have a deep connection with serial offending, in America and elsewhere. Even a cursory internet search leads straight to their catalogue of horrific acts.

Wayne Adam Ford walked into the Humboldt County Sheriff's Department in Eureka, California in early November 1998[57], presenting

---

[57] https://apnews.com/article/dc0353b0dc1562d71daa1d28ca9afd34, Trucker Confesses to Murder, Associated Press, November 6th 1998, Jeff Barnard.

officers with a severed women's breast. It belonged to Patricia Tamez, a twenty-nine-year-old woman from Victorville whose body had been found alongside the I-15, floating in the water of the California Aqueduct near Hesperia, two weeks before. Patricia, whose middle-class life had fallen prey to crystal meth addiction, was thought to have been a sex worker at the time of her death. Her breast was missing when her body was found.

Ford, born in December 1961, was troubled by the break-up of his parent's marriage when he was ten-years-old, and is reported to have suffered two head injuries – one at the age of two, falling off a step, and a severe trauma at eighteen, when he was hit by a drunk driver[58]. The change in him after the latter incident led to violent behaviour which resulted in several stays in mental health facilities. His arrests in the early eighties were for numerous assaults on sex workers, animal cruelty, and the attempted rape of a fifteen-year-old girl. Following a familiar pattern, he joined the marines and was honourably discharged, started truck driving, married and divorced, and then married again in 1994 - having a child a year later and divorcing a year after that. He lost custody of his son in the process and turned to sex-workers in earnest. On October 17th 1997, he killed for the first time, dismembering a sex-worker who remains unidentified and leaving her remains to be discovered by a duck hunter near Eureka. His second victim, Tina Gibbs, was a Las Vegas sex worker, the third an Ontario woman, Lanett White, who had been buying groceries near a truck stop and was found in an irrigation ditch in the days which followed. Tamez was his last victim and, for Ford, this was the end of the road. He confessed to his brother then handed himself in. Parts of his victims were found in the freezer at his trailer and there is a suggestion of evidence he had tried to cook some of them. He is currently on death row in San Quentin.

Ford has offered numerous excuses for his murders, from alcohol to hatred for his second ex-wife, but it is apparent that his issues were pre-existent,

---

[58] https://criminalminds.fandom.com/wiki/Wayne_Adam_Ford, Wayne Adam Ford, Criminal Minds Wiki

and deep, violent misogyny was a fixed part of his personality - he referred to women as "bodies with breasts[59]." Displacing blame for his own actions to his ex-wife is in-keeping with the weak and damaged psychology which had manifested even before he joined the marines.

Edward Surratt was born in Pennsylvania in August 1941[60]. He came from what was apparently a good family with no underlying issues but fell into a pattern of crime in the 1950s, which eventually led to his incarceration for assaulting a police officer. Despite this, his family paid for him to go to university after release, which he did in Ohio until 1963 - at which point he dropped out and drifted until he was drafted in 1964. During his service he was involved in violence and was dismissed in 1965 but re-enlisted in the marines in 1966, having bankrupted the family business after his father's death. He was sent to Vietnam and fought in the Tet Offensive, eventually being discharged in 1970 with a Gallantry Cross and Purple Heart. Post-Traumatic Stress Disorder set in despite him marrying and finding a job as a truck driver in North Carolina, and in 1974 he was convicted of the attempted rape of a thirteen-year-old boy. He was again imprisoned but served less than four years.

While working for a trucking company based in Charlotte, North Carolina, he frequented towns and cities in both Ohio and Pennsylvania and came to the attention of law enforcement who were investigating almost thirty unsolved murders. There was not sufficient evidence to pursue him, at first, though this changed in early June 1978 when he was found driving the car of a murder victim who had been savagely beaten to death with a baseball bat in his South Carolina home. Surrat was pursued, there was a shoot-out, and he escaped. His involvement in a series of home invasion murders was tracked by fingerprints and credit card receipts across Pennsylvania and Ohio

---

[59] https://www.spectator.co.uk/article/the-lancet-and-the-problem-with-women, The Lancet and the Problem With Women, The Spectator, 25th September 2021, Steerpike

[60] https://en.wikipedia.org/wiki/Edward_Surratt, Edward Surrat, Wikipedia, CC BY-SA 3.0

and he was eventually captured in Florida, in July 1978, when he committed another home invasion and fell asleep on a cocktail of drink and drugs after tying the family up and sexual assaulting one of the teenage daughters. As Surrat lay passed out, the father of the family slipped his bonds and called the police. By the end of October 1978, Surrat had been sentenced to over two-hundred years in prison and has continued to confess to additional crimes through his imprisonment, admitting to six more murders in 2007 and more still in 2021 – though he was not prosecuted due to his impossibly long term already being in place.

While the truck driving facilitated Ford's victim acquisition in a similar way to Rhoades, relying on wilderness and vulnerability, Surrat was different. Mobility was key but his method was distinct, in that he relied on the trucking routes but not the truck itself as a scene or the desolation of the highway for disposal. The inherent vulnerability of hitchhiking or sex-work did not matter to him. Material acquisition and exhilaration appeared to be his drivers.

Timothy Jay Vafeades, however, was a slightly different story.

Fifty-six-year-old Vafeades was truck driver out of Utah who kidnapped, imprisoned, and tortured multiple women [61]. He called his truck the "Twilight Express," after his own obsession with vampires. While he never progressed to murder before his 2014 arrest, Vafeades kidnapped at least six women, held them hostage in his truck for long periods of time, sexually assaulted them, and filed their teeth down to points with a Dremel. He was caught when a weigh station check revealed that his bruised female passenger had previously taken out a restraining order against him. The outcome of this intervention is the polar opposite of what happened with Regina Walters many years before but, considering Vafeades eventual sentence was only

---

[61] https://sacramento.cbslocal.com/2016/11/09/trucker-who-kept-sex-slaves-in-trailer-on-long-drives-gets-20-years-in-prison/, Trucker Who Kept Sex Slaves In Trailer On Long Drives Gets 20 Years In Prison, CBS Sacramento, November 9th 2016.

twenty years after plea-bargaining, it is easier to conclude that little has really changed.

Bruce Mendenhall was another who targeted vulnerable women[62]. He grew up in Illinois and had never crossed paths with the law, living as a married man with two daughters in Albion. On June 26th 2007 he murdered sex worker Sara Hulbert in Tennessee after encountering her at a truck stop. He was caught on CCTV and, on July 12th the same year, was spotted at another truck stop by an eagle-eyed Detective Sergeant, Pat Postiglione. On searching his truck, the ghosts of Rhoades were there to see, as was the development of forensic technique over the years since - they recovered a plastic bag full of bloodied clothes, a gun, gloves, tape, a nightstick, and sex toys. Samples taken from the items revealed the DNA of five different women. Mendenhall has been implicated in the murders of Symantha Winters (Tennessee), Jane Doe (found at the Flying J truck stop in Indianapolis), and Lucille Carter (Birmingham, Alabama). He has also been linked to investigations into seven other murders after abruptly ceasing any co-operation with authorities when, while in prison, he tried to use insurance money from his wife's death to take out hits on witnesses in his murder trial.

Meanwhile, far from America's network of interstate roads, Volcker Eckert stalked the roads of Europe[63], murdering at least nine women across East Germany, France, and Spain between 1974 and 2006.

Born in 1959, by the age of nine he had become sexually attracted to a doll belonging to his sister and this became a damaged psychology woven into his offending. At the age of fifteen he murdered a female classmate by strangling her and successfully duped authorities into believing she had committed suicide. By the age of eighteen, he was stalking and strangling women in the street. Despite his MO being so well known, he was inexplicably not connected with the 1987 murder of teenager Heike

---

[62] https://murderpedia.org/male.M/m/mendenhall-bruce.htm. Murderpedia, Bruce Mendenhall.

[63] https://en.wikipedia.org/wiki/Volker_Eckert, Wikipedia, Volker Eckert, CC BY-SA 3.0

Wunderlich, who was strangled, stripped, and left exposed in a local wood. Later that year he assaulted another teenager, but she survived and his psychiatrist identified him from a sketch circulated in the local newspaper. Eckert was sentenced to twelve years for this but was released after just six years of them, in 1994, commencing his career as truck driver in 1999. Between 2001 and 2006, he kidnapped, murdered, and mutilated sex workers along his pan-European trucking routes. He was eventually caught through CCTV, in similar circumstances to Mendenhall and, on searching his house, photographs of the victims and cuttings of their hair were found. He was using them as dolls.

Eckert committed suicide during his trial, on the 2nd of July 2007.

The last case I will mention here is that of Keith Jesperson. Born in 1955, he became known as the "Happy Face Killer" after drawing so-called smiley faces on his taunting confessional letters to the media[64].

From a documented abusive family background, Jesperson strangled animals as a child and used the same method on his victims. Over the years, he has made bold claims of murdering almost two hundred women but has only ever been connected to eight, which I believe speaks more to the fragile need for recognition which drove the letters. He was, once again a family man – married with three daughters, once again had divorced before his spree began, and – once again – had attempted to join law enforcement but failed due to injury. Between 1990 and 1995, the truck driver killed eight women across Washington, Oregon, California, Florida, Nebraska, and Wyoming, starting with Taunja Bennett. He picked her up in a bar and murdered her at his rental home. His series ended with Julie Winningham – his long-time girlfriend. It appears that ego prompted his letter writing, when police initially arrested, charged, and convicted the wrong people – Laverne Pavlinac and John Sosnovske – with Taunja's murder. His daughter,

---

[64] https://en.wikipedia.org/wiki/Keith_Hunter_Jesperson, Wikipedia, Keith Jesperson, CC BY-SA 3.0

Melissa Moore, has spoken out about her father's crimes and was instrumental in the disturbingly intimate podcast, *Happy Face*[65].

These cases are the reason we have seen horror films such as Jeepers Creepers, creating caricatures of something all too real just to titillate and entertain. But these movies create a layer of detachment from reality which does not truly exist. Monsters are real. They are under our beds and driving along our roads. Through fiction, though, we give the killers and society an out: the fiction inspires the fact and not vice versa. We provide ourselves with a reassuring narrative that bad people do not simply exist, we only create them with TV – which means we all have control. This is not true; it is just one of the comfortable lies we tell ourselves to make the world more palatable.

The truth is no secret, however. Because of cases like Rhoades, and those which preceded and followed, the FBI have tried to invest in combatting the reality which is left dulled by the fiction. The Highway Serial Killings Initiative was launched in the early 2000s[66], creating a database of hundreds of female victims found murdered at or near truck stops across the US. Alongside it, they maintain data on truckers linked to killings and sexual offences and claim to have used analysis of the data to solve dozens of cases.

The initiative itself is a natural extension of ViCAP and the BSU and I have no doubt it grew from the legacy of the Rhoades case, given my insight into Greg's career and the influence of Roy Hazelwood. This is good, necessary work, but I found myself angry with it. The unit chief, now retired, told the LA Times back in 2009: "We don't want to scare the public and make it seem like every time you stop for gas you should look over your shoulder. Many of these victims made poor choices, but that doesn't mean they deserved to die." My anger came straight from the classic line about

---

[65] https://open.spotify.com/show/2nSjQByMjsSLCVMaarlGxV, Happy Face Podcast, Spotify

[66] https://www.latimes.com/archives/la-xpm-2009-apr-05-me-serialkillers5-story.html, FBI makes a connection between long-haul truckers, serial killings, Los Angeles Times, April 5th 2009, Scott Glover

victims leading high-risk lifestyles. As long as we live in societies which allow people to exist day-to-day without a safety net, this is lazy, and I am not sorry for saying that. The suggestion is repeated in the FBI's public study notes [67], which state most of the victims are women: "living high-risk, transient lifestyles, often involving substance abuse and prostitution. They're frequently picked up at truck stops or service stations and sexually assaulted, murdered, and dumped along a highway."

There is an uncomfortable echo. The killers themselves are quick to blame women - for divorce, for being *Lot Lizards*, for being *Bodies With Breasts* - and that is not far removed from saying they live high risk lifestyles and make bad choices. If the phrase "she was asking for it," is even in the same time zone as law enforcement thinking, the thinking is wrong and must be called out. It is too easy to displace the responsibility for offending and provide reinforcement to this concept that somehow victims might be to blame for creating an opportunity and the hard truth remains that the offenders are the problem. The gaps in society which people fall through are the problem. My conversation with Della told this story, about those things which are too terrifyingly large to deal with and ignoring them leads to perverse outcomes.

A misguided reaction to the Couzens case in the UK has arisen from very similar thinking. The Home Office proposed that lone women can call a new, triple-eight telephone number if they feel unsafe, the national telephone provider British Telecom is building an app which women can use to register when they are alone and taking a journey, and one local police force has proposed an app women can use to request CCTV monitoring of their route home. These courses of action not only fail to deal with the problem raised by the murder of Sarah Everard – namely that Couzens was using real ID and a real policing power when he kidnapped her – but creates a host of other vulnerabilities. One is a false sense of security: CCTV

---

[67] https://www.fleetowner.com/operations/drivers/article/21695112/truckers-make-ideal-serial-killers-fbi, Truckers make ideal serial killers: FBI, Fleet Owner, May 23rd 2016, Larry Kahaner.

operators already struggle to monitor city centres and causing a split of attention across multiple subjects while leading women to believe they are entirely safe and under constant watch is dangerous. Another is the ability of organised crime and intelligent criminals to divert resources away from locations, leaving them free to commit offences. Additionally, emergency phone numbers are already straining under the weight of demand - between 999, 101, and online reporting, they regularly result in unreported crime and have done for years. The last issue to mention is by far the biggest: victim surveillance, which creates a central repository of information on the whereabouts and habits of vulnerable women, is less safe than properly analysing offending and offenders, and providing real suspect control and public advisory alerts. Worse still, such a database, in the wrong hands such as those of Couzens, provides qualified targets.

Victim profiling can work, if the intention is to plan a tactical response to protect them and reduce the risks they are exposed to - and if the real capacity exists to put it in place. Unless that is real, the result is only ever going to be a loop back to "many of these victims made poor choices." Creating impossible to service applications or phone numbers, is creating more layers of things which cannot prevent offending on top of a system which already cannot prevent offending. This exposes a growing addiction to, or hyper-reliance upon, instant technology which sparkles and shines but achieves little more than a diversion of funds from things which do work but are much more difficult to implement. If crime could be fixed this way, we would already be living in Utopia, but we do not. The App Store and some PR does not hold the answer.

The foundation of my problem with all of this, I suppose, is the weight of the value judgment which is attached to misapplied victimology. A lump of lead tied to victims by people who do not fully understand that others are already drowning, whether because they themselves are on dry land and far from the water or have been given a set of waders in the form of legal authority or academic funding. The other aspect to it is what I have come to think of Amity Island Effect - by which I mean authorities know there is at least one shark in the water, tell everyone to swim anyway, and then criticise them for not getting out fast enough when something goes wrong and the sirens sound. In many ways, the *Jaws* analogy holds more broadly in the public true crime world too: amateur shark hunters are everywhere, jumping on a variety of boats no matter how risky it is to themselves and everyone else. Very often, while the wrong shark is being held up for public spectacle, the real predators swim quietly on about their deadly business.

Over the course of looking into the Rhoades case and all that comes with it, I have developed my own operational theory about offenders and the risk profiles which surround them. Specifically, it centres on the offenders most likely to leave unidentified victims or long discovery delays behind them, modelled on Rhoades and tested against the other cases. Quite by accident, the theory generated its own acronym: DOE.

Earlier this year, I won and worked on a government contract as part of the national security vetting programme. This work focused on identifying real-world warning signs set against a developed framework to determine how much risk a person posed to departmental and national security. I will not discuss this in any detail, due to the nature of the project (as you might expect), but those same skills have a natural carry through to the work required to identify serial offenders and mitigate the risk of harm. Doe Theory, as it is, starts with possible outcomes, namely: No Harm, Verbal Assault, Minor Assault, Kidnap and False Imprisonment, Serious Assault and Sexual Assault, and Homicide. Each of those outcomes is simple and already well-documented enough not to require a huge supporting risk framework being created from scratch. Each is also easily understandable, irrespective of jurisdiction. The risk framework, divided into three categories, connects directly to the outcomes - with each element scored individually as low, medium, or high risk.

The three categories - Damage, Opportunity, and Evasion - relate to the offender, not the victim. Damage would include physical trauma, mental health issues, lived trauma, life experience, financial hardship, whether they experienced military service, whether they applied for authority roles, whether they suffer PTSD, any offending history, relationship status, and any child custody issues. Opportunity would include the regularity of exposure to distance from home and known faces, regular autonomy or lack of immediate supervision or control, access to vulnerable societal segments, access to areas with an absence of CCTV or other control measures, privacy and mobility or interchangeability of accommodation, and access to secluded areas. Evasion would include cross-jurisdiction travel, clean down opportunities, forensics awareness, opportunity if not deviating from expected travel patterns, and presence in searchable databases. Where the risks across the DOE categories are high, a subject is more likely to be connected to a serious outcome. A simple continuum runs alongside, with higher risk in all categories increasing the likelihood a victim would be harder for authorities to identify or would be discovered later, impacting investigations.

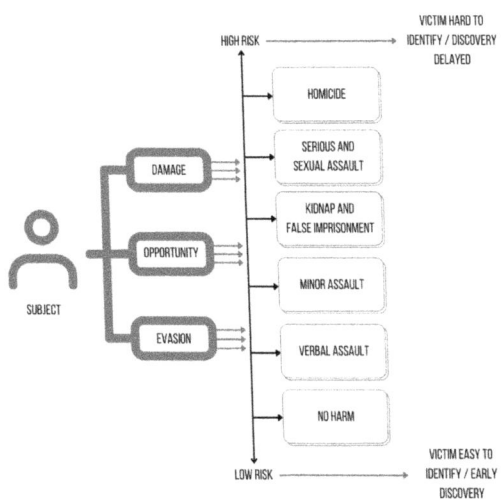

Figure 1: Doe Theory Risk Model, simplified version, October 2021, Patrick J.

The model is also reversible, meaning the trail of breadcrumbs can be followed from an unidentified victim or late discovery, through the risk categories to a category of subject or, even, a named subject – providing the data exists.

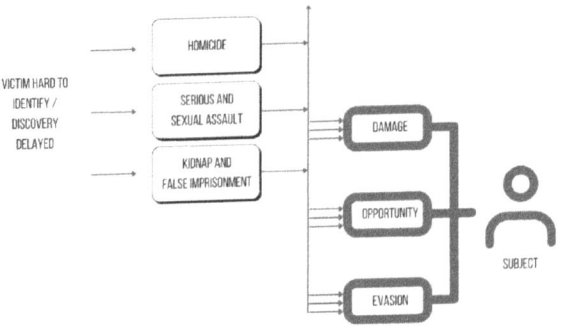

Figure 2: Doe Theory Risk Model, inversion, October 2021, Patrick J.

While it may have been tempting to include a second continuum which looks at the likelihood of a subject knowing a victim, one good look at Jesperson's last murder and a brief reflection on the red-mist effect on Rhoades, indicates this might well be fool's gold - as people unravel, they tend to buck trends and expectations. An unquantifiable risk is a high risk, so there is nothing to lose by accepting unknowns exist.

This working model folds into a much larger piece of work I did not, at least at first, know I was even doing. A solution which has grown out of the ground of the Rhoades case where I planted my feet. It is not just Doe Theory or the Themis system as standalone responses, they are branches of something much bigger. Something solid, deeply rooted, and evergreen.

There is nothing I can do to bring back the girls and women who have already lost their lives, it is not within the power of anyone on this Earth, but we can and must try to learn from the injustice of what was done to them and use those lessons to change the future. I know this a departure from what is expected when someone explores anything connected to true crime – I should probably pitch a tent on lawn somewhere minutes after a crime occurs and create a Tik Tok account to broadcast my every wandering thought - but my philosophy has long been that we should plant trees for others to sit in the shade of. And this tree, grown from genuine understanding of the Rhoades case and all its implications, should be able to do that job long after all the despicable killers are dead and gone.

- Broken Roads -

THE ROAD

It feels like a long time ago, the day I first sat staring at the photograph of the girl in the truck and had that long conversation with Pamela. Since then, I have come to fully understand the true horror of Robert Ben Rhoades and his predatory offending. He was a despicable beast but, at least now, a much clearer portrait of what he did and how he was caught by pure chance exists.

While exploring his case, I have discovered other tragic deaths too. Victims of monsters unknown, some of whom remain unidentified to this day. The girl in the pasture won't leave me but appeals and referrals have rendered nothing so far and others, like Marsha, have received no justice despite the passage of decades. The broken roads of America are haunted by stories of people who did not deserve to die, let alone be denied the peace of recognition. The problems which lead to these situations are tangible, however, and this means they can be fixed.

Mending what does not work, unfortunately, must start with creating a definitive timeline for the truck driver, from Council Bluffs to Menard Correctional Facility. This allows for identification of the potential intervention points – the times he could have been stopped or diverted - and, also, allow a full search to be conducted for other potential victims. As with most things investigative, this involves significantly more administration than driving fast or kicking down doors. It is another one of those time-involved processes which do not provide an immediately gratifying result. That is real police work though, vastly different from the way it is portrayed or discussed. One too many times in recent months I have listened to true crime podcasts or watched YouTube videos in which hosts vomit their minds, describing how they would do this or that, when they would be better off staying out of the way in almost every case. Perhaps that sounds harsh, and maybe I am angry with the sensationalised way the murder of innocent people has become a spectator sport. But perhaps I am justified. The Colosseum is a monument to humanity at its worst, not an aspirational endpoint.

The truck driver's timeline clarifies relatively well, though in some cases specific dates are simply not known and, in the case of the foreman who witnessed Rhoades with Regina, the location cannot be readily confirmed. The murder of Judith Pleas in Council Bluffs has been included, as it the clearest early offence which may one day prove to be connected to him in some way.

Best Date	Event	Location
22nd November 1945	Robert Ben Rhoades born.	Council Bluffs, Iowa
1964	High school yearbook photo ("The Monticello")	Council Bluffs, Iowa
24th February 1966	Father, Ben Rhoades, deceased amidst sexual assault allegations	Council Bluffs, Iowa
18th February 1970	Second marriage	Council Bluffs, Iowa
1970s	Truck driving career begins	Council Bluffs, Iowa
10th August 1973	Judith Pleas reported missing	Council Bluffs, Iowa
14th October 1973	Judith Pleas found deceased	Council Bluffs, Iowa
1984	Pamela Milliken journey with Rhoades	Winnipeg, Canada
1985	Separated from Debra Davis	Houston, Texas
1985	3 months uninterrupted truck driving	Presumed National
14th February 1986	Married Debra Davis following reconciliation	Houston, Texas
1989	Alleged to have raped Debra Davis, marriage ends	Houston, Texas
January 1990	Patricia Walsh and Douglas Zyskowksi dropped at Six Flags Atlanta by friends	Atlanta, Georgia

January 1990	Patricia Walsh and Douglas Zyskowksi staying in Tuscaloosa	Tuscaloosa, Alabama
21st January 1990	Douglas Zyskowksi's body found	Sonora, Texas
27-29th January 1990	Patricia Walsh murdered after captivity period	Fillmore, Utah
31st January 1990	Shana Holts picked up by Rhoades at truck stop	San Bernardino, California
4th February 1990	Regina Walters reported missing from home	Pasadena, Texas
5th February 1990	Shana Holts escapes, scared to street ID Rhoades	Houston, Texas
March 1990	Depot foreman sees Regina with Rhoades	Unconfirmed
12th March 1990	Call to Regina's father	Jewett, Texas
16th March 1990	Call to Regina's father	Oklahoma City, Oklahoma
17th March 1990	Call to Regina's father stating her hair was cut and she was in a barn	Ennis, Texas
1st April 1990	Lisa Pennal picked up at truck stop	Buckeye, Arizona
1st April 1990	Lisa Pennal rescued, Rhoades arrested	Casa Grande, Arizona
6th April 1990	Warrant executed at Rhoades' apartment	Houston, Texas
29th September 1990	Regina Walters' body found	Greenville, Illinois
1st October 1990	Patricia Walsh's body found	Fillmore, Utah
16th October 1990	Det. Trammel receives Det. Sheeley's bulletin	Pasadena, Texas
3rd March 1991	Ricky Jones' body found	Lamar County, Mississippi
February 1992	Rhoades interviewed in prison	Arizona
14th February 1992	Rhoades served Illinois extradition papers	Arizona
27th March 1992	Illinois proceedings begin	Bond County, Illinois

11th September 1992	Rhoades sentenced to imprisonment in Illinois	Bond County, Illinois
1992	Douglas Zyskowksi identified	Sonora, Texas
13th July 2001	Rhoades' Illinois appeal denied	Menard, Illinois
2003	Patricia Walsh identified	Fillmore, Utah
2005	Extradition to Utah vacated for Texas trial	Houston, Texas
1st July 2008	Ricky Jones identified	Lamar County, Mississippi
2012	Rhoades pleads guilty and convicted for Walsh and Zyskowksi murders	Ozona, Texas
2015	Pamela Milliken sees photograph	Alberta, Canada
2019	Pamela Milliken speaks to media	Alberta, Canada
2021	Rhoades still serving sentence in Menard Correctional Facility	Menard, Illinois

The timeline allows a map of his final spree to be drawn, providing insight which is both essential and terrifying. With Douglas Zyskowski's body discovery as the starting point (upwards arrow), Rhoades's 1990 offending took him on a round trip of over five thousand miles as the crow flies. The journey ended with Lisa Pennal's rescue in Arizona (downwards arrow). His offending territory between January and April of 1990 was staggering - over six hundred thousand square miles, an area over six times the size of the United Kingdom. Using a demographic analysis on this primary offending zone, the population within that area is now over forty-eight million people. The trucker was a needle in a haystack in the very literal sense.

Taking the clear visual together with facts of the case, the logical hypothesis is that Rhoades was offending from home-base and selecting victims opportunistically as they presented themselves on the road. The route all but confirms his admission that Patricia Walsh was murdered and left by the roadside as he made his way south, picking Shana Holts up almost immediately afterwards before taking her back to his apartment. With the variety of clothing found in the flat, it seems very likely that Shana was not the only victim taken there.

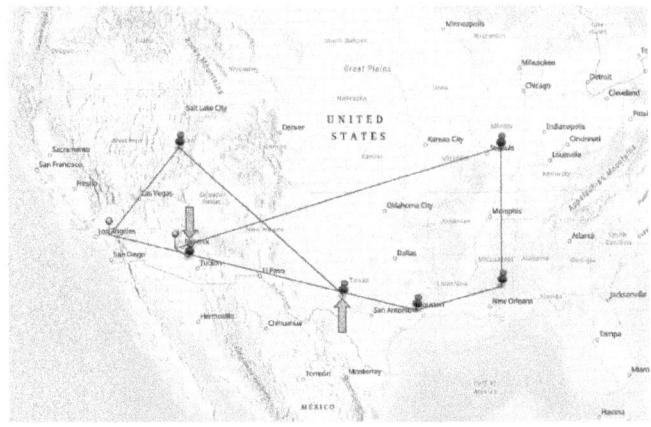

Figure 3: Rhoades' Spree, Mapped in ESRI ARCGIS, October 2021, Patrick J.

As he picked up two couples within the space of only months, it is understandable that his offending period is thought to have spanned a much longer timeframe. This was clearly something which needed testing and having a large dataset on hand made doing so possible. Starting with a blank map, I plotted Rhoades' 1989 trucking route, which ran from Seattle in the north-west corner all the way to Columbus at the most easterly point - a crooked smile running across America, tracking the Interstates across Washington, Oregon, California, Arizona, New Mexico, Texas, Oklahoma, Louisiana, Mississippi, Arkansas, Tennessee, Alabama, Georgia, Kentucky, Missouri, and Ohio. Interstates 84, 82, 5, 10, 40, 55, 70, 65, 75, 20, 59. 49, 12 and the highways in between.

With the base map in ESRI set to navigation, America's freight lanes glowed yellow with too cheerful blue and red shields dotting them, while the spaces between cities showed as pale green emptiness. The scale of the US is bewildering at times, more so when you know those cheerful looking lines are littered with unidentified bodies. I traced the ghostly voids along the interstates, mapping areas between population centres ideal for an offender like Rhoades, then overlayed the thirteen-thousand unidentified bodies from the NaMus data set, filtered to show cases with an estimated year of death between 1987 and 1990. Anything falling within the empty areas had at least the potential to be a Rhoades case, pending closer inspection.

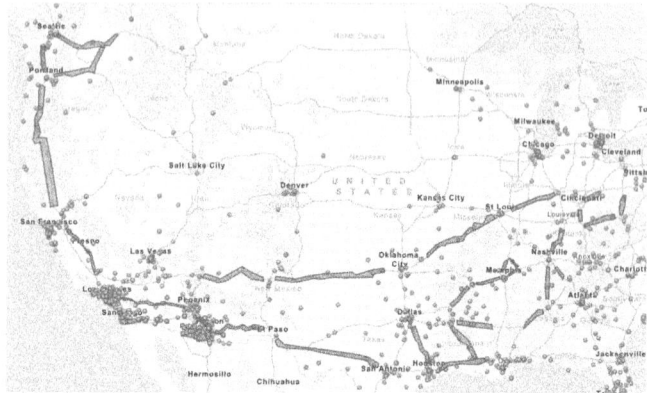

Figure 4: Rhoades' '89 Route, Mapped with NaMus data in ESRI ARCGIS, October 2021, Patrick J.

There were seventy-five unidentified person cases on that list, fifteen of them female, nine of them listed as "unsure," and the rest male. The easiest starting point – and yes easy is allowed, even within a process like this – was to go through the cases in which the sex could not be determined. Two of them, both in Chehalis, Washington, were marked as "cranium found in storage with no records," which pointed towards a well-documented problem with evidence retention. The rest of them were partial skeletal remains and nothing even remotely suggested a link to Rhoades. Records relating to females were not much more informative or likely - the majority were partial skeletal remains found in areas known for transient or migratory deaths. The male records were in similar shape but with a larger volume of deaths following vehicle collisions (trains and trucks). The most noteworthy discovery, near Seattle, was that of a male skeleton at the entrance of an animal den.

Across the United States, a huge volume of cold cases are being publicised in varying formats, across thousands of individual web pages. The best unified resource I have found to date is the Project: Cold Case[68] database which holds summary details of almost twenty-five thousand cases nationwide. A search was conducted for all cold cases reported between January 1st 1987 and January 1st 1990, which returned four-hundred-and-fourteen records. The records are slim, with most featuring the phrase "No Narrative Given," meaning the circumstances are being held back. This rendered immediate analysis futile from the outset but nothing in those cases immediately leapt out or spoke to me as being linked to Rhoades.

The research is not definitive, that should probably go without saying, but it exposes the potential of an alternative view. Namely that Rhoades offending began after the alleged rape of Debra Davis – his effective break point, which occurred in 1989 – leading to a rapidly escalating and self-destructive single spree which began with Patricia Walsh and Douglas Zyskowksi and ended with Lisa Pennal, albeit only due to his arrest. While this might not be comfortable to accept, and there is certainly a host of reasoning which suggests his offending spanned a much longer period, challenging any key assumption is a healthy approach in any investigation. To assume makes an ass of u and me, the saying goes.

Effectively, if you step away from the conventional wisdom, you are left with two serviceable hypotheses with can be set side-by-side and weighed:

1) *Rhoades may have killed somebody earlier in life, around the time his second marriage began to break down, potentially Judith Pleas. He became fixated with BDSM as a way of reliving the murder but kept himself under control day-to-day, offending clandestinely throughout his life - even while married to Debra Davis, who was servicing most of his needs until the alleged rape. He had committed multiple similar murders over a period of years by the time he was caught.*

---

[68] https://database.projectcoldcase.org/

2) Rhoades came from a traumatic childhood background and in later life became fixated with BDSM. While married to Debra Davis, who was servicing most of his needs until the alleged rape, he was not committing offences – though he may have engaged prostitutes and personal ads while on the road. Following the rape incident and the departure of his compliant partner, he lost self-control and filled his needs in a pattern of escalation – most likely unreported rapes and assaults - until the spree occurred. He lied to the victims about previous offences as part of his narrative to gain compliance through fear.

There are pros and cons to each hypothesis and the process would be to follow every line of evidence to its conclusion in line with the checkable facts, provable lies mantra. Without a decent account from truck driver himself, that process will be nigh on impossible and it is not helped by the chaotic and incomplete nature of the information and crime data available. I should also add that there is another option which must appear at the very beginning of every single case with an identified suspect - that being they are completely innocent. As well as seeking the evidence to prove a case, it is equally important to follow every lead which points the other way (within reason and rational thought, of course). In the case of Rhoades, however, there is already sufficient evidence to rule out innocence in respect of the victims he is serving time for killing, but it would need to be applied to any future cases which are potentially linked to him – for example a cold case investigation into the murder of Judith Pleas.

With Robert Ben Rhoades, the purpose of the differing hypotheses is to try and understand his *why* – the reasoning behind the established facts in the timeline. My personal view, for what it is worth, is that the truth is somewhere in between the two explanations. I think it is probable he did kill someone in the early to mid-seventies, and absolutely believe the case of Judith Pleas should be reviewed with him in mind – as a bare minimum for elimination reasons. I believe he carried trauma from childhood through his life and this affected him deeply, changing his perception of normal and acceptable. It appears likely that truck driving allowed him to indulge fantasies with sex-workers and hitchhikers and this became less and less healthy or controllable over time. I suspect that he was already spiralling when he met Debra but, to a degree, the nature of their relationship satisfied many of his urges, at least for a time. I feel that, after their marriage broke down, he lost control and believed he could take whatever he wanted, so his behaviour rapidly escalated from paying for kinky sex to playing out the fantasies he became obsessed with after his willing partner was gone. Given the description of anal rape provided by both Debra Davis and Shana Holts, it begs questions as to whether Rhoades was reliving the event with Debra and seeking a different outcome, or reliving an extra-marital experience – pre-dating Debra's rape - which became his template.

I have chosen my words deliberately for a reason: *probable, think, believe, likely, suspect, feel*. They differentiate my own levels of surety and distinguish between what I infer from the evidence gathered and analysed and what comes from intuition and confirmation bias – something we all have and ignore at our peril. I think of this as personal fair dealing, as it allows you to express your thoughts while rationalising where they come from to keep you on the straight and narrow. Being honest with yourself is as important to the quality of an investigation as maintaining chain of custody in physical items, because facts and evidence should always steer your thinking and it should never be the other way round.

The bottom line at the end of this process is that we may never get a clearer view of Rhoades rationale. We might never be able to fully resolve the hypotheses. One major barrier to establishing the precise truth about Robert Ben Rhoades is that the evidence pertaining to *why* have never been tested at trial. This is a common issue which occurs when a plea-bargaining system meets capital punishment, incentivising what are probably best described as perverse outcomes – in the sense that the reality of what happened is distorted by the dealings to put it to bed. A wealth of study and commentary on this exists and it is not my intention to rehash it here, but a summary from Cornell Law School[69] is useful. They say: "Some commentators oppose plea bargains, as they feel that plea bargains allow defendants to shirk responsibility for the crimes they have committed. Others argue that plea bargains are too coercive and undermine important constitutional rights. Plea bargaining does require defendants to waive three rights protected by the Fifth and Sixth Amendments: the right to a jury trial, the right against self-incrimination, and the right to confront witnesses."

In a nutshell, plea-bargaining gives some offenders a way out from certain things they have done, and allows authorities a speedy, headline-friendly conclusion which does not test the quality of their case or the investigation behind it. Add in the death penalty and what you are left with is little more than "If you don't agree to this we will kill you." When put like this, in its simplest form, plea-bargaining does not sound much like justice. I freely admit I look at this from a perspective shaped by the absence of death penalty outcomes, combined with strict rules around the treatment of suspects and investigative procedures, but I also see it as coming from a position of power - which works to increase the quality of investigations leading to conviction.

The learning from the Rhoades case, from the things we *can* confirm, is a very different matter - the unknowns are fewer and the concrete provisions, which could stop someone like him from offending in future, or reduce the number of victims either unidentified or going with years without justice, are clear. There are still opportunities to explore whether he committed additional offences too, which is where I think the end of this should begin because this represents the low-hanging fruit in terms of commitment, action, and administration.

Despite what might perhaps be perceived as a series of dead ends in the available data, the ask is a fairly simple one. If departments and offices have missing person cases involving couples or lone females who were hitch-hiking between 1979 and December 1989, the cases can be assessed together

---

[69] https://www.law.cornell.edu/wex/plea_bargain, Plea Bargain, Cornell Law School, Accessed 6th November 2021

and compared to Rhoades's movements and victim profiles. In addition to missing persons, any unidentified person case - whether male or female - found within close proximity of an Interstate and with an estimated date of death between those dates, in particular those with signs of .22 gunshot injury, ligature strangulation, or improvised garotte, can be assessed together. Lastly, cold case homicides and sexual offences between those dates, particularly those involving recognisable elements derived from the contents of Rhoades torture kit, should be assessed together. This means cases where living victims mention: a truck, a truck driver, a charming man with glasses, the names Dusty, Robert, or Whips and Chains, a horsebit, a neck chain which loops to hand and ankle restraints, a double-ended sex toy, BDSM, cutting hair and shaving pubic hair, genital or nipple piercing, whipping, photography and story-posing, being asked to wear provided clothing, and anal rape. In deceased males it means .22 gunshot injuries and a discovery site within a short driving distance of a truck stop or interchange. In deceased females it means bodies in close proximity to the roadside in wilderness areas or found in abandoned buildings in such areas, cropped hair, shaved pubic hair, piercing to the genitalia and nipples, restraint marks on the wrists and ankles, whip marks on the torso and legs. Signs of vaginal and anal trauma, ligatures or ligature marks to the neck, and improvised garottes.

Rather than dally or put things off for another day, I spent the few minutes needed to create a pre-referral briefing for law enforcement officers and created a page at the Cold Case Live website[70] to collect any referrals agencies and offices may wish to make. Simple, fast, effective solutions are key and a resource like this comes with a tiny administrative burden for a potentially significant pay off.

As I said, this was the low-hanging fruit and the solution has been implemented. Having done this, I reflected briefly on that national cold case recording problem and the limitations of the current system - some of it

---

70 https://coldcase.live/rhoades-case-referral/

driven by the hold-back practice which preserves or shields the investigative approach from the eyes of the outstanding suspect. In for a penny, in for a pound, I invested some extra time I had not intended on using in designing and deploying a unified database. I called it NCCD, which stands for National Cold Case Database. It follows the same "simple is best" approach of the Rhoades case referral process, not actually asking for circumstances to avoid the "narrative not given" trap, instead using category dropdowns to facilitate rapid statistical and geographical analysis. Adding a case takes less than a minute for registered law enforcement officers and none of the data gathered compromises an investigation's integrity. Solutions should be meaningful, rapidly deployable and – most importantly – serve a genuine purpose without creating an intrusive burden, and this meets these criteria. It is available through the Cold Case Live website[71], first made live on the day I built it in November 2021.

The more complicated elements are all that is left, and no matter how much it might be easier to put them off and retire at creating a database, to do so would be a cheat or a cop out. The first of the more complex pieces was identifying the points at which an intervention with Rhoades was needed and explaining what actions could have been taken at those points. The purpose is not to look backwards with perfect hindsight, but to develop a concept of what can be done with other individuals in future to act as a brake, preventing a transition to offending. The timeline, that dull but essential administrative exercise, had already done most of this work and the clearest intervention points with Rhoades were:

Best Date	Event	Location
24th February 1966	Father, Ben Rhoades, deceased amidst sexual assault allegations	Council Bluffs, Iowa
1970s	Truck driving career begins	Council Bluffs, Iowa
1985	Separated from Debra Davis	Houston, Texas

---

[71] https://coldcase.live/nccd

1989	Alleged to have raped Debra Davis, marriage ends	Houston, Texas
31st January 1990	Shana Holts picked up by Rhoades at truckstop	San Bernardino, California
5th February 1990	Shana Holts escapes, scared to street ID Rhoades	Houston, Texas
March 1990	Depot foreman sees Regina with Rhoades	Unconfirmed
17th March 1990	Call to Regina's father stating her hair was cut and she was in a barn	Ennis, Texas
1st April 1990	Lisa Pennal picked up at truck stop	Buckeye, Arizona

Formative trauma is recurrent across serious offending profiles, though it cannot be stressed enough that many survivors of abusive and traumatic childhoods do not themselves go on to offend. However, the immediate appearance of a traumatic event – of a dual nature in Rhoades' case – provided me with the first solution.

The death of a parent or the wake of a familial abuse allegation is a therapeutic opportunity and, had Rhoades been offered or mandated counselling at that point, it may well have allowed a shift in his psychology to take place. At school age the obvious strategy for such interventions is through the education system, which has direct access to an almost captive audience. With someone slightly older, considering Rhoades was twenty-one at the relevant time, that dynamic shifts. Workplace interventions remain less than likely – and it is important to be realistic on that – but two other clear opportunities do present. The first is a point of entry intervention in the military - given that many offenders gravitate towards service after formative trauma, often causing problems while there. The logic of implementing trauma therapy as part of the onboarding process, especially if it reduces poor behaviour of personnel and can act to prevent post-service offending, is obvious. The second intervention point lies with law enforcement. When one family member is accused of a serious crime it is traumatic for the others involved and, whether we like it or not, policing comes with a duty of care to everyone in or close to the process. Very rarely are families involved in the offending, but they do have to pay consequences for selfish acts of another family member and, all too often, those family members have also been victims of the same person. Subsequently, the provision of a therapeutic intervention at point of contact with law enforcement, thinking mostly about child abuse cases, could well act to prevent future offending. In addition, it could also result in the exposure of evidence of unreported offending leading to a weightier conviction. Saving one life in future is worth the upfront investment and, in terms of a policy solution, it is easy to communicate and implement, whether nationally or at a state or municipal level.

The second point of intervention, at the start of a truck driving career, is another clear opportunity and ties directly Doe Theory and the principle of through-life vetting. It is a career in the high-risk category per se, so introducing due diligence which steps a little beyond the expected background checks is simply a sensible societal measure. The execution of vetting is also not the complicated mess it is often thought to be - a simple electronic record completed at the point of application, which uses bespoke algorithms to score risk, is a five-minute intervention with a limited cost implication and low administration. Updating those records once a year does not shift the equation and, if combined with real-time reporting of driver-specific stops, arrests, and other law enforcement interventions – all capturing geographical information, suddenly an open door for serial offenders is transformed into a near unstoppable prevention mechanism. Yes, the implementation of mandatory vetting would require a legislative intervention but trust in business is a valuable commodity and a voluntarily obtained accreditation of vetted drivers would only benefit a logistics business by enhancing its reputation. Industry also has a deal of freedom to introduce contractual terms without the controversy of new law.

Much in the same way as the Rhoades referral mechanism and NCCD are designed to create a minimal burden for maximum return, driver risk vetting is a low input, high mitigation activity with clear gains for society, law enforcement, and businesses. So, again following the principle of creating rapidly deployable solutions, I invested the time in designing a software system called DRiVet (Driver Risk Vetting) as a standalone package with a low access cost. For law enforcement agencies it will be accessible as a module of the Themis system. For industry the cost of an annual, standalone subscription will be less than ten dollars for up to fifty drivers, or twenty cents a head per year. With 3.5 million drivers in America, it is not designed to get anyone rich, but it is designed to pay its own way in contributing to public safety. The commercial version of the DRiVet system, with the fully integrated communication channels between industry and law enforcement will be launched in 2022, as early as I can possibly make it happen. In the interim, I have created a lightweight version which allows an individual assessment to be generated without recording the subject information. It is a fast and to use form, asking a small number of questions, which returns a simple risk statement, and can again be found at the Cold Case Live website[72]. The commercial system will feature a questionnaire and consents for completion by the vetting subjects, a management database for industry, and a law enforcement access module which requires appropriate authorities to gain decrypted access to private data.

Relationship breakdown was the third intervention point in the Rhoades case but this one has less of a direct opportunity for intervention. When people split up, there is rarely an agency or authority involved as life just happens and it is not always the start of a murder spree. While on the one hand DRiVet would pick up the change of relationship status and adjust the automated risk score appropriately, a deeper analysis into social media content and other publicly available electronic information (PAEI) would be

---

[72] https://coldcase.live/drivet

too intrusive to implement – stepping clearly into mass surveillance, considering such a system would need to monitor the whole population all the time. This leaves a more generalised opportunity which would take the form of public safety announcement styled work and probably sits best with charities or NGOs. The intervention would be relatively simple, targeting males aged twenty-five to fifty-five with behaviourally designed messaging, directing them to a resource designed to steer them healthily through relationship breakdown. This could be a website, an app, or physical resource centres. The desired outcome would be healthy acceptance of the end of the relationship and a focus on productive rather than destructive behaviours (for example, joining a club). Diversionary interventions like this are particularly effective because, if you saturate a population segment with both a solution and unhealthy behaviour to look out for in their peers, the knowledge is retained, the group begins to self-police and a change in what was is known as Collective Common Sense takes place. In practical terms, this means that people in a slice of society change the way they think by talking about issues. The theory originally came from a psychologist called Serge Moscovici[73] and the principle is both functional and powerful - it is something I use in the day job regularly to create positive behavioural change.

The alleged rape in 1989 was another key intervention point. This is again complex, as it would have relied entirely upon reporting of the offence.

Sexual violence is still a drastically under-reported crime, in particular when it occurs within a pattern of domestic abuse, and stigmas and disbelief – such as those faced by Shana Holts or Lisa Pennal – sadly do still exist in law enforcement, no matter how much progress is made. Even in such an environment, the opportunities to drive change and create solutions are still present. Mandatory domestic abuse prosecution without the through-trial support of the victim is a much more common occurrence nowadays, internationally. This has broken through of the cycle of abuse in many cases

---

[73] La Psychanalyse : Son Image et Son Public, Published by Presses Universitaires De France, Paris, 1976, Serge Moscovici

and allowed victims to make new lives, while the people who tormented them have finally faced a justice they never believed was coming. To bolster this, to make sure the true scale of sexually motivated crime is known, understood, and factored into both policy creation and resource allocation, the solution area which stands out to me is the mechanism for victims to report what happened. This is incredibly difficult to address because there are a variety of barriers to overcome - psychologically, victims of sexual violence tend to be deeply affected and there are a range of responses which present themselves, from deep PTSD to misplaced shame or embarrassment. Having to relive what happened when making a first report, then a detailed statement, then in court is incredibly oppressive for victims. Attending a Sexual Assault Referral Centre (SARC) or other such facility for intimate examination is, in and of itself, trauma on top of trauma. Then there are trust issues with authority and whether investigators will believe the victim or, in some areas, whether the officers are somehow connected to the offenders through corruption - the under-recording of serious sexual offences was one of the key issues I raised back during the whistleblowing and examined in a different context in Mexico. It is an area I know too well for comfort.

Ultimately, unrecorded crime helps offenders get away with what they have done, so it is necessary to find a way through. This is something I have wrestled with for years and, only now, have I come to what feels like the answer. It starts with accepting that every victim deserves to be heard but not every victim will want to put themselves through the full onwards trauma of supporting prosecution. This leaves a gap which is not effectively filled by current reporting and recording systems, contributing to eighty percent of sexual offences never being documented. The logical response is the provision of a confidential, secure, direct reporting mechanism which lets the victim input as little or as much information as they want, ensures that the information needed to prevent serial offences is captured, and does not add the intimidating pressures of statement taking and physical examination as standard. The result is an immediate barrier removal and creates a starting point from which rapport could be built with victims over time.

The practical aspects of this solution relate to the design of a secure, confidential reporting module for the Themis system which can be accessed directly by the victims at any time they feel comfortable enough to make the report. The system takes them carefully through a process designed to capture the information which matters, closing offending windows in an entirely new way. Given the highly sensitive nature of the data gathered, I built a function which encrypts the information at the point the victim writes it and only releases the content they agree to release to people authorised, by them, to retrieve it. Even the analytical process within the system is designed to work with the data in encrypted form. To me at least, this solution presents a rare transformational opportunity to save people from further and future trauma and to make sure the true picture of sexually motivated crime is documented.

This topic area ties directly to the failed street identification procedure which allowed Rhoades to drive away from his attack on Shana Holts too. None of that was Shana's fault, she should never have been asked to do it and procedure has changed over the years to prevent such circumstances, but repetition never hurts: the officer at the scene had probable cause, what we would call reasonable suspicion here, and should have exercised it. To avoid argument or ambiguity, the clear solution to this issue lies at policy level, in introducing legislation which allows suspects to be detained in custody for the purpose of a properly executed identification procedure. This would balance the rights of the victim and the offender and empower police officers to take direct, proportionate action in a pre-defined procedure which can specify constitutional rights. This is a simple fix and would be fully supported by decent people, I have little doubt. A technology option to support such a change would be to create a secure app for law enforcement agencies allowing an officer at scene with the suspect to capture live images, forensically store them, and transmit them to the officer with victim, protecting the latter from direct exposure to a potential offender while recording their reaction as part of the evidence. Specific, simple, purposeful.

The truck stop pickups of Shana Holts and Lisa Pennal, and the sighting of Regina Walters by the depot foreman all present one intervention opportunity really: the ability to identify who is with a driver and whether they are safe with them. Imagine the DRiVet system taken to the extreme, with high-risk drivers prevented by law from carrying passengers, and all drivers obliged to carry a red, yellow, or green vetting mark on their trucks, denoting whether there is a high, moderate, or low risk operator behind the wheel. Hitchhikers and sex-workers would make significantly different decisions, and highway patrol officers would be better informed before even approaching the vehicle. Even without going to that depth, simply carrying out spot checks at truck stops would make a massive difference – as it did at the weight station, with Vafeades and his victim. Another novel approach, specifically addressing the depot foreman's failure to report what he saw, would be to introduce a delivery note system which identifies who is expected to be with the driver and requesting either a notification to the logistics company or that a call to check things out with local officers is placed. One line on a template form could have saved Regina's life and may save somebody else.

The last point of intervention in the timeline was the phone call to Regina's father.

Though Detective Trammel traced the call later, and telephone technology has shifted significantly in the decades since, there is scope to introduce solutions which can be deployed to make such connections faster. Whether that be telephone companies forcing caller ID and location reporting from the moment a missing person is reported, with real-time reports sent to law enforcement agencies, or the provision of any-time access to truck GPS systems, the technological assets and capabilities are with us. Sometimes, the only barrier is knowing what to ask for and from whom.

I found myself asking if Rhoades could have been stopped by these interventions. I had written them out quickly, thinking out loud almost. Without a pause for further thought, I believe the answer is yes. Chance and luck still would play their part, I have no hesitation in adding, but every completed or even threatened intervention would have removed the equilibrium of his control and reduced the comfort he felt which acted as psychological permission to offend. The simple act of undermining his self-confidence and introducing less certainty into his thinking would have worked. I felt that very strongly, even though I know there is no such thing as a perfect solution and I had proposed no magic bullets. But, with all of these things in place, the probability of Rhoades doing what he did is reduced substantially.

The cross-jurisdiction and inter-agency issues which affect information sharing and pattern analysis, the time lapses between discovery and identification of victims, and the broader societal issues which put people in his path, are the topics I have had mixed feelings on writing about. On the one hand, there was professional excitement, on the other this was always the biggest, scariest bit of the solution process to articulate. Much as Doe Theory grew organically from the ground of the Rhoades case, as I mentioned before it is only a branch. The tree itself is what I have come to call Fixing Broken Roads, a nod to the now very well-known Fixing Broken Windows theory of reducing crime by addressing environmental factors in high crime areas.

Fixing Broken Roads is a whole of society approach to the problem, designed to increase public safety, reduce offending opportunity, and mitigate the risks which will exist no matter what else is changed. There are certain elements of it within my gift to address directly, which I set out briefly using adaptations of the SMART process[74] to keep things sensible and steer me away from impossibility. Other pieces in the jigsaw require the

---

74 SMART – Specific, Measurable, Achievable, Realistic, Timely

input and action of law enforcement agencies, public services, the government, and legislators at a state and national level – which also means the support of the public is prerequisite. While looking into the Rhoades case was a highly emotive experience, this is the business end and those emotions which helped construct the landscape must be set aside to successfully navigate it. This is a colder approach, but this is also valuable as it shuts down tunnel vision and personal bias, both of which lead to knee-jerk responses which are either destined to fail or may create unintended consequences.

There are three elements to the Fixing Broken Roads approach. These are Subject Risk, Victim Environment, and Safety Strategy. The elements work together to achieve one purpose: the prevention of serious cross-jurisdiction crime to improve public safety.

Subject Risk addresses offending behaviour through early intervention and encapsulates through life mitigation measures, taking onboard all the learning from Rhoades and what he did. The purpose is to introduce a combination of forks in the road at which offending behaviour can be diverted, and to place barriers at the points it cannot. For the sake of clarity I wrote the practical example as a timeline, using Rhoades as a template:

Event	Intervention	Owner	Type	Outcome
Potential Child Abuse	Removal From Danger / Harmful Environment	Social Care/ Education/Law Enforcement	Fork	Subject removed from exposure to harm, trauma reduced.
Family Impact Arising From Police Contact	Trauma Counselling	Law Enforcement	Fork	Subject learns to deal with stressors / trauma in a healthy way.
Entry To Military	Vetting and Pre-Entry	Military	Fork	Subject addresses trauma and

	Trauma Therapy			learns to deal with stressors in a healthy way.
Exit From Military	PTSD Therapy / Vetting Aftercare	Military	Fork	Subject deals with in-service trauma and is provided with healthy mechanisms.
Starts Truck Driving	Initial Subject Vetting and Through-life Vetting	Industry	Fork / Barrier	Highest risk subjects rejected, opportunity removed. Other subject behaviour tied to norm compliance and constantly monitored.
Relationship Breakdown	Diversionary PSA	Government / NGOs	Fork	Subject diverted towards to healthy behaviours and activities. Population awareness created.
Domestic Abuse Event	Arrest and Prosecution	Law Enforcement / Prosecutors	Fork / Barrier	Subject offered rehabilitation and placed under direct control.
Resumes Truck Driving	Vetting Risk Updated	Industry / Law Enforcement	Fork / Barrier	Subject opportunity removed.

| Conviction After Further Offending. | Sexually Violent Predator Designation | Law Enforcement / Medical | Barrier | Subject placed under direct control measures while risk posed. |

One piece of the puzzle I took direct ownership of is subject vetting. This is exactly what the DRiVet system is designed to – providing that crucial risk assessment at the point of entry into a high-risk career and tracking that subject for the whole of their employment lifecycle. The other measures are far from complicated but do require a combination of funding and policy intervention. For example, it may be necessary to review the threshold or circumstances in which taking a child into protective custody, or to introduce a formal definition of "police contact" to determine when a duty of care needs to be exercised and create the funding package for therapeutic interventions.

In practice, adjusting the safeguarding threshold for specific circumstances could see the introduction of a definition such as:

> *a) A child under the age of eighteen should be removed from the family home where the Collective Authorities hold a reasonable belief that serious sexual abuse of The Child or The Children, or another member of the same family of which the child is likely to be aware, has occurred and may continue, and that remaining in the family home or with other close relatives, may expose the child to the risk of new harm or further harm.*
>
> *b) The child may be removed for a maximum period of two weeks and placed in appropriate care by the Primary Agency pending a judicial review as to whether the removal should be extended or made permanent based on the Primary Agency's representations.*
>
> *c) Where an extension is granted, it shall not be for a period of more than three months, pending a further judicial review when that time period expires – at which point a further extension may be requested or the removal made permanent by the same court.*

> *d) Reasonable Belief is a belief that would be held by an ordinary and prudent person in the same circumstances.*
>
> *e) The test of whether the child is likely to be aware of harm to another is subjective, based on the individual circumstances of the case and the construction or layout of the family home.*
>
> *f) The test as to whether the child may be exposed to risk of harm is subjective, based on the individual circumstances.*
>
> *g) The "Collective Authorities" are Child Protective Services, the child's School Safeguarding Panel, and the appointed Safeguarding Officer for local Law Enforcement. The Primary Agency is Child Protective Services.*
>
> *h) Harm is physical or psychological.*

Multi-agency safeguarding is a common practice and this definition changes very little, rather adding a few specific details which clarify certain meanings - what will happen, how long for, and what the process is. This is not rocket science, and nor should it be, but it needs to be executed properly and the necessary conversations to implement a legal definition are high level. The ideal situation would be that such a definition is adopted uniformly across the country to ensure no postal code lottery effect began to manifest.

A similar approach is also suitable for the formalisation of duty of care following police contact, taking particular note of the general knowledge principle that the rational brain is not fully formed until the age of twenty-five – meaning change can still be preventative rather than corrective.

Such a definition could be:

> *a) Where a person under the age of twenty-five is exposed to a traumatic or stressful event or series of events arising from law enforcement contact, the primary law enforcement agency involved is subject to a special duty of care for that person for three months after the event or three months after the last event in the series.*

b) The test as to whether an event is traumatic or stressful is based upon what the ordinary, reasonable person would perceive to be traumatic or stressful in the individual circumstances, e.g. the arrest of a parent or sibling for serious offences.

c) Events arising from law enforcement contact are defined as events which could not have occurred but for the actions of a law enforcement officer or agency, e.g. an arrest.

d) Special duty of care is defined as the positive offer of and, if accepted, provision of free-of-charge access to three one-hour sessions of trauma therapy with a qualified independent counsellor.

The potential offset with this intervention, in terms of the cost of subsequent investigations alone, significantly outweighs the scale of up-front investment. On top of that, moving law enforcement into a structured duty of care stance actively works to cement and - in some cases - repair trust relationships with communities. The impact of police contact is generally understood, internationally, and focused on negative outcomes such as deaths in custody or suicides following incidents, but there is a real opportunity to start drawing positive lines which reduce future offending. It should be grasped with both hands.

This is an inexhaustive look at the type of work which can be done to address the Subject Risk strand, leaving plenty of scope for innovation at a local, regional, national level.

Victim Environment is a more complex area and a key driver which should sit behind thinking on it is a move away from the "they exposed themselves to a high-risk lifestyle" rhetoric and a shift towards a risk mitigation approach. Over time, this will drive lasting behaviour change, so the starting point is to recognise the relevant risks people are exposed to and deal with them, following up with work to address why those risks manifest to begin with. Think of it as building a safety buffer around potential victims without needing to engage personal judgments and confirmation biases. Structural bubble wrap to preserve something precious.

In the context of Fixing Broken Roads, the identifiable risks which need mitigating are a level of private exposure to potentially high-risk offenders and presence at locations with limited opportunities for acquiring assistance. The reasons for the manifestation of these risks can be summarised as: choice, substance abuse, financial hardship, or trauma. Choice might seem a surprising inclusion at first glance, but there is a simple truth behind it. Patricia Walsh and Douglas Zyskowski, for example, were simply hitchhiking to return from Bible studies and not for any other reason.

By setting out clearly what it is that needs to be addressed it is much easier to design impactive change, and several solutions leapt out at me immediately. DRiVet was one - the extreme option of outward identifiers of driver risk levels is highly valuable - and implementing spot checks at truck stops and delivery points is another. What I haven't touched on yet, however, is how drawing up new offences can be used to change behaviour.

Introducing the offence of Hitchhiking, if handled badly, would change nothing and just create something impossible to enforce. If handled well, however, with an appropriate penalty aimed at dissuasion, it would pay dividends. I have given this some thought and any offence design would need a robust definition with a behavioural outcome in mind, for example:

> *a) A commercial driver found picking up another person, or transporting or offering transportation to another person on or near an Interstate or Highway, without exemption or authorisation, is summarily guilty of an offence.*
>
> *b) A person guilty of an offence under this section is liable to the immediate suspension of their driving licences, commercial and otherwise, for a period of twelve weeks and may not legally hold motor vehicle insurance during this time.*
>
> *c) The driver will be escorted to the nearest place of safety to deposit the vehicle until such time it can be collected by a correctly licensed and insured driver.*

d) A person guilty of an offence under this section is also liable to fixed penalty of $1500 payable within twenty-eight days of the date of the offence.

e) Law enforcement, fire and rescue, and emergency medical staff travelling in marked vehicles and carrying out their lawful duties are exempt under this offence.

f) Vehicle recovery drivers may request exemption on a per case basis but must provide a verifiable justification for the circumstances.

g) A commercial driver may be authorised to carry a specific passenger prior to the commencement of their journey and the authorisation must be verifiable at the roadside.

h) A law enforcement official may issue temporary, conditional authorisation in an emergency situation.

i) A person found summarily guilty of this offence may appeal the decision in writing within 10 days of the date of the offence, requesting a judicial hearing in the jurisdiction of the offence.

Worded this way, a jeopardy is created (inconvenience, business interruption, loss of income, and disruption to private life) through an absolute offence, and there is little more powerful in steering behaviour than creating a potential personal loss - *Don't miss out!* your advertising screams, and now you know why. This may sound like harsh legislation but the logic is clear: the majority of people are simply going to comply with the law, leaving only people already inclined to break it doing so. This type of intervention is another which works on the Collective Common Sense psychology and, once the community adapts, it would start to self-police - meaning the few drivers left carrying hitchhikers would be identified in short order. Additionally, though the law does not target hitchhikers or potential victims, they would surrender the transport option more quickly, and a carefully targeted public safety announcement campaign would do the heavy-lifting. In one simple offence, ideally implemented at the national level for uniformity, the two core risks in the Victim Environment element are directly addressed, leaving the causes of manifestation – the first of which, choice, is dealt with directly by the legislation. This leaves substance abuse, financial hardship, or trauma as key causation to address, all of which might sound impossible, but it is necessary to consider that the problem at hand is a specific one with a limited geography. Providing pastoral care, recruiting people to recovery programmes, and even providing targeted grant support could be focused on those potential victims, for example sex-workers, frequenting truck stops and the small communities around them. Bit-by-bit, simply by providing that absent safety net highlighted by Della, potential victims are removed from danger and steered away from risks.

The final element in Fixing Broken Roads is Safety Strategy, currently informed by and reliant upon incomplete crime data. Cross-jurisdiction information sharing and pattern analysis sit firmly within this strand – both key issues which allowed Rhoades to offend in the first place. This is where Themis sits. This is what I had been working on and, finally, felt able to articulate. Themis is a software system – technically called the Thematic Incident System, but it has long since taken on the identity of her Greek namesake, the goddess of order and justice. While researching and writing, I spent a lot of time in the background prototyping, redesigning, coding, and testing, and the long hours and late nights were worth it.

The system allows officers and members of the public to report crime through a use-anywhere web interface which leads them through the process, capturing every piece of detail needed to automate ViCAP submissions and reduce the administration burden on agencies and officers, while increasing the volume of cases voluntarily reported to the FBI and increasing analytical accuracy at the federal level. Where officers are recording the crimes, they can predefine information sharing protocols and levels of redaction or holdback, with the system automatically generating press release and even social media bulletin text. Where victims are recording the crimes, the principles discussed previously apply. With all of the data held securely and encrypted at the point of entry, the system distributes key statistical and geographical information across jurisdictions in real-time and also creates detailed law enforcement circulars and briefings, as well as automating a number of other crime analysis and mapping functions. Internally, it can be used for case management too, with officers able to keep their investigation logs up to date, and it provides an end-to-end audit trail. Externally, and this is really exciting in my view, Themis provides automated public dashboards and creates automated public safety announcements and crime prevention advisories. I also worked hard to train the system to produce offender profiles at the point of data entry.

Over the years I have worked with various crime recording systems, from the black and white nightmare which was Scotland Yard's CRIS system, to the glorified MS Access database which stretched a criminal damage report into an exercise fit to test anyone's patience at Derbyshire. Themis is not like that. It does what it is supposed to do and removes work rather than creating more. One of the key aspects of the process was building in budget considerations, resulting in a five-seat licence being achievable at under a hundred dollars a month, putting technology in the same spending bracket as stationery, where it belongs.

The point of the whole exercise was to make sure that every one of America's twenty-seven-thousand agencies and offices could afford access to unified crime recording which helps identify offenders and put them away. Taken together, the end product is a fit for purpose tool made to improve public safety. Created to resolve the Safety Strategy element of Fixing Broken Roads. Additional modules have already been created – for example intelligence handling - and more will follow - such as the additional offence category recording and the full integration with DRiVet, which will match high risk drivers to potential offences as they are recorded.

There is still some work left to do – there always is – but the core system should be ready for launch in 2022 so it can get to work. Then, I kid myself regularly, I will take a break for a couple of months. I know perfectly well I will not. I am not built that way and there are so many cases which need attention. Too many.

When I set out to investigate Robert Ben Rhoades and his offending, I did not deliberately decide it would end in a package of solutions – either societal or technology based – but it has. It may not be closure in the traditional sense but it is a form of it, shutting the door on future offenders and potentially saving lives.

Every time I had a moment of doubt or hesitation in this process I took a quiet moment to think about the women and girls on the highways and in the fields across America.

They are not ghosts.

They are the reasons to do better.

AFTERWORD BY GREG COOPER

This Book

This work represents a disturbing but accurate account of one of the most notorious serial killers to have ever traversed our national Interstate Highway System. The author, James Patrick, has done a masterful job in presenting the "5 W'S and 1H ", (Who, What, When, Where and How) for this case study. James' intent is to educate, inform, and instruct both law enforcement and the public about a very dark side of humanity that preys upon the vulnerable. He effectively examines investigative considerations to identify, pursue and apprehend these roaming predators, thereby preventing further victimization. Moreover, he identifies behaviors that elevate a potential victim's risk level to the "point of no return."

Paradigm Shift

The details presented herein are unnerving and will leave an indelible mark on your psyche. As you travel alone, along a sparsely populated highway, you will never again completely enjoy the same level of serenity often associated with uninterrupted drives. If you are like me, you have enjoyed that quiet, undisturbed "floating time." Until now, it has allowed you to escape from your hectic life into uninterrupted random thoughts while enjoying a hypnotic state of relaxation. Not anymore. Now, when passing by an abandoned barn on a rural and isolated highway, an interstate hitchhiker, stranded motorist, or semi-truck gliding down the roadway, you will be jerked out of that "roadway nirvana" into a stark recollection of the case details of this book. You will be questioning and doubting, speculating, and even challenging certain situations and circumstances, or people. Heretofore, such casual observations may not have even caught your attention, much less occurred to you as strange, suspicious, or troubling. From now on you will be seeing life through a different pair of lenses. You are transformed and you are not the same person as you were before reading this book. In fact, armed with this new perspective, you may very well save your life, a stranger or someone you care about.

As a former FBI profiler, Supervisor of the FBI's Criminal Profiling, ViCAP and Arson/Bombing Programs, instructor for the FBI National Academy, Chief of Police, and now as the Executive Director of the Cold Case Foundation, I enthusiastically endorse this book and highly recommend it to you.

Interstate Highway

In 1954, President Dwight D. Eisenhower appointed General Lucious D. Clay to head a committee designated with proposing an interstate highway system plan. Clay summarized the purposes for constructing such an ambitious system accordingly:

"It was evident we needed better highways. We needed them for safety, to accommodate more automobiles. We needed them for defense purposes if that should ever be necessary. And we needed them for the economy. Not just as a public works measure, but for future growth".

Eisenhower sent Clay's proposal to Congress and after subsequent negotiation and compromise between the House and Senate, it concluded with the passage of the Federal Highway Act of 1956. Interestingly, our Interstate Highway System was formerly known as the Dwight D. Eisenhower National System of Interstate and Defense Highways. All told, there are about 4.09 million navigable roadways across our 50 states. The central beating heart of this system is the nation's 47,432 miles of Interstate Highways.

America's railway system had been the primary means of conducting national transportation of passengers and freight. With the passage and construction of the Interstate Highway System, the railroad system declined sharply. But the trucking industry skyrocketed! Now, the trucking industry has come to dominate the freight industry in the later portion of the 20th century.

The significance of trucking is reflected in the adage: "If you bought it, a truck brought it". The national supply of goods and services depends entirely upon trucks to distribute vital cargo from initial manufacturing to final delivery. A key component to making this possible are the estimated 3.6 million professional commercial truck drivers traversing our road systems who deliver seven days a week, twenty-four hours a day. The nation is grateful for an effective transportation system and dedicated professionals who make up the key components responsible for delivering goods and freight that keeps our commerce vital and thriving. However, as in all professions intended to do good there are unfortunate examples of an "exceptional" employee who will exploit a position of public confidence by turning it to evil. Regrettably, the trucking industry is not excluded and has its exceptions.

The reader will note that one of the major motivations and purposes for the Interstate Highway System was referenced above in General Clay's summary wherein he specifically includes the national "need for defense purposes". While the purpose of the interstate was intended for the public good, safety and welfare of this nation, it is also ironic that there are those who have exploited its benefits for evil designs.

FBI's Highway Serial Killing Initiative (HAK)

In 2009, the Federal Bureau of Investigation (FBI) released the report entitled the Highway Serial Killings Initiative (HSK). This analysis reflected the results of a five-year-long research project investigating the unsolved murders of prostitutes, hitchhikers, and stranded motorists compiled in the FBI's ViCap national database (Violent Criminal Apprehension Program). It consisted of examining over 500 murder victims from along or near highways, who were primarily women living high risk, transient lifestyles, often involving substance abuse and prostitution. Such "high-risk" victims are often picked up at truck stops and service stations and are sexually assaulted, murdered, and dumped along a highway. The initial investigation resulted in identifying at least 10 suspects, predominantly long-haul truck drivers believed responsible for some 30 homicides. It has grown significantly from there.

Such studies do not conclude or even mean to imply that "long-haul truck drivers" dominate the population of serial killers. Not at all. There is no suggestion of a "trucker" personality that has a predominate disposition or propensity to serial killing. To my knowledge, there is no such effort nor professional interest in suggesting or researching such a hypothesis.

As a criminal profiler, when initially analyzing a crime, I first look at victimology. I don't start my analysis with the question, "Who did this"? Initially, if the information is available, I start with "Who is the Victim"? When a victim has been determined to be living a "high-risk" lifestyle, i.e., a prostitute or hitchhiker who willingly places themselves in harm's way, etc., preliminarily it suggests that they have most probably been a "victim of opportunity." Meaning that the offender often selects the victim by taking advantage of the immediate set of circumstances, situation, and environment that the victim willingly enters. For example, if a female hitchhiker or prostitute willingly accepts a ride with an unknown male truckdriver who has proprietary control of the driver/passenger compartment and with deadly motives, she is at an immediate disadvantage and at risk of being restrained or worse by a potential offender. To use the "spider and the fly" analogy, he has deceitfully snared the victim into his web of power and control. It is the interactive nexus between victimology and the environment, situation, and circumstances that the predator uses to their advantage while elevating the victim's risk and minimizing their own. The more that is understood about the victim and their lifestyle, the more is revealed about the offender.

-Broken Roads-

In some cases, the very motivating factors for pursuing the long-haul trucking profession, i.e., freedom and independence, ability to set their own hours, privacy, independence, open road travel, interstate travel, and minimal supervision can be used to facilitate the commission of various forms of criminal activity. The mobile nature of offenders, the unsafe lifestyle of victims, the significant distances and multiple jurisdictions involved, and the scarcity of witnesses and forensic evidence increase the risk for potential victims and reduce the risk of identification and apprehension for human predators. Like it or not, the working environment and conditions for the professional truck driver sets the stage and opportunity for a travelling predator on the hunt to successfully commit crimes against high-risk and vulnerable targets.

Enter Robert Ben Rhoades

I have never met Robert Ben Rhoades face to face. But I know him and have been "associated" with him and his "work" for 30 years. Special Agent Roy Hazelwood, my highly esteemed colleague of the FBI's Behavioral Science Unit, first introduced him to me, under a unique set of circumstances.

I joined the FBI with the ultimate aspiration of becoming an FBI Profiler. That dream was realized in the summer of 1990, when renowned FBI Unit Chief John Douglas, who would become my mentor and close friend, selected me to fill one of three newly authorized "criminal profiler" positions. I was assigned to what was then called the Investigative Support Unit (ISU), housed sixty feet below ground at the FBI Academy in Quantico, Virginia. ISU, currently labeled the Behavioral Science Service Unit (BSSU), was made famous in the classic movie, "Silence of the Lambs", which arrived at the theaters a few months after I arrived at the ISU. ISU consisted of three programs: Criminal Investigative Analysis Program (CIAP) where the criminal profilers were located; the Violent Criminal Apprehension Program (ViCAP) and the Arson and Bombing Program (ABIS). I was initially assigned to CIAP and trained by a cadre of "Who's Who" FBI Special Agents responsible for bringing international acclaim and notoriety to the field of criminal profiling and the FBI's inaugural role in its development.

I was one of three agents who had been selected for the new post and we were in a "probationary" status for a year following our arrival at the FBI Academy. We were required to successfully pass through a yearlong training program before being officially sanctioned as an FBI criminal profiler. The training consisted of a rigorous academic curriculum and attendance to a series of "case reviews" presented by senior profilers. Additionally, we were each assigned incoming cases and required to present our analysis to a board of profilers who tested our knowledge, skills, and abilities.

After two years of serving as a criminal profiler, the Behavioral Science Unit (BSU) recruited me to concurrently instruct an "Abnormal Psychology and Criminal Profiling" course for the FBI National Academy. BSU consisted of various instructors including FBI agents who conducted various research projects and instructed select courses to international law enforcement professionals who were attending the FBI National Academy.

As one of the newer members of the Unit, I was thrilled and privileged to be recruited to instruct at the FBI National Academy, while also continuing my assignment in CIAP as a profiler. While I was gathering material and developing the curriculum for the course, I needed a unique and instructive case study that would effectively illustrate an example of classic serial killer. I approached Special Agent Roy Hazelwood who was recognized as both an excellent profiler and one of the premier instructors at the FBI Academy. He was also renowned for his research and respective professional publications on serial rapists and serial rapists who kill.

Roy was also one of my instructors who had mentored me in the art of criminal profiling during the first year of required training for newly appointed profilers. I asked Roy if he had a case that I could use in my class as an example of a serial killer. Roy "introduced" me to Robert Ben Rhoades. Roy explained that Rhoades, a long-haul truck driver, was a classic example of a serial killer and sexual sadist who was responsible for the torture, rape, and murder of several victims. He related that the case dramatically illustrated Rhoades' method of operation including victim selection, pre-offense, offense, and post-offense behaviors. Roy presented me with the Regina Walters case, included as a principal case detailed in this book.

Regina Walters

Over the last thirty years, I have presented Regina's horrific story to thousands of law enforcement officials and college students. I have given presentations to audiences attending the FBI National Academy, hundreds of law enforcement training courses, several colleges and universities and a myriad of professional conferences.

I have continued to represent Regina by relating her tortuous journey long after retiring from the FBI. I have considered it a solemn responsibility and privilege to extend her life by relating her legacy to as many people as possible.

My purpose for presenting her case has been to dramatically illustrate the challenges that a roving serial killer poses to the public and law enforcement. I emphasize key components for successfully investigating, identifying, and apprehending these human predators in what I call the "3-C's": Communication, Cooperation and Coordination, between law enforcement agencies who are investigating homicides, missing persons, unidentified remains and rapes with serial characteristics. Additionally, by relating her account, she vicariously lives on by helping law enforcement solve similar cold cases and prevent other victims.

Full Circle

I had a life before the FBI. I started my law enforcement career as a Provo City (Utah) police officer. Provo is seated along the I-15 corridor at the base of the majestic Wasatch Mountain range and home to Brigham Young University. After working there in various assignments and completing a graduate degree I decided to expand my professional horizons. I had applied to the FBI and thought an offer was imminent but was placed "on hold" due to a federal hiring freeze.

Consequently, I took a divergent path. At 27, young, ambitious, and looking for an intermediate opportunity, I searched for a challenge that would further my professional aspirations. That opportunity came along when I was hired as the Police Chief in the small rural community of Delta, UT. Delta is in Millard County, the largest county covering an expansive southeastern portion of the state. Delta was experiencing an infusion of growth related to the coal fired energy expansion of the 80's which resulted in the construction of the Intermountain Power Project (IPP), about fifteen miles north of Delta. I considered this as a great opportunity and challenge. As the new Police Chief my, primary charge was to prepare for the anticipated growth, social impact and corresponding demand for public safety services by organizing a police department capable of responding to and managing the effects of that impact.

There were only two police departments in the county at that time, the Millard County Sheriff's Department and the Delta City Police department. We relied on a close and cooperative working relationship with the Sheriff's department to augment our resources. Sheriff Ed Phillips was highly respected throughout Millard County and the state of Utah. He was among the first to welcome me in my new job and graciously extended his friendship and department's resources in support of managing the task ahead. It was due to our department's close working relationship with the Sheriff and members of his department, with the consistent support of the Mayor and City Council that were responsible for the effective public safety services during those transition years.

-Broken Roads-

Approximately two and a half years later, Delta was beginning to experience the natural side effects of a "Boom-Bust" cycle, often associated with the completion of large projects that bring a significant increase in population. In short, I felt that my primary objectives for Delta were approaching completion. We doubled the size of our department, recruited and trained some exceptionally qualified personnel, and completed the construction of a new police facility in the new City Administration Building. Moreover, as a department we effectively managed the increase for services in a professional and responsive manner while maintaining the historical community atmosphere that the citizens and city administration desired.

I was becoming restless and considering a search for another professional challenge. Also, my curiosity had been recently peaked over the status of the FBI's hiring freeze that had interrupted my hiring expectations with them before I accepted the appointment as Delta's police chief. I had recently attended a three day "Criminal Profiling for Law Enforcement" course, instructed by two FBI agents, Kenneth Lanning, and Bill Hagmaier, held at Salt Lake Community College.

After attending that course, I was mesmerized by the subject matter and the role of an FBI criminal profiler. I vividly recall that as I walked back to the parking lot and just before entering my car, I experienced an "Ah-Ha" moment. I had a distinct impression, an absolute conviction and persuasion that this was the job for me. From that moment I knew what my principal professional purpose was, and I was committed to pursuing it until I accomplished it. This focus revived my interest in the FBI.

Coincidentally, while considering my options, I received a phone call from the FBI who advised that the hiring freeze had been lifted and inquired if I was still interested in a career with the FBI. The timing couldn't have been more perfectly orchestrated and that's why I lean more on destiny rather than coincidence.

-Broken Roads-

I entered FBI New Agent's Training in April 1985 and graduated from the FBI Academy in August. As indicated above, in August 1990, five years and two FBI Field Offices later, I was selected to fill one of three newly authorized positions, as an FBI criminal profiler.

In 1995, I retired from the FBI, after serving as the Acting ISU Unit Chief, ViCAP National Program Manager, FBI National Academy Instructor and FBI Criminal Profiler, and returned to Provo, Utah as the Chief of Police. I continued to present the Regina Walters case to various law enforcement audiences and was invited to give a presentation at the upcoming annual Utah Police Chiefs and Sheriffs conference held in St. George, UT. In preparation for the conference, I considered that it may add some additional insights if I could interview Rhoades about Regina. Rhoades had been convicted for Regina's abduction and murder in 1994 and was incarcerated at the Menard Correctional Facility in Chester, Illinois.

Arrangements were made to talk with him over the telephone…it didn't go too well. During our conversation, I brought up Regina Walters and her boyfriend Ricky Lee Jones. It went downhill from there. He proceeded to rant and rave spitting out protests and personal derogatory attacks against Regina. He also blamed her boyfriend Ricky for killing her, claiming his own innocence.

I listened to this psychopath for as long as I could, and finally couldn't take anymore. I knew I wasn't going to get anywhere with him and so I decided to share with him what I personally thought of him, including that I would do everything I could to make his life as miserable as possible…and much more. The "conversation" ended abruptly by him throwing his phone across the room. The prison guard picked up the phone and asked me WHAT I said to Rhoades for him to react that way. I explained that it was "confidential" between Rhoades and me and better left that way.

-Broken Roads-

As the saying goes, "Best laid plans". While my intentions were good, there wasn't much of anything to add after the telephone visit with Rhoades, so I gave my customary presentation.

When I was setting up, I was delighted to see the familiar face of Millard County Sheriff Ed Phillips along with his customary Stetson hat, among those attending my presentation. It had been over ten years since we had worked together while I served as the Delta Chief of Police.

I proceeded to share Regina's story with the group including her victimization by Robert Ben Rhoades. With the dramatic impact of crime scene photos, I highlighted the maps reflecting Rhoades long haul truck route in 1984, 1987, 1988, 1989 and 1990. Just as I was emphasizing that Utah was included among the many states that he traversed in 1990, I notice a hand raise up in the back of the room. It was Sheriff Ed Phillips. He related that he had a cold case of an unidentified female who had been murdered and whose remains were discovered in a rural area of Millard County in 1990. After the class, we continued our discussion and concluded it advisable for him to follow up with the FBI and other law enforcement agencies associated with Regina's case. Not to be distracted, and consistent with their reputation for dogged investigations, Sheriff Phillips and his team of investigators pursued that lead until they solved their cold case. No longer a cold case, it was determined that the victim was Patricia Candace Walsh, also included in this book.

While my role in solving Patricia Walsh's case may not have the investigative flair dramatized in a true crime documentary, it was a critical piece that set things in motion to solve her case. It further underscores the principles of the "3 -C's": Communication, Cooperation and Coordination between law enforcement agencies, particularly when investigating serial killers. Had Regina Walter's case not been presented at the Utah conference, Walsh's case is likely to have remained among the over 200,000 cold case homicides archived in law enforcement agencies across the United States. In an indirect way, Regina also has contributed to solving the Walsh case and possibly many more. And as an added personal bonus, little did I know at the time I made the promise to Rhoades, that I would be able to contribute to making his life as miserable as possible. That gives me great personal satisfaction.

The Cold Case Foundation

I have served in the law enforcement profession for 45 years. It has been a privilege and an honor to have represented several organizations in various assignments. As law enforcement representatives, I believe that our primary clientele are victims of crimes whose rights have been violated. I submit that we are duty bound to honor them, both living and dead, by vicariously representing them in our pursuit for justice in their behalf.

The United States Declaration of Independence identifies three examples of unalienable rights given to all humans, "Life, Liberty and pursuit of Happiness", which governments are created to preserve and protect. Furthermore, as documented "in the US Constitution, the people, through our government, seek to form a more perfect union by establishing justice, ensuring domestic tranquility, providing for the common defense, promoting the general welfare, and securing the blessings of liberty to ourselves and our posterity".

Also, the Constitution of the United States identifies the four main purposes of government, namely: to establish laws, maintain order and provide security, protect citizens from external threats, and promote the general welfare by providing public services.

I don't see anywhere in these documents that suggest either the unalienable rights or the purposes of government to protect them are conditioned upon a person's (i.e., victim of crime) mortality. In other words, such rights and the government's responsibility to protect them extend beyond the person's life. And there is no apparent presumption that there is a financial burden associated with that extension.

As a result of my personal philosophy outlined above and my combined experience working with federal, state, and local law enforcement on interpersonal violent crimes, particularly as it relates to cold cases, an idea was born.

A disturbing study of the FBI records found that since 1995 the national average of solved homicides in the United States is only about 64%...leaving 36% of murders unsolved annually. Approximately 5,700 killers get away with murder every year. Such an amount of unsolved Cold Case murders has a compounding financial and workload effect on police departments and respective personnel assigned to work them.

To address this challenge, some police departments can dedicate Cold Case detectives while others simply must do the best they can with limited resources in manpower and scarce funding. Disturbingly, this has a national compounding effect resulting in an estimated aggregate of over 200,000 unsolved cold case homicides nationally.

We know that many Cold Cases are solvable. And the primary key to solving them is that they must be WORKED. It is not for lack of interest that cases turn cold and seemingly forgotten; they are never forgotten by victims' families, or the investigators assigned to them. As a society, and certainly as law enforcement professionals, we must ensure that the victims of these cases are never forgotten. Additionally, we must insist that such cases are never at the mercy of insufficient funding or otherwise available resources. Law Enforcement's desire to resolve Cold Cases is ever present, but often the resources and budget to solve them are not. Considering these challenges an idea emerged for providing resources (at no expense) to victims, their families and law enforcement in support of their efforts to resolve cold cases. In 2014, we established the Cold Case Foundation (CCF), a 501c3 nonprofit to address these concerns.

The mission of the Cold Case Foundation is to support law enforcement agencies in their efforts to successfully resolve the following types of unsolved cases: Homicides, Missing Persons, Unidentified Remains and Sexual Assaults with serial characteristics. This is accomplished primarily through funding, consulting, training, networking, and victim support.

I have been amazed by the cadre of retired and working professionals considered experts in their own fields, who have joined us in this great cause. We currently have over 120 volunteer members of our Investigative Team of Consultants, with various levels of expertise and disciplines including, Law Enforcement, Forensic Science, Forensic Digital Technology, Forensic Psychology, Crime Analysis, Social Science, Criminal Profilers, Medical Examiner/Coroner, Fire Science/Arson, Victims Advocacy, Media, Search and Rescue, Legal Professionals, Graphologists, Statement Analogy, etc. Collectively, they have provided thousands of hours of case consultation pro bono to law enforcement organizations, victims, and their families.

CCF is supported by private and public donations, and we are pleased that all donations have been devoted to operational case work expenses. All personnel are volunteer, nonpaid staff.

We are dedicated to stopping the deadly compounding effect of cold cases and providing hope and resources to families affected by violent crime. The Cold Case Foundation is committed to raising public awareness and creating partnerships to assist and provide law enforcement whatever resources are needed to bring about closure.

If you are interested in the Cold Case Foundation mission and how you can help in this effort with your time and/or resources, please visit our website at coldcasefoundation.org.

Gregory M. Cooper, 20th January 2022

-Broken Roads-

WITH SPECIAL THANKS

Pamela Milliken.

Della.

Dr. Lawrence J. Simon.

Greg Cooper.

Dean Jackson.

Andrew Jackson.

Dr. Todd Grey.

Dr. Alison Schechter.

Francine Bardole.

Melissa Lee-Patrick.

-Broken Roads-

GET INVOLVED

By buying this book you are already supporting the work of the Cold Case Foundation.

If you want to do more, you can visit www.coldcasefoundation.org and donate directly or go to www.coldcase.live and sign up for a supporter's membership. In exchange, you will get access to blogs, articles, podcasts, web series, and online training courses, all accessible within our custom-built social media platform. Members get access to the Cold Case Live app and join a growing international community of people who want to make a difference.

Stay safe.

-Broken Roads-

ABOUT THE AUTHOR

James Patrick is an intelligence specialist who served as a police officer for a decade. On leaving Scotland Yard he was commended by the British Parliament. He now focuses on threat mitigation and intelligence analysis, specialising in the digital and information landscapes.

He served as a police officer from May 2004 to October 2009 in the Derbyshire Constabulary, where he qualified as a Sergeant under the OSPRE Part 1 and 2 examination regimes. During this time, he was commended for his work as an intelligence officer. In October 2009 he transferred to the Metropolitan Police Service in London and received three commendations in September 2010 for bravery in apprehending an armed suspect, leadership and fortitude at the scene of a fatal fire, and bravery at a life-threatening incident. In 2012 he was recruited by the Assistant Commissioner to work on a new strategic department following his presentation of a predictive policing model and enhanced intelligence briefing system.

During his time as a specialist analyst for Scotland Yard he discovered the mass under-recording of serious sexual offences and serious acquisitive crime. He eventually acted as a whistle-blower, sparking a Select Committee inquiry by the British Parliament which exposed thirty years of crime figure manipulation across the country. As a result, the way crime is recorded and investigated in England and Wales was permanently changed and government-imposed targets were abolished. The Committee's final report commended James before Parliament, stating: *"We are indebted to PC Patrick for his courage in speaking out, in fulfilment of his duty to the highest standards of public service, despite intense pressures to the contrary."* He retired from the force in 2014 after the inquiry concluded and then Home Secretary, Theresa May, made a commitment to revise the treatment of whistle-blowers in policing due to his case.

He is now the director of a company providing specialist analytical and intelligence products and services, working with clients globally. He has particular expertise in PAEI, interpreting data patterns or anomalies, and in identifying investigative opportunities in both complex and incomplete evidential scenarios. He is the Director of Intelligence at the Cold Case Foundation.

-Broken Roads-

www.ingramcontent.com/pod-product-compliance
Ingram Content Group UK Ltd.
Pitfield, Milton Keynes, MK11 3LW, UK
UKHW041330100225
4527UKWH00040B/242